COMPUTER TECHNIQUES IN ENVIRONMENTAL SCIENCE

COMPUTER TECHNIQUES IN ENVIRONMENTAL SCIENCE

R. P. OUELLETTE
R. S. GREELEY
J. W. OVERBEY II

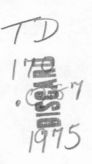

PETROCELLI / CHARTER   NEW YORK 1975

Library of Congress Cataloging in Publication Data

Ouellette, R   P   1938–
    Computer techniques in environmental science.

    Includes bibliographical references.
    1. Electronic data processing—Environmental pro-
tection.   I. Greeley, R. S., 1927–   joint author.
II. Overbey, J. W., 1941–   joint author.
III. Title.
TD170.O87   1975   363.6   74-23805
ISBN 0-88405-281-8

CONTENTS

FOREWORD

This book is addressed to the environmental scientists slowly drowning in the data generated by research, regulatory, and enforcement groups around the country.

This is not a cookbook. It does not provide easy answers to difficult problems. The book is seen as a guide to the intelligent user.

There are seven chapters. The first provides an overview of the environment and provides a preview of where computers could be used effectively. Chapter 2 is an introduction to computers. It is probably naïve to the specialist and too sophisticated for the non-initiated. Here again, this chapter provides the guidelines and the starting point for further studies and is a compressed refresher for the initiated. Chapters 3, 4, and 5 address the use of computers in monitoring functions, control activities, and scientific and administrative applications. This is the heart of the presentation, where general principles, successful applications, and useful lessons are derived. Chapter 6 provides practical guidelines on how to perform a requirement study, a systems analysis study, a specification for procurement, and the implementation planning for acquiring a computer. This is essentially a model suggested to the reader. Chapter 7 attempts to integrate the first six chapters into the needs and alternative solutions to environmental data systems problems.

We would like to acknowledge *The American Scholar* for granting permission to quote from "The Disappearing Optimist" by Rene Dubos.

We further acknowledge the kind authorization of *Datamation* to use a previously published article in their magazine as the basis for Chapter 7.

We wish to thank the MITRE Corporation and its management for providing a stimulating intellectual environment where this book was born; MITRE also provided us with the necessary graphic arts and typing support. Mrs. Jean Reynolds did most of the typing for the almost infinite series of revisions we required.

We wish to thank all those who helped with suggestions and review—in particular, D. M. Rosenbaum, R. P. Pikul, M. M. Scholl, and A. Biswas.

Most of all, we wish to express our appreciation to our wives and children without whose understanding this book would never have been produced.

CHAPTER 1

INTRODUCTION TO ENVIRONMENTAL SCIENCE

"I . . . hope that modern man will learn to manage intelligently and constructively the new ecological system created by technology." Rene Dubos, The American Scholar, *Spring 1971*

Environmental science has become a topic of great public and academic concern. In 1969 the National Environmental Policy Act became law. In 1970 the Council on Environmental Quality was created in the Executive Office of the President, and the Environmental Protection Agency was formed. During fiscal years 1970, 1971, and 1972 over $3 billion was appropriated by the U. S. Congress for pollution-control programs, including over $300 million for research and development in advanced control techniques.[1] Actual outlays in fiscal year 1973 were $1.9 billion and are estimated at $3.1 billion for 1974.[2] At last count 35 state governments had established environmental agencies, and over 270 local governmental agencies monitor and attempt to control pollution.[3, 4, 5] Industrial expenditures for waste-treatment equipment have increased to a level of roughly $5 billion per year.[6] Private environmental and conservation groups have seen their membership increase 40 percent in a single year. The number of such groups is now estimated at about 4,000.[7] Over 150 four-year colleges and universities have established majors or programs in environmental science, and several departments of environmental engineering have been set up.[8]

One reason for this recent concern is that pollution has become so visible. A brown cloud of smog greets the air traveler as he lands in many American cities. Suds and scum float past the boater on lakes and streams. Mounting piles of trash spill over municipal disposal

1

sites. Such sights remind everyone that our surroundings are being polluted at a serious rate. Hopefully this degradation is not irreversible and can be largely alleviated by scientific and technological developments and their vigorous application by private and governmental actions.

This book will describe some of the roles computers can play in the research and technology involved in understanding and controlling our environment. These roles include monitoring, process control, and data processing for administrative and scientific purposes. Computers can switch on remote sensors from central locations and interpret and store the return signals as measures of ambient environmental quality or emitted constituent concentrations. On the basis of these or other measurements, computers can signal valves to open or close in complex sequences throughout an industrial facility to control process streams for maximum efficiency. Governmental administrators can request extensive data to be rapidly processed and summarized by computers for program evaluation and control. Scientists developing mathematical models to simulate diffusion and flow in the real environment can exercise these models on computers to explore conditions that cannot be attained or measured in practice. Complex laboratory equipment can now be computer-controlled and the data automatically processed.

Despite the potential for widespread use of computers for these applications, the actual number of computers in such use is relatively small. Most sensor data is recorded by hand or measured from strip charts. Few waste-process streams are automatically monitored and controlled. Most administrative use of computers is in business applications such as payroll. Although mathematical modeling and simulation are widely carried out on computers, there are many technical problem areas where models could be utilized but are not. Relatively few laboratories are automated.

The cost savings and other benefits to be obtained from computer techniques have been amply demonstrated in many fields. However, the realization that environmental science can profit from computer techniques has been slow to develop. One of the primary reasons for writing this book is to illustrate the applications of computers in specific cases and to describe the cost savings and benefits so that other professionals in environmental science may reap improvements in efficiency, economy, and capability to simulate or control the environment.

The First Annual Report of the Council on Environmental Quality [9] describes the environment as follows:

. . . Interdependent living and nonliving parts make up ecosystems. Forests, lakes, and estuaries are examples. Large ecosystems or combinations of ecosystems, which occur in similar climates and share a similar character and arrangement of vegetation, are biomes. The Arctic tundra, prairie grasslands, and desert are examples. The earth, its surrounding envelope of life-giving water and air, and all its living things comprise the biosphere. Finally, man's total environmental system includes not only the biosphere but also his interactions with his natural and manmade surroundings.

It is clear the term *environment* can be used to encompass essentially all conceivable attributes and interactions in the universe. Similarly computer techniques can be used in countless ways to investigate, simulate, or control these attributes and interactions. It is helpful, therefore, to focus on specific portions of the environment by way of example rather than to attempt a comprehensive survey of applications. We shall provide examples of computer techniques primarily in the areas of air pollution, water pollution, and solid waste. We shall also consider applications of computers for monitoring, process control, scientific calculations, and administrative purposes. We shall conclude with a discussion of the role of computers in national environmental policy- and decision-making.

PRESENT STATE OF THE ENVIRONMENT

The environment is quite imperfectly measured and understood, even in terms of just air pollution, water pollution, and solid waste. Extensive monitoring and simulation studies of environmental variables will be needed to allow pollution-control strategies to be applied effectively. Even where relatively accurate measurements exist for the past hundred years or more, reasons for the observed levels and effects are held to be tentative at best and predictions for just the next 30 years are questionable.

Some aspects of air pollution appear to be improving in urban areas in the United States. Settleable dust and sulfur dioxide concentrations are decreasing due to the institution of control programs and to the elimination of soft coal as a residential and industrial heating fuel over the last 30 to 40 years.[10] However, even with a high degree of control of sulfur dioxide emissions, the increase in power generation required to meet power demand to the year 2000 and beyond may well result in significant increases in sulfur dioxide and particulate concentrations in the future. The effects of these pollutants have not been thoroughly demonstrated, although some factor probably related to air pollution causes the death rate from lung cancer in large cities to be twice that in rural areas.[11]

The U.S. government has taken on the responsibility for controlling pollution from the automobile and other mobile sources. The governmental program adopted in the Clean Air Amendments of 1970 sets very stringent standards on the allowable emissions from automobiles to be reached in the 1976 or 1977 model year. Every new car is to be equipped with emission-control devices and given a 50,000-mile warranty on the equipment. This equipment must decrease pollutants by roughly 90 percent from 1970 values.[12] As a matter of fact, carbon monoxide and total oxidant pollution from automobiles already have shown a decrease since 1967, the year pollution-control equipment began to be required on all new automobiles.[13] Although older cars will still be on the road, the incidence of smog in most cities should be substantially decreased by 1985, and carbon monoxide concentrations will be decreased except perhaps in the heaviest traffic by that time. If exhaust controls were placed on used as well as new cars, minimum levels of pollution could be reached by about 1980.[14] Long-term forecasts show that even with this extent of control of automotive pollution, growing population and increased industrial activity may well cause levels of unburned hydrocarbons, nitrogen oxides, oxidants, carbon monoxide, and other pollutants to approach 1970 levels toward the end of the century. Therefore, at that time control of emissions from trucks, buses, construction equipment, motorcycles, industrial operations, spillage from gas-tank filling, as well as other minor sources will have to be controlled to maintain the air quality achieved by 1985.[15]

It should be noted that the health effects of air pollutants from automobile emissions are not known for certain at this time. The eye irritation produced by smog is certainly unpleasant, and many doctors feel that heavy exercise during high smog conditions could cause health difficulties. The health effects of carbon monoxide at 50 parts per million, a level frequently reached in heavy traffic, have been documented as resulting in impaired ability to judge time and in impaired vision.[16] Measurements of 100 parts per million have been made in some cases in very heavy traffic, and the effects at this level have definitely shown impaired performance on simple physiological tests within a very short exposure.[17] However, no conclusive evidence has been shown that levels up to 50 parts per million or more actually contribute to auto accidents.[18]

Long-term trends in water quality in some U. S. rivers and lakes have been measured from 1861 to the present time.[19] These measurements indicate that despite accelerated pollution-abatement efforts in recent years, the waterways studied do not appear to show a decline in their waste burden, much less a return to the levels of 70 or more years ago. Contributing to the pollution of our waterways are municipal and industrial wastes, sediment runoff from urban, rural, and surface-disturbed areas, and spills of oil and hazardous materials. Today 13,000 communities, containing 68 percent of the nation's population, are served by municipal sewer systems. Yet of this "sewered population" 14 percent receive no treatment. That is, raw sewage from these people flows into the rivers. And 46 percent receive inadequate treatment. Over 1,000 communities outgrow their treatment systems each year. Major water-using industries are believed to discharge about three times as much waste as is discharged by all of the sewered population, and the amount is increasing at about 4½ percent per year, or three times the rate of increase of the population. This industrial waste includes an unknown amount of chemicals of all kinds.[20]

Sediment produced by erosion contributes at least 700 times as much suspended material to our rivers and lakes as sewage discharges. This erosion comes from marginal farms, river banks, highway and home construction, and surface mining. The latter source has been estimated at 94 million tons of sediment per year.[21] Reported oil spills increased 30 percent in number from 1968 to 1969, and accidental discharges of poisonous chemicals such as cyanide and various pesticides have been implicated in fishkills, many of them massive.[22]

The U. S. must now dispose of over 150 million tons of solid wastes per year. With the increased control of air emissions and water effluents together with an ever-increasing population and increase in industrial production, this could increase to over 250 million tons by 1980. Many cities are running out of areas for solid-waste disposal. Many incinerators are being required to close to decrease air pollution. No easy solution to this disposal problem—nor any economic capability to extract valuable materials or to recycle waste products—has been developed.[23]

General levels of radiation to which the population is exposed have been decreasing due to the ending of most atmospheric nuclear weapons tests. However, background levels could rise again by 1975 to 1980, with the construction of many large nuclear power plants.[24]

ENVIRONMENTAL SCIENCE FOR IMPROVING ENVIRONMENTAL QUALITY

The word *science* means possession of knowledge as distinguished from ignorance or misunderstanding. The scientific method involves the recognition and formulation of a problem, the collection of data through observation and experiment, and the formulation and testing of hypotheses. If we are to halt further degradation of the environment and start improving environmental quality, we will need to make environmental science a significant part of every governmental, business, and private activity. As noted above, the problem is well recognized because it is so apparent. On the other hand, the problem needs much further formulation in terms of the impact of emissions and effluents on the health and well-being of the biosphere. Environmental science will, at the same time, involve the collection of extensive data under carefully controlled conditions and the establishment of a variety of experiments both in the real world and through simulation in order to understand the variety of interactions that occur in nature. Finally, the various hypotheses put forth to explain these interactions must be tested with further controlled experiments and simulations.

The recognition and formulation of the environmental problem can be seen to start with monitoring the environment. Computers can be valuable if not essential for every stage of the monitoring process. There are in existence several automated monitoring systems for air and water pollution that involve computer control. For instance, New York State has a Burroughs 3500 computer system in Albany that directs both air and water sensors in over a dozen sites throughout the state to send their data on a regular basis over a telephone network to a direct-access file, magnetic tapes, and printers. When pollutant levels reach specified values, the computer signals an alert.[25] Along the Ohio River there are some 17 water-pollution-monitoring sites, which are polled and recorded on a routine basis by a computer system.[25]

Handling the data from current monitoring programs in the United States is already an immense task. For instance, the National Aerometric Data Bank currently contains about 500 million characters on a magnetic tape file. A computer file-management system is used to gain access to the file, to sort through the desired data, and to print out desired forms in graphical and summary reports.[26] It is unlikely that this amount of data could possibly be handled in timely fashion without the use of computer techniques.

In formulating specific aspects of the problem statistical techniques are essential. For instance, the effects of air pollution on human health have been investigated recently with the use of statistical correlation techniques.[11] Again the computer is an invaluable tool for carrying out the regression, sensitivity, and correlation calculations in order to relate specific levels of pollutants to specific health effects. Currently there is a great deal of emphasis on the economic effects of pollutants. Data being gathered can be rapidly sorted, summarized, and printed to determine the specific cost of pollution in each area of the country.

Many experiments with the environment are too complex or would have too many unknown factors to attempt to carry them out in the real world. In these cases it is appropriate to simulate the real world using computer techniques. One major effort in this regard is the attempt to understand the weather using a simulation of complete global weather patterns. This simulation is being conducted on the largest computers available by the National Center for Atmospheric Research and the Environmental Research Laboratory of the National Oceanic and Atmospheric Administration.[27] More localized simulations involve various computer models for determining the fate of specific pollutants from various sources in a city, the dispersion and diffusion through the air, and their ultimate impact on ambient air quality. With these models it is possible to change completely the basic flow patterns, which would be impossible in practice, and to investigate the effects of marked changes in the input parameters.

A great deal of monitoring depends upon physical, chemical, and biological samples being taken to a laboratory and investigated in detail. Many of these laboratory techniques now involve sophisticated instrumentation such as an emission spectrograph or the gas chromatograph. Many laboratories now have computers connected to these instruments to direct their step-by-step procedures, to receive the data from each analysis, and to print out the data in summary format. It is further possible to connect each instrument and its computer to a central computer or alternatively to use a large central machine to operate and receive data from an entire laboratory full of instruments. Such laboratory automation is being installed at the National Air Surveillance Network Laboratory in Research

Triangle Park, North Carolina.[28] The accuracy of sampling, the control of the data, and the speed of analysis are all improved with computer techniques.

The actual control of pollution will depend ultimately on measures taken at every smokestack or drainage pipe where the emissions and effluents can be controlled. Furthermore, many industrial processes may need to be modified to a large degree to prevent continuing pollution of the air or nearby streams. Some industrial executives have found that by paying attention to effluent and emission streams they can actually recover materials and, if not make a profit, at least pay for part of the installation of the pollutant-control devices. Many modern plants are now computer-controlled, and the emphasis on reducing emissions and effluence will lend greater emphasis to continuing automation in industrial facilities. It has been possible for some time to sense temperature, pressure, flow rate, chemical composition of various process streams, etc. on a minute-by-minute basis. In the past recorders were placed throughout the plant with strip or circular charts on which the sensed variables were recorded. These charts then had to be monitored frequently by a maintenance and control operator and renewed every few hours or once a day, posted in some log, and stored. Now it is possible to have a computer sense these instrument readings, process the data, check the data for high or low values, and pick them out as desired. It is further possible to have a complete control loop as the computer sends signals to open or close valves to modify the process stream to maintain the facility at its most efficient settings. As an example, Seattle is installing a "Computer Augmented Treatment and Disposal System (CATAD)" for treating its municipal sewage.[29]

Finally, in the control of pollution there is a need for administrative access to data and reports on a wide variety of environmental control programs that have recently been initiated. The administrative use of information has been slow to utilize computer techniques. One exception is the STORET system of the Office of Water Programs of the Environmental Protection Agency. Data from thousands of water-quality monitors throughout the country is entered into this data bank situated in Washington, D. C.—in some cases through the use of teletype input over telephone channels. The data is entered in a standardized way and can be retrieved from computer terminals located not only at the Environmental Protection Agency headquarters in Washington, but also at the Regional Environmental Protection Agency headquarters throughout the country. The most current data on stream quality for any stream being monitored can be obtained within a very few minutes using this system.[30] Yet to be developed, however, is a comprehensive administrative system that would provide the Environmental Protection Agency Administrator and assistant administrators with current data on all of their budgetary items, their grant and research programs, as well as on the quality of the air, water, and land. The environmental program administrators at other levels of the federal, state, and local governments as well as in private industry could similarly make use of such a system for providing the necessary information on which to base their decisions with the most reliable up-to-data data.

There may be other applications of computer techniques in environmental science that would be of tremendous benefit in improving environmental quality. This book will concentrate on several techniques that are currently in use and that can clearly show the benefits to be gained by using that remarkable device we know as the modern electronic computer.

REFERENCES

1. Matthew J. Kerbee, ed., *Your Government and the Environment, An Annual Reference,* Vol. 1, Appendix V, p. A5-2. Output Systems Corp., Arlington, Va., 1971.

2. *Air/Water Pollution Report,* Vol. II, No. 6, p. 51. Business Publications, Inc., Silver Spring, Md., 1973.

3. *Environmental Quality,* The First Annual Report of the Council on Environmental Quality, p. 214. U. S. Gov't. Printing Office, Washington, D. C., 1970.

4. *Environmental Quality,* The Second Annual Report of the Council on Environmental Quality, pp. 37-77. U. S. Gov't. Printing Office, Washington, D. C., 1971.

5. *Environmental Quality,* The Third Annual Report of the Council on Environmental Quality, pp. 180-192. U. S. Gov't. Printing Office, Washington, D. C., 1972.

6. *Annual McGraw-Hill Survey of Pollution Control Expenditures.* McGraw-Hill Publication Co., New York, 1973.

7. *Environmental Quality,* The Fourth Annual Report of the Council on Environmental Quality, pp. 373-403. U. S. Gov't. Printing Office, Washington, D. C., 1973.

8. *The New York Times 1972 Guide to College Selection.* Quadrangle Books, Inc., Chicago, Ill., 1972.

9. *Environmental Quality,* The First Annual Report of the Council on Environmental Quality, pp. 6-7, U. S. Gov't. Printing Office, Washington, D. C., 1971.

10. J. Ludwig, et al., "Trends in Urban Air Quality." *Trans. Am. Geophysical Union 51* 5, p. 468, May 1970.

11. L. B. Lave and E. P. Seskin, "Air Pollution and Human Health." *Science* 169, 723-731 (1970).

12. *Clean Air Amendments of 1970,* Public Law 91-604. U. S. Gov't. Printing Office, Washington, D. C., 1971.

13. *Environmental Quality,* The Third Annual Report of the Council on Environmental Quality, p. 7, U. S. Gov't. Printing Office, Washington, D. C., 1972.

14. *Transportation Energy and Environmental Issues,* The MITRE Corp., February 1972, M72-25, p. 30.

15. *Profile of Air Pollution Control,* County of Los Angeles, Calif. Air Pollution Control District report for 1971, p. 46.

16. R. R. Beard and G. A. Wertheim "Behavioral Impairment Associated with Small Doses of Carbon Monoxide." *Am. J. Pub. Health* 57, pp. 2011-2012, November 1967.

17. *Air Quality Criteria for Carbon Monoxide.* U. S. Dept. of Health, Education and Welfare, pp. 8-14, 15, Washington, D. C., 1970.

18. *Ibid.,* pp. 8-20, 21.

19. Wm. C. Ackerman *et al.,* "Some Long-Term Trends in Water Quality of Rivers and Lakes." *Trans. Am. Geophysical Union* 51 (6):516, May 1970.

20. *Clean Water for the 1970's,* A Status Report, p. 4. U. S. Dept. of the Interior, Washington, D. C., June 1970.

21. *Ibid.,* p. 10.

22. *Ibid.,* pp. 8-9.

23. *Environmental Quality,* The Fourth Annual Report of the Council on Environmental Quality, p. 204. U. S. Gov't. Printing Office, Washington, D. C., 1973.

24. *Environmental Trends: Radiation, Air Pollution, Oil Spills.* p. 4. The MITRE Corp., MTR-6013, 1971.

25. See Chapter 3 for more complete description of these systems.

26. See Chapter 5 for a more complete description of the NADB.

27. Warren M. Washington, "On the Possible Uses of Global Atmospheric Models for the Study of Air and Thermal Pollution." Chapter 18, in *Man's Impact on the Climate,* p. 265. The MIT Press, Cambridge, Mass., 1971.

28. Private communication.

29. See Chapter 4 for a more complete description of this system.

30. See Chapter 5 for a more complete description of STORET.

CHAPTER 2

INTRODUCTION TO COMPUTERS

This chapter will provide the reader with the elements of computer technology essential for the understanding of subsequent chapters. The reader interested in furthering his knowledge in the area of computer technology is referred to more extensive texts.[1,2] While not exhaustive in coverage, this chapter is intended as a guide to the most relevant matters in this fast-growing field of knowledge.

Computers are electronic tools for rapidly handling large quantities of numbers or varying electrical signals. Keydata Corporation[3] currently lists 395 different makes and models of central processors available in the free world. These range in size from a 4,000-word minicomputer to a 572,000-word large scientific machine, and they range in speed from a few hundredths of a microsecond to over ten microseconds per processing cycle. They may be designed primarily for business applications or for scientific use; they may work on digital or analog signals (or both in a hybrid); and they may rent from $180 to over $155,000 per month. Clearly, choosing the proper computer for the intended application at minimum cost is a complex job that requires an understanding of both the applications and the hardware and the software available.

The value of a computer lies in its capability to manipulate numbers or a complex set of instructions to provide a useful result at less cost than could manpower or a prewired electronic circuit. This basic criterion must be borne in mind whenever computer techniques are being considered for an environmental science application.

COMPUTER PROCESSES

There are six primary processes involved in computer technology: *data acquisition, communications, data entry, data storage, data processing,* and *display* or *data output.* These processes are illustrated in Figure 2.1. The computer itself normally is considered to include the data processing units. The data entry, storage, and display equipments are called *peripheral devices,* although they are normally in the same location as the computer. However, many modern systems have the data entry and display device remote from the computer.

Data Acquisition

Any mechanical signal or voltage difference can be converted by appropriate electronic devices into machine-readable impulses. Many computers are connected through appropriate input buffers directly to environmental monitoring sensors. Sensors are available for monitoring a wide variety of environmental variables. For instance, sensors currently on the market can automatically measure temperature, pH (or acidity), conductivity, dissolved oxygen, reduction-oxidation (or redox) potential, turbidity, dissolved organic matter, and various specific ions in solution which constitute water pollutants, as well as sulfur dioxide, nitrogen oxide, ozone, hydrocarbons, radioactivity, and other pollutants in the air.

Sensor signals can be generated in either digital or analog form. In an analog signal the voltage or current amplitude or the frequency varies in some direct prescribed manner with the variable being sensed. A digital signal represents the varying parameter with a series of coded pulses indicating the value of the parameter at each successive instant of time. Analog and digital signals can be interconverted readily. An analog data acquisition subsystem could, for example, include the sensory amplifiers or signal conditioners, appropriate calibration and control equipment, an input scanner, and a multi-channel tape recorder. A digital data acquisition system would probably include the sensors, signal conditioners, calibration and control equipment, an input scanner, an analog-to-digital coverter, and a digital tape recorder or memory unit. Either the analog or digital systems could be connected directly to a suitable computer. Data-acquisition subsystems are illustrated in Figure 2.2.

In many cases data is obtained manually from charts or from manual records or calculations. The data must be collected, formatted, and entered into the computer through some type of input device

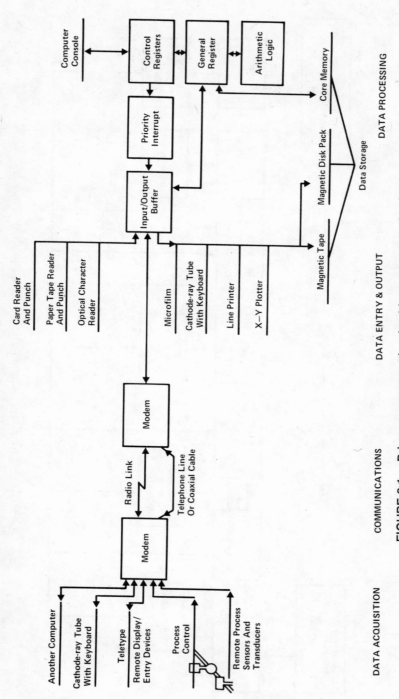

FIGURE 2.1. Primary processes involved in computer technology.

DATA ACQUISITION   COMMUNICATIONS   DATA ENTRY & OUTPUT   DATA PROCESSING

13

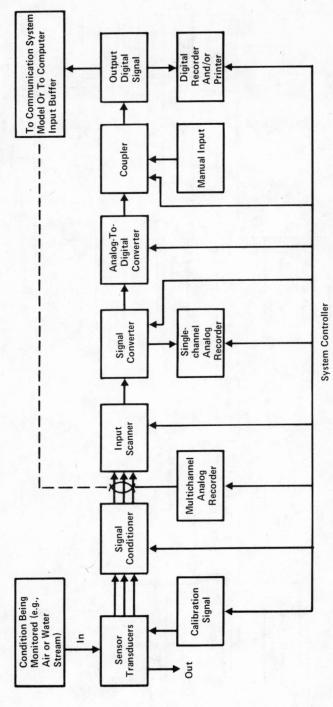

FIGURE 2.2. Block diagram of a data-acquisition system.

14

(see *Data Entry* below). Data can also be entered from a manual keyboard, often remote from the computer, or from another computer.

It should be noted that operation of the computer and of the data acquisition subsystems are very interdependent and require careful consideration of the system requirements and specifications before purchase.

Communication

Communication is herein defined as that part of an overall system that permits exchange of information. The field of communication is extensive, and the reader is referred to other texts [5, 6] for more in-depth study.

Figure 2.3 illustrates the essential components of a single-path communication link between two computers or between a remote terminal device and a computer. It consists of the two data-acquisition subsystems or a remote terminal (or another computer), the modulator-demodulator (modem), the channel to another modem, and the computer. The simplicity of a single link is deceptive, however, and the planning and design of a cost-effective complete communications system involves consideration of many complex factors. These are illustrated in Figure 2.4, which depicts the major elements of an overall communications system design in the form of a treelike diagram.

System architecture involves deciding on a method of connecting the locations originating or receiving data. The simplicity of direct point-to-point connections must be weighed against the possible efficiency and economy of a switched network.

Transmission is the process that involves accepting data from a source, converting it to a form compatible with the transmission medium, dispatching it to its destination, and reconverting it to its original form at the receiving end.

The transmission medium is the physical path over which the information is exchanged. There are several media typically employed, including: common carrier telephone lines, coaxial cables, microwave or lasers for line-of-sight applications, cable/microwave combinations, and high frequency radio transmission, either direct or via space satellite repeater stations.

The data rate expressed in bits per seconds (BPS) is a measure of the throughput capacity of the communication link. The transmission mode is the electrical representation of the signal being transmitted. Both analog and digital signals are encountered.[8] The most commonly

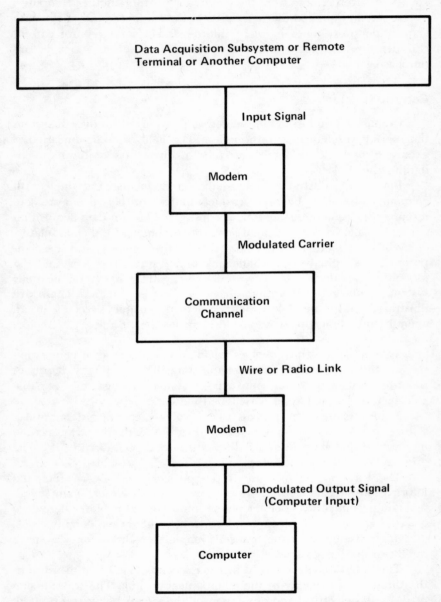

FIGURE 2.3. Essential components of a single-path communication link.

16

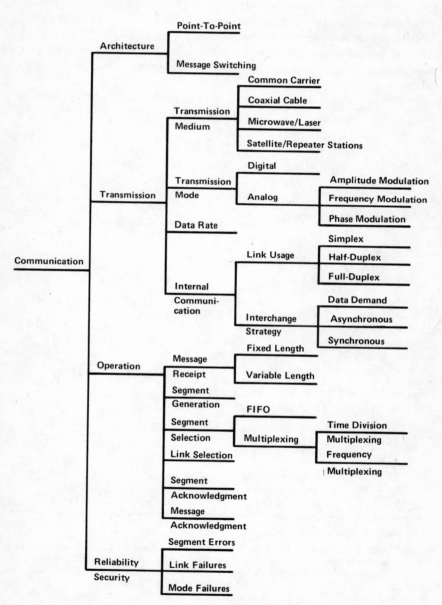

FIGURE 2.4.   Communication alternatives.

17

used data transmission medium is the common carrier telephone line. Table 2.1 lists the commercially available services.

The interface device between the digital electronic data processing equipment and the communications media linking remote terminals and the central processor is the modem (Figure 2.3).[10, 11]

Some common techniques employed in analog data transmission are amplitude modulation, frequency modulation, and phase modulation.[11]

The link usage defines the extent of the internodal communication

TABLE 2.1

Currently Available Common Carrier Communications Offerings
Useful for Data Transmission

National Switched Networks	Data Transfer Rate in Bits per Second
Networks	
Telegraph-grade	
TWX (AT&T Tariff FCC No. 133)	45–150
Telex (WU Tariff FCC No. 240)	50
Voice-grade	
Message toll Telephone (AT&T Tariff FCC No. 263)	1,200–2,000*
WATS (AT&T Tariff FCC No. 259)	1,200–2,000*
Broadband exchange (WU Tariff FCC No. 246)	1,200–2,400
Dataphone 50 (AT&T)	50,000
National Leased Network (AT&T Tariff FCC No. 230, WU Tariff FCC No. 231)	
Telegraph-grade	45–180
Voice-grade	1,200–9,600*
Broadband	
12 voice channels (Series 8000)	50,000
60 voice channels (TELPAK C)	250,000
240 voice channels (TELPAK D)	500,000

SOURCE: Mathison & Walker, ref. 9.

* One of the factors limiting the data-transfer rate on a given communications channel is the performance characteristics of the modem interface device at the endpoints of the line. In the near future commercially available modems will allow data-transfer rates of 3,600 bps on switched, voice-grade lines. Modems operating above 4,800 bps on voice-grade lines are infrequently used today because of their high cost and sensitivity to time-varying channel characteristics.

abilities (considering a communication network as made of nodes and links). There are three ways in which two nodes can be interconnected: (1) the simplex method permits transmission in one direction, (2) the half-duplex method permits two-way communication but only one direction at a time, and (3) the full-duplex method supports communication in both directions simultaneously.

There are basically two interchange strategy data transmissions: synchronous and asynchronous. Asynchronous data comes over the transmission line one message at a time. This is essentially a start-stop method or mark-space technique at the beginning and end of transmission. Synchronous transmission feeds a continuous stream of data with some coding on how the message is to be reconstructed. This last technique avoids the intervening start and stop bits. Data demand technique is a form of asynchronous transmission in that a pulse or message is sent out requesting or triggering a return transmission within a specified time slot.

System operation decisions involve detailed evaluation of the types of messages to be transmitted. The generation, receipt, and

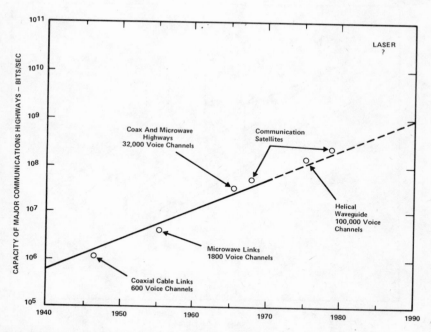

FIGURE 2.5. The sequence of inventions in telecommunications. *(From J. T. Martin, ref. 5)*

acknowledgement of messages and segments of messages, and the method of intermingling or "multiplexing" message segments versus the "first in, first out (FIFO)" method are among the operating elements involved.

Finally, the reliability and security error rate must be estimated, since the parameter will affect the required transmission link quality, the coding scheme, and certain equipment specifications. Security of the data may be important in some industrial applications where process stream concentration and flow rates may be company proprietary.

Complicating the system design is the rapid trend of innovation in the communications industry. The phenomenal growth projected for U. S. telecommunications will have major impacts on the capabilities, technological applications, system implementation, and cost for computer systems in environmental science. For instance, Figure 2.5 suggests that the combination of invention, utilization, and invest-

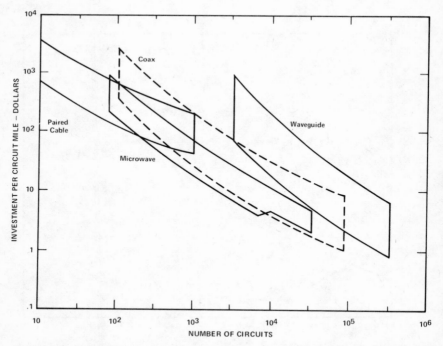

FIGURE 2.6.   Cost trends in terrestrial transmission. *(From J. T. Martin, ref. 12)*

ment has driven the expansion of telecommunication highway at such a rate as to multiply itself by six each ten years ever since 1850. There is no apparent diminution of this trend. In fact, the use of lasers for communications may provide a major step increase capability before the turn of the century. Figure 2.6 illustrates cost trends in terrestrial transmission. Wire-paired cable will be the predominant mode of telephone transmission for the next 10 to 15 years on routes with less than 500 to 15,000 circuits. For large intercity type trunks coaxial cable may be the lowest in cost because its higher construction cost is divided among 15,000 to 18,000 circuits per cable.

The American Telephone and Telegraph Company (AT&T) predicts that 90 percent of its long-haul circuitry in 1980 will be via coaxial cable. Beginning in the late 1970s helical-waveguide trunks may be introduced with capacities greater than 80,000 telephone terrestrial transmission over routes longer than 900 to 1,400 miles.

Data Entry

When a sensor signal in the form of a demodulated signal arrives at the computer, an input buffer allows the signal to be matched to the computer cycle without losing data. A priority interrupt control device on the computer detects the incoming signal and initiates the interrupt action to notify the computer that data is arriving and to allow for the data to be accepted from the buffer according to its priority in the computer operations scheme. When the computer is busy doing jobs other than input, the data is stored in the buffer. When the computer is ready to accept data, the buffer contents are read out. Naturally the computer size, the buffer size, and the priority interrupt scheme must all be designed to handle the specific sensor data load.

As noted above under *Data Acquisition,* much data exist on paper charts or records or in the mind of a person desiring certain computer actions. The data or instructions must be entered into the computer through some type of direct-input device. Manual keypunching of cards is still the method in general use in spite of its low speed, high manpower cost, and high error rate. The technique is the obvious choice when dealing with small volumes or when a routine ongoing operation can justify establishing a permanent staff of keypunch operators. The compounded problems of increasing cost and input volume have given birth to a variety of equipment aimed at reducing the computer input bottleneck. Typical devices of this nature include: (1) keyboard-to-tape (paper or magnetic) devices;

(2) direct-keyboard-entry devices; (3) mark-sense readers; (4) optical character readers; (5) microfilm readers.

The codes used in formatting the data for computer entry are worthy of note. Generally the computer uses digital data in binary form. However, frequently numbers are read into the computer in a preliminary program in binary coded decimal form or in Hollerith code (the latter named after the inventor of the punched card). Neither of these formats is quite as efficient in transferring information as pure binary. For transmission of sensor signals over telephone or telegraph wires, the widely adopted ASCII code is generally used. This is even less efficient than binary code decimal, although the difference in efficiency is generally negligible.

Currently, in most large systems, input data is read from the entry device onto magnetic tape in a preliminary step. Then, when the central processor is ready, the data can be transferred very rapidly from the tape to the computer core for processing.

Data Storage

Storage [13] is the process by which data is recorded in a more or less permanent fashion. Storage devices vary in capability and organization and are usually evaluated in terms of cost, access time, and storage capability.

For our purpose we will divide storage into three categories: mainframe core, or direct access memory; remote access memory, and off-line storage.[14] Mainframe memory space in the computer core on magnetic elements, films, or large-scale integrated "chips" is generally limited since the operating computer program must be accommodated together with the data actively being processed. Data in core storage is available essentially within one cycle time of the computer, generally less than a millionth of a second (a microsecond). A large machine will hold several hundred thousand binary numbers in core storage at any one moment, some representing instructions and some data.

Remote-access memory is maintained on randomly addressable devices such as disk packs or drums. Commercial devices currently hold hundreds of millions of binary numbers with access times in the range of milliseconds. Magnetic tapes represent both remote-access memory in sequential form with access time in the range of hundreds of milliseconds (tenths of seconds) and permanent off-line storage. Each tape can hold billions of binary numbers and tape libraries exist with up to a trillion (10^{12}) stored numbers. Recently, with the advent of the minicomputer, magnetic tape cassettes and cartridges have become popular. Perforated paper tape is still used extensively for both on-line and off-line data storage. It is useful for small or short jobs where inexpensive and visible data recording and entry are desired.

Off-line storage otherwise is maintained on punched cards. The permanence, ease of storage, visibility, and ease of sorting make cards a very useful and flexible storage medium.

In this section we have discussed the types of physical devices available for storage of information. The devices available within a computer installation have great impact on the techniques employed in the data processing, file-structure definition, and data management systems that can be utilized. On the other hand, in the rare event when specific hardware components can be selected for a particular application role, greatest efficiency can be achieved by simultaneously trading off hardware capabilities and costs against anticipated data

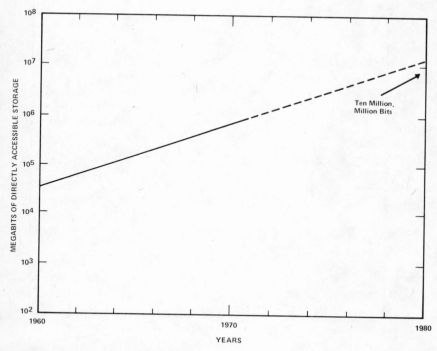

FIGURE 2.7. On-line files directly accessible to the computer. *(From J. T. Martin, ref. 12)*

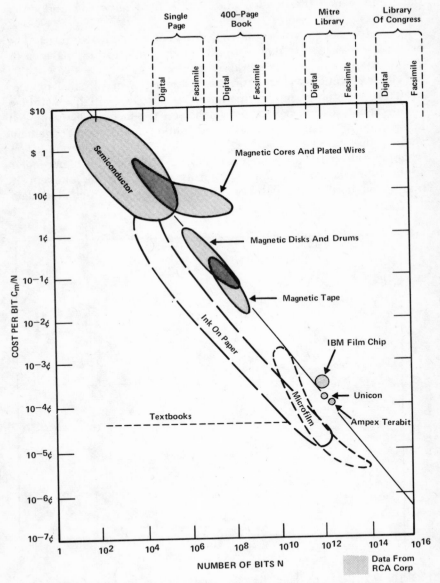

FIGURE 2.8. Trend in cost per bit. *(From P. N. Everett, ref. 15)*

processing storage requirements. This fact will become more evident after the reader completes the next section.

The future trends of machine-readable storage are toward larger on-line storage capacity with shorter access times. The trend in storage capacity is illustrated in Figure 2.7. It is estimated that by the end of the decade, more than ten trillion bits (10^{13}) will be able

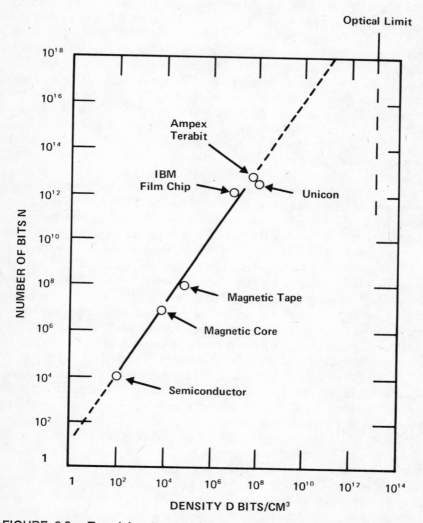

FIGURE 2.9. Trend in storage density. *(From P. N. Everett, ref. 15)*

to be directly accessible to a computer. The costs and capabilities of some typical devices are illustrated in Figure 2.8. The trend in storage density is illustrated in Figure 2.9.

Data Processing

The manipulation of data to structure it into files or restructure existing files and to compute or extract information from them is known as data processing. The set of instructions that causes the computer "hardware" to operate is known as the "software." Generally commercial machines have a basic set of operating instructions written in so-called machine language, which can be inserted into the machine from cards or magnetic tape to organize the electronic structure of the registers and memory for handling the data processing function. Except for certain machine-language programs that make use of the electronic structure of the machine to be very efficient, most software is written in a higher level language.[16, 17, 18] The most commonly used language for scientific work is FORTRAN (Formula Translator), while business applications generally use COBOL (Common Business Oriented Language). Other widely used general-purpose languages include BASIC, PL/1,[19] APL, and ALGOL.[20] Special-purpose languages have been developed such as GPSS and SIMSCRIPT for simulation [21] and Mark IV for large-file manipulation and maintenance.

In many cases the most important measure of data processing capability in a computer is the throughput in characters or bits per second. Figure 2.10 illustrates the past and future trends in this measure. Environmental applications that would find this measure important include the simulation of worldwide weather patterns, currently being carried out on a very high-powered machine by the National Center for Atmospheric Research, and the analysis of nationwide air and water pollution data, not yet underway.

One frequently ignored aspect of computerized environmental system is the process of updating system data. Much planning and presystem design analysis is often given to the process of data coding, computation, retrieval, and display. Unfortunately, less thought is put into the data collection implications of updating stored data.

The cost of maintaining data banks is high since much central processing unit (CPU) time and many system resources are utilized in this system function. Regardless of the magnitude of this cost, it does not include the cost that results if the data base becomes unused, even if not unusable. The confidence that a user has in the contents of the entire data base is greatly reduced when he finds

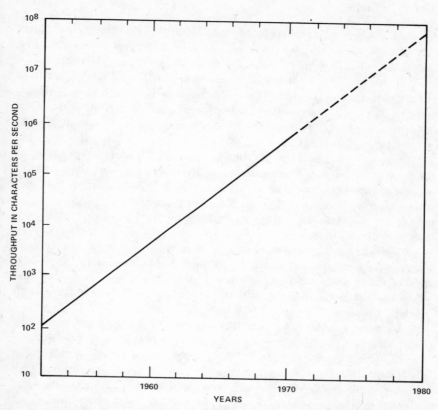

FIGURE 2.10. Computer power throughout trends. *(From A. H. Canada, ref. 22).*

even a few errors or data that does not agree with his personal expert knowledge of conditions.

The ultimate use of the data, analysis, and information system greatly affect the choice of file structure and data representation. In the design of algorithms and computer programs the data organization in computer memory and secondary storage (tapes and disks) can greatly affect both the efficiency and complexity of the algorithms. An appropriate data organization can make the performing of certain operations rather simple, while an inappropriate organization can make those operations extremely costly by wasting the system throughput capability.

File Structures

The inherent characteristics of individual data files—which must be considered in the selection of an efficient design and method of organization—are activity, size, growth, volatility, and retrieval.

ACTIVITY. The number of records to be processed during a run in relation to the total number of records present influences the design of the file. Data sets having low percentages of activity should be designed so that any record can be found quickly without having to examine all records of the file.

SIZE. For small files the design and method of organization is of little consequence, since processing time will be short regardless of the organization. For large files the method of organization becomes important if processing time is to be kept reasonable.

GROWTH. The file design should anticipate the growth rate over a given period of time.

VOLATILITY. The frequency of insertion and removal of records from a file measures the volatility of the file. The design and organization of static files, which have a low update frequency, are less critical then the design and organization of volatile files, which have high update frequency.

RETRIEVAL. The nature of the request for information contained in the file greatly influences the design and organization. When many records must be located to fulfill a single information request, the ability to obtain the necessary records quickly without examining all records, is desirable. Frequently requested information that requires calculation should be anticipated to eliminate redundant computations.

The above characteristics will vary among the individual files. Each file's requirements and characteristics should be examined to select the data structure and file organization most appropriate. These characteristics will also impact on the record content, the file sequence, and the selection of storage media.

There are many methods of organizing data files. They differ in the procedures used to create, integrate, and maintain the files as well as the efficiency with which they perform these tasks. Some are independent of special hardware and software, while others require unique capabilities of the hardware and can operate only with special software features. Two methods of file organization are sequential and indexed sequential organization.

SEQUENTIAL. This type of file organization, strictly speaking, is a positional organized file in which records are arranged according to a collating sequence of the data identification items, (record keys) that are unique. This organization makes the most economical use of storage since it is a simple organization (that is, the organization has only one structural pattern).

As long as the sequence in which access is required conforms to the file-organization sequence, record access is rapid unless a large number of records must be skipped. To access in a sequence other than file-organization sequence requires either a reordering of the file or exhaustive searching of the file for each record desired. Both alternatives involve time-consuming operations. Maintenance of such a file is straightforward. The file is completely written with inserted records placed in their correct sequence.

INDEXED SEQUENTIAL. This type of file organization is a sequential file with indexes that permit rapid access to individual records. More storage is required for indexed sequential files than for strict sequential, since storage space is required for the keys. Also, overflow storage areas (which can amount to as much as one-third of the file size) must be allocated for record insertions.

By reference to the record indexes, individual records can be quickly located when access is required in a random sequence. However, when records are accessed in sequence with few records being skipped and in the file-organization sequence, access time is slower than with strictly sequential files. Although maintenance of indexed sequential files does not require rewriting of the entire file, whether or not maintenance time for an indexed sequential file exceeds that of a strictly sequential file depends on the file volatility. For a small to moderate volume of insertions and alterations, maintenance time for this file organization is less than that of the strictly sequential.

Data Management Systems

An information management system (IMS) is a formal, organized approach to handling, coordinating, and enhancing data and information. This system differs from a management-information system (MIS). The IMS aims to satisfy information demands of multiple organizations, whereas the MIS aims to serve the managerial personnel of a single organization.

Inherent in each of the above systems is a data base management (DBM) system. This system controls the maintenance and utilization of stored data for various reporting and analytical purposes. A variety of generalized DBM systems exists from commercial software vendors which can easily be installed on most computer systems.[23, 24, 25, 26, 27, 28, 29]

With any data bank of a respectable size and complexity, the need for generalized and specialized language for updating and file maintenance is obvious. The National Aerometric Data Bank with more than 500 million characters uses MARK IV * for file structuring, file updating, file maintenance, and report generation. Actually there are over a hundred data management systems being marketed today, largely as proprietary software. These include, besides the MARK IV, IBM's NIPS and IMS, TRW's GIM, MRI's System 2000, Cambridge Computer Associate CCA 104 System.

The capabilities of most management information systems leave much to be desired from the standpoint of supporting management decisions. Most executives—even those with expensive computer systems—privately admit to keeping their own file on index cards or a little black book. The problem is that it is extremely difficult to predict what information the executive truly wants and will use. Experiments and demonstrations have been attempted with interactive techniques that allow the executive to query a data base by means of a keyboard and an index displayed on a display screen driven by the computer. No successful systems of this type are yet in operation outside of the military and NASA.

Time-Sharing and Computer Network

Because of the large initial cost of computers and the consequent need to keep them fully utilized in order to operate in a cost-effective manner, many corporations are turning to the use of time-sharing services. Time-sharing, or time-slicing, is a technique whereby a computer serves a large number of people at once. Each user has the impression that he is the sole user of the remotely located hardware. Besides saving time and money, time-sharing sets up a dialogue between users and the machine. Time-sharing computers, because of the interactive nature of their operations, are heavily used for program testing and debugging as well as for short programs and quick turnaround service.

The priority interrupt and input-output buffer capabilities developed to facilitate time-sharing also permit job entry from numerous remote terminals. There are some experimental data bases available in which the remote terminal user can search the data base, extract data, create his own files, manipulate them, make calculations, and restore data to the file. These sophisticated techniques will surely

* Proprietary System of Informatics, Inc.

become more important as the usage of environmental data becomes extended.

In order to augment the power of a remote time-sharing service, the concept of a computer network was advanced. The largest commercial network currently is the CYBERNET ® of the Control Data Corporation, a nationwide distributed network composed of heterogeneous computers, mainly CDC 6600s and 3300s linked by wideband communication lines. The CYBERNET is intended to make the computer utility concept available to all of its commercial users by offering the following services: "supercomputer" processing, remote access, multi-center network, file management, and applications library and support. Load sharing, data sharing, program sharing, and remote service on any available computer or on a specified computer are possible.

Other networks being developed include: (1) the MERIT network, a cooperative venture among Michigan State University, Wayne State University, and the University of Michigan; (2) the TSS network, serving IBM 360/67 computers at IBM Watson Research Center, Carnegie-Mellon University, Princeton University, Bell Telephone Laboratories at Lewis and Ames; (3) the TUCC, a cooperative venture among Duke University, North Carolina State University, and the University of North Carolina; and (4) the Advanced Research Projects Agency (ARPA) network, serving a wide variety of machines at over 32 locations across the country.

Through either local time-sharing services or these extensive networks, almost any conceivable computer capability is within reach of the environmental scientist.

Data Display or Data Output

The process by which data is made intelligible to the human using the machine is called data display. A wide variety of devices from the simple typewriter to the sophisticated cathode-ray tube (CRT) technology is available. A common classification is to separate hard copy output from devices not providing a permanent record. Typical output is provided through the teletypewriter for low-speed and small-volume output or through the line printer allowing output ranging from a few hundred to more than a thousand lines of output per minute.

Printers are also available for producing computer-generated graphs and charts. These "x-y" plotters can be quite sophisticated and are generally run off-line, that is, they are operated from data stored on magnetic tape while the computer is busy with primary processing tasks.

The cathode-ray tube (CRT) [30, 31] finds its full value as an interactive terminal allowing the display of complex schematics, flow-charts, and geometrical projections besides the more standard upper- and lower-case letters and numbers. The CRT terminal is most important because it forms an effective man-machine interface.

Computer output microfilm (COM) [32, 33] is the newest ally to computer with its smaller bulk, high recording density, easy manipulation, and reproduction; the microfilm is taking a place of increasing importance among the more traditional output devices. An added advantage is that, with microfilm output speed is increased. This is not to be neglected in a computer world where most jobs are input/ output bound.

Many specialized software packages have been developed to facilitate the use of these devices. Some are sufficiently generalized to be application independent, whereas others are so oriented to a specific display application that transfer to another application is difficult, if possible at all.

The hardware requirements of these packages vary from as few as 35K to a few hundred thousand bytes of main computer memory as well as tape drives and disk units for secondary storage. Typically these packages are coded in higher-level computer languages, but often machine-language subroutines are employed to take advantage of special or unique capabilities of the system for which the package was developed.

CONCLUSION

It is worth repeating that computers are electronic tools for rapidly handling large quantities of numbers or varying electrical signals. In acquiring a computer system careful analysis and planning are required, starting with identification of the basic, essential requirements that need to be met and continuing through the specification, installation, testing, and, finally, operation of the complete system.

REFERENCES

1. D. Eadie, *Modern Data Processors and Systems.* Prentice-Hall, Inc., Englewood Cliffs, N.J., 1971.
2. M. Sherman, *Programming and Coding Digital Computers.* John Wiley & Sons, Inc., New York, 1963.

3. *Computer Characteristics Review,* Vol. 10, No. 3. Keydata Corporation, Watertown, Mass., 1971.

4. R. F. Tomlinson, ed., "Geographical Data Handling." International Geographical Union Commission on Geographical Data Sensing and Processing, 1972.

5. J. T. Martin, *Telecommuncations and the Computer.* Prentice-Hall, Inc., Englewood Cliffs, N.J., 1969.

6. J. T. Martin, *Teleprocessing Network Organization.* Prentice-Hall, Inc., Englewood Cliffs, N.J., 1970.

7. B. M. Dawidziuk and H. F. Preston, "Comparative Evaluation of Modern Transmission Media for Global Communications." *Telecommunications Journal,* 38, 1971.

8. R. P. Witt, S. Barosin, and R. A. Culpon, "An Economic Comparison of Analog Versus Digital Based Common User Communications." The MITRE Corp., MTR-1930, August 1970.

9. Stuart L. Mathison and Philip M. Walker, *Computers and Telecommunications: Issues in Public Policy.* Prentice-Hall, Inc., Englewood Cliffs, N.J., 1970, p. 155.

10. Robert Toombs, "Considering Telecommunications? Select the Right Modem." *Computer Decisions* 3(7), 1971.

11. Paul Hersch, "Data Communications." *IEEE Spectrum* 8(12):47-60, 1961.

12. J. T. Martin, *Future Trends in Telecommunications.* Prentice-Hall, Englewood Cliffs, N.J., 1971.

13. David Mayne, "What's Next in Memories." *Datamation* 14(2):30-32, 1968.

14. H. E. Staehling, "Remote Access Storage Services." *Data Processing* 8:429-432, 1965.

15. P. N. Everett, "The Trend in Computer Memory Costs and Some Implications." The MITRE Corp., MTR-134, March 1972.

16. Bernard A. Galler, *The Language of Computers.* McGraw-Hill Book Co., New York, 1962.

17. Philip M. Sherman, *Programming and Coding Digital Computers.* John Wiley & Sons, Inc., New York, 1963.

18. James T. Golden and Richard M. Leichus, *IBM 360 Programming and Computing.* Prentice-Hall, Inc., Englewood Cliffs, N.J., 1967.

19. Frank Bates and Mary L. Douglas. *Programming Language One.* Prentice-Hall, Inc., Englewood Cliffs, N.J., 1967.

20. Charles Philip Lecht, *The Programmer's Algol: A Complete Reference.* McGraw-Hill Book Co., New York, 1967.

21. Francis E. Martin, *Computer Modeling and Simulation.* John Wiley & Sons, Inc., New York, 1968.

22. A. H. Canada, S. J. Turner, N. A. Wilson, "Some Comparative Trends in Telecommunications." The MITRE Corp., WP-9795, January 1972.

23. Robert V. Head, "The Elusive MIS." *Datamation* 16 (10), September 22-27, 1970.

24. Charles W. Nevendorf, "New Dimensions in Management Information." *Data Processing* 6: 42-69, 1967.

25. Frederick G. Withington, "Trends in MIS Technology." *Datamation* 16(2), 1970.

26. Carolyn J. Byrnes and Donald B. Steig, "File Management Systems: A Current Summary." *Datamation* 15(11):138-142, 1967.

27. J. Gosden and E. Raichelson, "The New Role of Management Information Systems." The MITRE Corp., MTP-332, April 1969.

28. J. P. Fry, et al., "Data Management Systems Survey." The MITRE Corp. MTP-329, Rev. 1, May 1969.

29. John B. Glore, "Major Problems of Generalized Data Management System Development." The MITRE Corp. M70-56, February 1970.

30. John A. Murphy, "Interactive ERT Terminals. I. Full Graphic CRT Terminals and Systems." *Modern Data* 4(6):44-55, 1971.

31. Robert A. O'Hare, "Interactive ERT Terminals. II. Alphanumeric ERT Terminals and Systems." *Modern Data*, 62-75, July 1971.

32. Charles P. Yerkes, "Microfilm a New Dimension for Computers." *Datamation*, 94-97, December 1969.

33. Anthony D. K. Carding, "Microfilm: EDP's Newest Ally." *Administrative Management*, 38-48, April 1970.

CHAPTER 3

THE USE OF COMPUTERS
IN MONITORING

MONITORING THE ENVIRONMENT OF THE NATION

Environmental monitoring is one of the keys to effective management of environmental quality. Monitoring support is essential in most stages of pollution abatement—from initially identifying environmental problems to finally providing direct evidence in enforcement actions. Decisions based upon monitoring results are far-reaching, requiring a comprehensive data base that is both accurate and reliable. This means that strong and dynamic monitoring programs are desirable at all levels—local, state, and federal.

At the outset various important terms should be defined. *Surveillance* is a broad term that describes the detection of conditions; in the environmental field it describes the detection of violations and is thus source oriented. *Ambient monitoring* is related to the quality of the environment and is more area- and/or receptor-oriented.[1] In this book surveillance and ambient monitoring will often be aggregate as monitoring and defined as the process of collecting environmental data for decision-making.

Active monitors are those that emit energy and detect the energy reflected, refracted, etc., from the environment and/or pollutant. A passive monitor only detects properties of the environment and/or pollutant using other sources of energy, such as the sun, to illuminate the target.

Remote monitors, which may be active or passive, do not come in contact with the target of interest. In-situ monitors are in contact with the target of interest. Platforms, such as aircraft, boats, towers, buoys, satellites, etc., do not dictate the classification (remote, in-situ) of the monitor; this point is sometimes overlooked and causes confusion.

35

Finally, there are in-situ monitors that may have remote data links (such as telemetry). It is to be understood that the nature of the communication link does not specify the classification of the monitor.

Monitoring includes the following types of activities: field sampling and measurement of environmental quality, emissions, and effluents; laboratory analysis of field samples; operation of technical information systems and data analysis; measurement sensor and technique development and testing; instrumentation and methodology standardization and quality control.

Monitoring Purposes and Needs

We see at least four basic types of monitoring systems currently in use (Figure 3.1).[2]

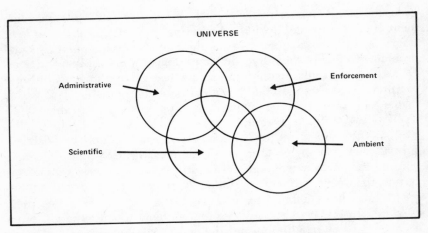

FIGURE 3.1.   Overlap in monitoring systems.

A surveillance system collects data in support of surveillance, compliance, and regulatory activities; this tends to be a source monitoring system. An administrative system collects and uses environmental data in the cycle of planning, budgeting, and assessing the impact of control programs. An ambient monitoring system collects data to determine the status of the environment. It usually contains a baseline-defining component and an early-warning aspect for episode conditions. Finally, a research and scientific system is aimed primarily at supporting effects studies. This system supports research activities including the identification of new pollutants, the in-depth study of problem areas, and the establishment of cause-effect relationships. A great number of variations and refinements can be conceived. We believe that the above taxonomy will be useful in the following discussion.

Data collected by means of monitoring programs provides the raw material that can be translated into valuable information for: (1) the continuing assessment of the effect of pollutants and pollution on man, the natural and the modified environment; (2) the detailed study of pollutant formation, interactions, synergism, and patterns; (3) the development, establishment, review, and enforcement of criteria, ambient standards, and industry performance standards; (4) The evaluation of the effectiveness of adopted control procedures and preventive measures (control devices, institutional modifications, monies, etc.); (5) planning resources used and product and process changes in order to minimize environmental impact; (6) Defining the need, direction, and intensity of future research programs.

Monitoring Programs

Currently monitoring programs (Table 3.1) are applied to all media and at all levels of our political-jurisdictional system. A number

TABLE 3.1

Some Federal Monitoring Programs

AIR

Continuous Air Monitoring Program (CAMP) [5, 6]
National Air Surveillance Networks (NASN) [7]
    Total suspended particulate network
    Membrane filter sampling network
    Gas sampling network
    Precipitation network
    Mercury sampling network
    Radiation alert network
    Anderson impactor network
    Metals and fractions information
Emission Data Information

WATER

Water Quality Control Information System (STORET) [8, 9]
    Fishkill information

Beach and shellfish bed-closings information
Water-quality standards
Water-quality measurements
Municipal-waste inventory
Municipal-waste implementation plans
Municipal-waste treatment-plant operation and maintenance information
Municipal-waste treatment construction grant needs assessment
Municipal-waste treatment-works contract awards
Voluntary industrial-waste inventory
Refuse Act Permit Program industrial-waste information
Federal Power Commission thermal-pollution information
Industrial-waste implementation plans
Manpower and training information

SOLID WASTE

Survey of community solid-waste products

RADIATION

Pasteurized milk network
Institutional diet network
Surface water network
Radiation alert network

PESTICIDES

Pesticides in water
Pesticides in air
Human tissue levels
Fishkill

SOURCE: Bisselle et al, ref. 1.

of federal monitoring networks are in operation; state and local agencies contribute heavily to the monitoring efforts; and special studies are sponsored by a variety of interested groups. The role played by the Environmental Protection Agency by comparison with state agencies can be derived by comparing the number of active stations in 1973 (Table 3.2).[3]

Extensive surveys of monitoring activities in the U. S.[4] and around the world have been completed. We will not repeat this material here, but will provide a rapid overview of monitoring in the major medias.

TABLE 3.2

Number of Active EPA and State Monitoring Sites

Media or Pollutant	Number of Sites	
	EPA	STATE
Air	826	4785
Water	128	680
Pesticides	2298	275
Solid Waste	—	—
Radiation	492	7614
Noise	—	—
Totals	3744	13,354

SOURCE: Blacker & Burton, ref. 3.

Air

There are over 9,000 state and local air polution measuring sites in the United States, in addition to the various sites shown in Table 3.3.[10] Of six air pollutants for which ambient standards have been issued by EPA, only two—SO_2 (sometimes sulfation) and particulates —are monitored on an extended geographical basis.[10]

Water

Water monitoring antedates, is more widespread, more diffuse, and more complex than, air monitoring.

There are approximately 24,000 water quantity (hydrological) stations and 15,000 water quality stations (chemical combination), which are operated by local, state, and federal agencies (Table 3.4). Note that quality and quantity parameters are often collected at the same time. The monitoring stations currently cover approximately 44,000 stream miles, 5,000 miles of Great Lakes shorelines, and 4,000 miles of coastlines and estuaries.[11]

Pesticides

The dangerous effects of pesticides are a problem in all three media. The currently minimal monitoring of pesticides in air is conducted by EPA and also by the FDA in eight northeastern states.

TABLE 3.3

Federal Air-Sampling Networks

Hi-Vol Network	suspended particulates; 247 sites; 26 samples/site/year
Membrane Filter Network	suspended particulates (no glass filter interference); 50 sites
Particle Size Network	particle size distribution; 11 sites
Gas Sampling Network	several gaseous pollutants; 197 sites; 26 samples/site/year
Precipitation Network	dissolved air pollutants in rainwater; 16 sites
Mercury Network	airborne mercury; 53 sites
Condensation Nuclei Network	one site
Radiation Alert Network (RAN)	airborne radioactive particles and radioactive contamination of rainwater; 73 sites; continuous daily sampling; this network may be phased out due to decreased atmospheric nuclear testing
Pesticide Network	airborne pesticides; 12 sites collecting but method for analysis has not yet been fully developed; in future, 40–60 sites

SOURCE: Bisselle *et al*, ref. 4.

Pesticide monitoring in water and on land is performed much more widely and more frequently than in air. A number of governmental agencies are involved in the National Pesticides Monitoring Program.

Radiation

A description of the major radiation surveillance and monitoring programs conducted in the United States, Canada, and Mexico has been published.[12] More than 42 networks measuring radioactivity in milk, food, air, water, and other material have been compiled.

Recent court decisions relating to the necessity of the Atomic Energy Commission to file complete environmental-impact statements regarding power plant construction suggests greater requirements for monitoring radioactivity and water temperatures in the vicinity of power plants.

TABLE 3.4

Summary of Water-Data Acquisition Stations, 1970

Agency	Surface-Water Stations	Water-Quality Stations	Groundwater Stations	Areal Investigations Miscellaneous Activities
Agriculture	132	46	—	76
Commerce	983	65	—	16
Defense	1,888	771	880	91
Interior	18,239	5,920	23,376	1,312
AEC	—	614	362	—
EPA	—	630	—	114
TVA	133	141	172	61
Other	149	46	—	1
Federal subtotal	21,524	8,241	24,790	1,671
Nonfederal	2,322	6,443	4,174	95
Total	23,846	14,684	28,964	1,766

SOURCE: Blacker & Burton, ref. 3.

Solid Waste

Information on solid waste is mostly concerned with volume, amounts, composition, and source. For planning purposes responsible agencies would like to know the composition of domestic and industrial refuse at specific locations for large urban areas as well as for rural locations. Often monitoring consists of physical sorting of garbage, which is costly and time-consuming, and subsequent recording of volume, composition, weight, etc. Scales are sometimes used in measuring loads at incinerator and landfills. In cases of industrial refuse the data is likely to be obtained from sampling surveys utilizing interviews or written questionnaires.

Noise

Recently the problem of noise pollution has received a great deal of attention, but an organized, carefully conceived monitoring program does not exist. The Bureau of Community Environmental Management has undertaken a few urban surveys, but these are mostly subjective, and it would be difficult to make comparisons among cities on a year-to-year basis. The FAA is conducting monitoring in the vicinity of airports to support noise-abatement programs. The Department of Transportation also has several studies underway to determine the amount and effects of highway noise.

Subsidence

The detection and monitoring of small movements of the earth's surface is in its infancy. The mechanism responsible for the surface movement is settlement of land into subsurface cavities that were formed during underground coal mining operations.[13, 14]

Biogeochemical Cycles

There is much concern today about the health of ecocycles, and ecology textbooks inevitably include diagrammatic pictures of the transformations among the various physical, chemical, and biological processes involved. However, relatively little substantive knowledge exists on how, when, or where to measure accurately the "health" of such cycles. Biogeochemical cycles (such as nitrogen, water, oxygen, carbon, phosphorus) are recognized to be fundamental to the support of life on earth. These cycles are complex and are not yet fully understood. The amount of material transported and the vastness of the geographic scope (i.e., the surface of the earth) render any monitoring attempts currently impractical.

THE ROLE OF COMPUTERS IN MONITORING

While monitoring devices and networks are growing as fast as pollution itself, only a handful of monitoring systems make use of on-line, real-time data acquisition and processing systems. On the other hand, each and every one of the monitoring networks investigated uses some form of computer in the discharge of their function, though most applications are of an administrative or data analysis nature.

In order to give the reader a sense of "real world" we will describe actual operating systems as examples. Four types of systems will be described: (1) ambient monitoring system, (2) source monitoring, (3) remote sensing, and (4) laboratory automation. The chapter will conclude with an example of detailed specifications for an automated air-monitoring facility, comparing a single with a multisite system, and a comparative anatomy of alternative computer systems.

First we describe an integrated overall paper concept for computerized environmental systems. This concept will then serve as a model and as a road map for further analysis. The systems concept was developed for the Environmental Protection Agency and is only partially implemented.

NADIS. The National Aerometric Data Information Service, NADIS [15, 16], is a systems approach to collecting, storing, and retrieving data in order to provide a systematic and timely flow of environmental data to and from a central depository—for instance, EPA's National Aerometric Data Bank (NADB). However, the basic concept and operation of NADIS can be expanded beyond aerometric data to include other environmental data. The Administrator of the Environmental Protection Agency has been given the responsibility by Congress of carrying out the provisions of the Clean Air Amendments Act of 1970. To meet this responsibility the Agency must be responsive to all the air-pollution information needs of federal, state, and local governments, as well as to the general public.

Aerometric data, as defined and used herein, are air quality data, stationary-source emissions data, stationary-source inventory data, meteorological data, and mobile-source emissions data. For the sake of simplicity only air-quality data will be discussed in subsequent pages. Any data base, however, could be substituted. Air quality was chosen because that data base is in the most advanced stage of development and could serve as a basis and format for developing other data bases.

Before developing any system of handling air-quality data, goals must be set forth (Figure 3.2). The basic concept for NADIS is that all

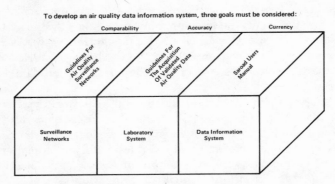

FIGURE 3.2.   Basic considerations. *(From R. P. Ouellette. J. Golden, & R. S. Greeley, ref. 15)*

air-quality data entered in the National Aerometric Data Bank will be comparable, accurate, and current. *Comparability* is determined by uniform surveillance techniques throughout local, state, and federal networks. The first concept is discussed in a document entitled "Guidelines: Air Quality Surveillance Networks." *Accuracy* of measurements is discussed in the guidelines document, "Guidelines for the Acquisition of Validated Air Quality Data." [17] The formating and coding scheme to be used is discussed in another guidelines document, "The SAROAD User's Manual." [18] This last document discusses the recording of data in a uniform format, the Storage and Retrieval of Aerometric Data (SAROAD) format. In the following discussion we will show how *currency* of the data can be assured by NADIS.

System Description. An overview of NADIS is presented in Figure 3.3. The headquarters for handling air-quality data will be the EPA's computer center in Research Triangle Park, North Carolina. Basic standardized software will be used in the National Aerometric Data Bank operations, whereby all air-quality data will be stored and processed in the SAROAD format. Each state will be connected to the computer by dataphone so that exchanges of data can be handled

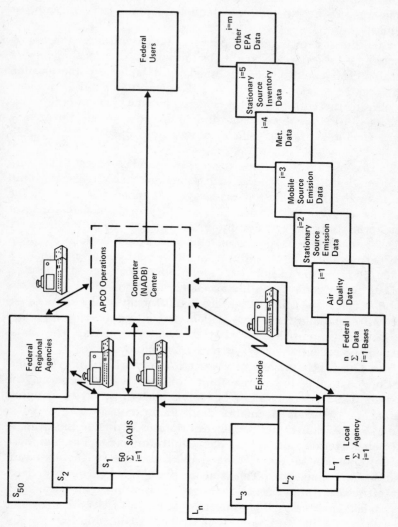

FIGURE 3.3. A NADIS overview. *(From R. P. Ouellette, J. Golden, & R. S. Greeley, ref. 15)*

45

expeditiously when necessary. Each of the ten federal regional offices will also have dataphone capability to query both the headquarters and the state center, the State Air Quality Information System (SAQIS). Depending on the type of information system required, local agencies may or may not have dataphone capabilities with SAQIS or headquarters.

When the system is fully implemented, EPA will have the option of querying during episode conditions the SAQIS or the local agency, if applicable. This could be accomplished via dataphone if the location undergoing the episode is so equipped. This is merely a more advanced procedure of the current practice of EPA, in which many cities have arrangements to telephone data during episodes to an Emergency Control Center in the EPA offices in Research Triangle Park, North Carolina.

During periods when there are no episodes, statistically summarized and validated air-quality data in the SAROAD format would be sent to the EPA computer center via dataphone or through the mails on such recording devices as magnetic tape, punched cards, or paper forms, whichever is appropriate for the agency concerned. These inputs would be processed and stored in the National Aerometric Data Bank. The central computer facility currently has an IBM 360/50 computer to store data and produce the necessary outputs.

Data in the NADB is readily accessible and structured for various types of query. The size of the data bank for air-quality data is expected to eventually reach five billion characters, covering all states and including approximately 10,000 monitoring sites. The data-management system MARK IV* is currently employed.

The Clean Air Amendments of 1970 explicitly state that air-pollution control is the responsibility of the states. Therefore, the SAQIS serves as the key building block for NADIS to gather comparable, accurate, and current air-quality data. Each state agency serves as the data-acquisition center within the state, and thus is the primary focal point. The respective state data-acquisition centers are responsible for providing necessary data-analysis support to the local air-pollution-control agencies. This is accomplished by utilizing standardized software possibly furnished by EPA or by employing the rapid-access facilities of NADIS. Through state, local, and federal cooperation technical assistance can be rendered within a reasonable time.

Every local surveillance program has three main functions to perform: (1) collect and validate data; (2) reduce it to SAROAD

---

* The MARK IV is proprietary software developed by Informatics, Inc., Bethesda, Maryland.

format; (3) transmit it to SAQIS. The exact nature of these functions depends on the degree of sophistication of the particular surveillance program.

Five classes of information systems have been defined within the NADIS concept.[19] The characteristics of each of the five classes are shown in Figure 3.4. Data transmission from surveillance networks ranges from highly sophisticated telemetry systems to completely manual systems utilizing high-volume (hi-vol) samplers and sulfation plates. Classes II and III have semiautomatic data-transmission capabilities during episodes. The class of information system required for a particular area is determined by factors such as potential for episodes, severity of episodes, size of agency, available personnel to operate the system, and geographical area covered.

The EPA returns validated air-quality data summaries to all state and local agencies on a scheduled or as-needed basis. In addition, agencies desiring to expand or improve their programs are able to receive standard software packages, on-the-job training for their staff, and consultation and technical assistance from EPA.

Valid air-quality data gathered in a particular state is reduced by SAQIS and forwarded in SAROAD format to EPA for entering into the NADB. Each quarter these data are summarized and returned to the appropriate agency or user. Because any data in the NADB is a matter of public record, the summary data can be circulated widely. The data summary for each state could be made available quarterly through the National Technical Information Services.

The EPA uses of the data include such activities as: showing progress of states toward meeting air-quality standards; enforcing Section 303, "Emergency Powers," of the Clean Air Amendments of 1970; supporting criteria document revision; identifying areas requiring intensified surveillance and abatement efforts; and developing comparable, accurate, and current air-quality data. In addition, EPA would be capable of responding to requests from the public, other government agencies, and state agencies, and would also be capable of developing data-acquisition guidelines for international studies.

The Current Operation. As part of the National Aeromatic Data Information Service (NADIS), five classes of air-quality information systems have been defined.[20] These theoretical classes have been used to catalog all existing air-quality agencies that operate surveillance systems. Approximately 223 air-pollution-control agencies currently record aerometric data, and all were part of our 1971 survey.[21] Most of these agencies operate a system with more than one site. The degree of sophistication of their surveillance programs varies greatly. Some systems sample manually once a month for one pollutant, while others sample with automated instruments for a number of pollutants every few minutes. The rest of the agencies have programs that operate somewhere between these two extremes. Each existing surveillance system has been assigned to the class whose specifications most closely matched those defined in Figure 3.4 (see Table 3.5). Table 3.5

Class	Instrument Characteristics	Data Transmission (Highest Order)		
		To EPA From SAQIS	To SAQIS From Local	To Local From Sampling Site
I	Automated	Dataphone	Dataphone	Online Telemetry
II	Automated	Dataphone	Dataphone	Manual Retrieval: (Dataphone Used During Episode)
III	Automated And/Or Mechanical	Dataphone	Dataphone	Manual Retrieval: (Warning System Used During Episode)
IV	Automated And/Or Manual	Dataphone	Mail	Manual Retrieval
V	Manual	Dataphone	Mail	Manual Retrieval

FIGURE 3.4.   Classification of NADIS information systems. *(From J. Golden & L. Duncan, ref. 19)*

TABLE 3.5

Present Local/State Information System Configuration

Total Air Pollution Agencies	245
Class I	12
Class II	9
Class III	0
Class IV	74
Class V	126
Unknown	2
Do not operate	22

was constructed from a knowledge of the air-quality data that the air-pollution-control agencies monitor and from information on the mode of data transmission from the local sampling site to the central data-acquisition facility. It was found, however, that most of the networks did not exactly meet all of the requirements for any particular class. Therefore, agencies have been placed into a specific class based on their "nearness" to that class. Those locations that have a mixture of surveillance systems—e.g., telemetered and hi-vol—were categorized by the higher class represented. A number of states (at least 12) already operate as SAQIS centers.

The National Aerometric Data Bank [21] contains some 400 million characters of air-quality data from some 9,000 sites throughout the nation. The data bank covers the period from 1965 to the present, with some data going as far back as the early 1950s.

Ambient Monitoring

Most computers are found in environmental monitoring of air and water. Tables 3.6 and 3.7 provide an overview of the major systems in operation today. It is expected that more such systems will be installed, with a series of automated monitoring networks eventually covering the major pollution centers. Despite variation in purpose, hardware, software, mode of transmission, and display features, these automated systems follow a basic pattern. A representative air and water monitoring will be described in some detail below.

A Case of Air Monitoring

Most computerized monitoring systems proceed with digitization at the remote site followed by digital-data transmission over leased phone lines to a central facility for data manipulation and storage.

Some conditions and/or applications make analog data transmission more desirable. The desire for live displays similar to a strip chart recording, short distance between remote stations and central terminal, high data rate associated with rapidly changing phenomena and the availability of analog front-end hardware are usually quoted as justifications for such systems. The slowly varying signals associated with environmental monitoring, the availability of solid-state analog to digital converters, and single or cascade multiplexers are capable of handling the typical data rates encountered. Except for very short distances (a few miles), there is no advantage of one mode of transmission over the other. In the final analysis the expertise of the in-

TABLE 3.6

Water-Monitoring Systems

Agency	Remote Stations	Transmission	Computer	Parameters	References
New York Department of Environmental Conservation	14	Digital, leased telephone line	B-500	DO, Cl, Fl, pH, conductivity, turbidity, temp., water stage height	28
Potomac			Data Logger		
ORSANCO	14	Digital, leased teletype grade line	IBM 1130	pH, ORP, DO, Cl, conductivity, temp; solar radiation	25,26,27
Florida Dept. of Air and Water Pollution Control	1	Digital dedicated telephone line	HP 2114B	DO, pH, conductivity, temp.	

TABLE 3.7

Partial List of Automated Air-Monitoring Networks

Agency	Computer	Number Remote Stations	Transmission Link	Transmission Mode	Wind speed/direction	Temperature	Humidity	Sulfur oxides	Particulate	Nitrogen dioxide	Nitrogen oxide	Total oxidants	Carbon monoxide	Hydrocarbons	Aldehydes	Hydrogen sulfide	Total oxides nitro.	Peripheral and Central Computer Equipment Characteristics	Reference
Los Angeles County	Litton 512	12	Telephone	Digital	X	X	X	X	X	X	X	X	X	X			X	Teleprinter, card punch, disk memory, display map, mag. tape	29
Wayne County (Detroit)	"	13	"	"	X			X	X	X	X	X	X	X				Teleprinter, mag. tape, data-display board	
St. Louis	"	8	"	"	X	X		X	X	X		X	X	X				Teleprinter, mag. tape	
Puget Sound APA	"	10	"	"	X			X	X				X					Teleprinter	
Columbia Willamette APA	"	8	"	"	X			X	X				X	X				Teleprinter	
Dade County	"	1	"	"	X	X		X	X	X		X	X	X				Teleprinter, mag. tape, lighted map, data-display board	30, 31, 32
Chicago	"	8	"	"	X	X		X	X			X	X						
State of Illinois (Primary)	"	4	"	"	X	X		X				X	X			X			
State of Illinois (Secondary)	"	8	"	"	X	X	X	X	X	X	X	X	X	X	X				
State of Delaware	"	4	"	"	X	X		X	X			X	X					Teleprinter	
State of Maryland	"	4	"	"	X	X		X	X			X	X					Teleprinter, mag. tape	
Province of Ontario	"	14	"	"	X	X		X	X			X	X				X	24K memory, 9-track Kennedy tape, ASR 35	33
State of Connecticut	Bristol		"	Analog															
New York State	B-3500	11	"	Digital	X	X		X	X	X		X	X	X					28, 34
New York City	PDP-8		"	Digital															
State of New Jersey	Spectra 70/45	17	"	Analog	X	X		X	X			X	X					Strip chart	
Allegheny County	IBM 1800		"	Analog	X	X	X	X	X	X		X	X		X			8K-16 bit memory, 1 million-bit disk storage	22, 23, 24
Netherlands	Philips-P9201	31	"	Analog				X										12K-16 bit memory, teleprinter	35, 36
Pennsylvania	IBM 1800	25	"	Digital	X			X	X			X	X					32K-16 bit memory, teleprinter, mag. tape, disk storage	37, 38
Denver	Climet Inst.	18	"	Digital					X										
El Paso	IBM		"	Digital				X											

vestigator and availability of hardware are deciding factors in selecting an analog or a digital system.

Since we will describe a digital system in water monitoring, an analog monitoring system will be described here.[22, 23, 24]

While analog transmission of environmental data does not appear to be the preferred mode of transmission, a sufficient number of systems exist to describe this approach. We have selected as our model the Allegheny County part of the Pennsylvania network.

This system is typical of many networks based on an analog data transmission. Differences exist, of course, since each system must be designed to meet local data collection needs and be built around existing capabilities and with specific budget constraints.

The Allegheny County of Pennsylvania approach is shown in block diagram form in Figures 3.5 and 3.6.

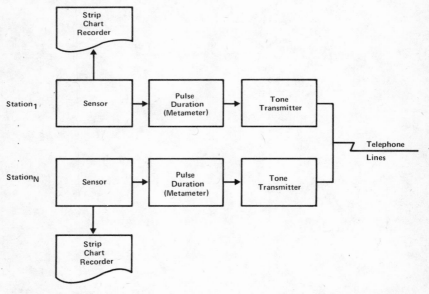

FIGURE 3.5.   The remote station. *(From E. L. Stockton & W. C. Shook, ref. 24)*

The central computer is an IBM 1800 model. This is a 40-microsecond, 8K, 16-bit words system operating under a time-sharing executive system and allowing for 12 levels of priority interrupt.

Seventeen remote stations continuously collect a variety of parameters, including: five particulates, hydrogen sulfide, sulfur dioxide, ozone, hydrocarbons, carbon monoxide, solar radiation, humidity, temperature, wind speed and direction.

The analog signals generated by the sensors are displayed on site on multipoint strip chart recorders. A pulse-duration metameter and a tone transmitter complete the electrical complement at each remote site (Figure 3.5).

At the central station (Figure 3.6), the tone receivers demultiplex the input signals and feed the component frequencies to slide wire receivers, in turn converting the pulses back to the original voltages.

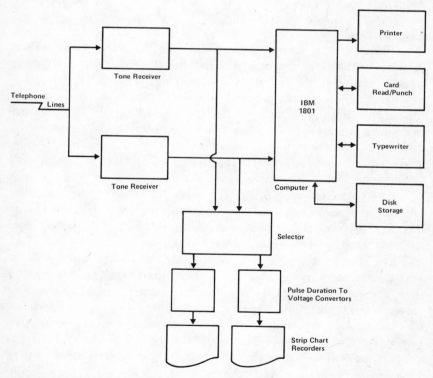

FIGURE 3.6.   The central station. *(From E. L. Stockton & W. C. Shook, ref. 24)*

The voltages activate strip chart recorders for display purposes. The computer reads the signals through digital input contact into an accumulator register. The remote sensors operate on a 15-second signal. At this point the computer software starts messaging the data, which is finally stored on direct-access storage devices and displayed numerically on a line printer.

Two Cases of Water Monitoring

The ORSANCO *Story.*[25, 26, 27] Probably one of the most successful attempts at water monitoring is the Ohio River system (ORSANCO), which comprises 961 miles of main streams and 19 major tributaries offering the entire spectrum of micro water habitats. The rapid industrialization along its rivers has resulted in all possible man-made point and diffuse discharges in addition to natural influences on the water system. Dilution from storage reservoirs, the operation of dams, and changes in rainfall and runoff further complicate the hydrologic picture.

The system is not an on-line, real-time data-acquisition system. An intermediate step is required to link the site data on paper tape to a traditional off-line data base and processing facility.

Seventeen stations, or robot monitors, mark the course of the river measuring the following water characteristics: pH, oxidation reduction potential (ORP), chloride-ion concentration, specific conductance, temperature, and solar radiation. Each remote station consists of flow cells and detectors, the actual electrical measuring instruments, and a recorder and transmitter.

Raw data from each of the 17 stations is transmitted to a central facility for processing, analysis, and indicated actions in order to comply with local water quality standards. The data is digitized prior to being transmitted over leased telephone lines.

The central station is built around an IBM 1130 computer. Tape and disk storages are available. The headquarter station interrogates each station sequentially over leased telephone circuits. The data as received from the station is immediately displayed on a teleprinter. The information is simultaneously punched on an 8-channel, one-inch paper tape that is subsequently fed to the computer. The digital computer is programmed to perform a variety of analysis on this raw data base.

Adding one level of sophistication and tying the computer directly on-line with the monitor via a leased telephone line is the case

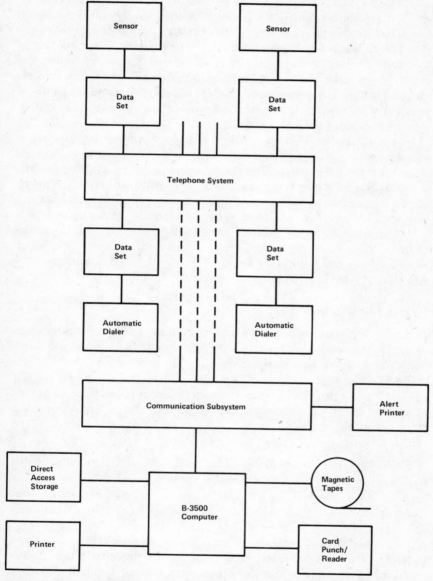

FIGURE 3.7. System diagram. *(From* Chemical Engineering, *ref. 29)*

of the New York State Surveillance System.[28] The data-processing configuration is diagrammed in Figure 3.7.

Three types of monitors in use are: (1) major monitor facilities, (2) minor monitor facilities, and (3) satellite monitor facilities.

Major Monitor Facilities. Major monitor facilities measure ten or more environmental parameters, transmitting the data digitally and directly to the central computer. The remote station is made up of the environmental sensors with their associated probes, reagents, and electrical circuits; the automatic sampler to collect a water sample for analysis by the sensor; and the functional command and control equipment, allowing the computer and/or the operator to control various components of the stations.

Minor Monitor Facilities. Minor monitor facilities are capable of measuring ten or less parameters. This monitor uses the same type of telemetry equipment as that used for the major monitoring facility.

Satellite Monitor Facilities. Satellite monitor facilities are small, compact, specialized stations within short distances of a major station. The data collected is usually transmitted via radio to a major station.

The central station built around a Burroughs B-3500 computer controls the remote stations. This is a time-sharing computer which allows other computer functions to be performed simultaneously while the system is collecting environmental data from the remote sites.

Source Monitoring

Few cases of source-monitoring systems using computers are currently operational. This is not to say that both manual and automatic devices are not in use to monitor air and water effluents from well-identified sources.

Below we describe two experimental setups to monitor the operating and emission characteristics of an electric power generating station and the emission from a coke-oven charging battery. These setups are quite elaborate since the facilities are used to test the effectiveness of experimental control devices. Simplified versions of these monitoring facilities would be used in routine process control or enforcement surveillance.

The Cat-Ox Process

The Catalytic Oxidation Project [39, 40] at Illinois Power is a joint project of the Environmental Protection Agency and the Illinois Power and Light Company to test the Monsanto Catalytic Oxidation Process to remove SO_2 emitted from power plant stacks. The system has been installed at the Wood River facility of the Illinois Power Company in Alton, Illinois.

The purpose of the test program is to evaluate a flue gas SO_2 cleaning device and to collect basic information on its performance under a wide variety of operating conditions. Because of the number of parameters under study and the volume of data involved, it was felt that an automatic data-acquisition system was essential. The data-acquisition system selected, besides meeting the technical requirement of supporting the entire test program, needed to be rugged enough to operate under adverse conditions of high temperature, noxious gases, and unpredictable weather.

The catalytic oxidation process is one of a family of flue gas SO_2 removal systems. In this process the sulfur dioxide in the gas stream is converted, in the presence of a catalyst, to SO_3. This last chemical is combined with water to form a diluted sulfuric acid, which must be disposed.

Figure 3.8 shows the flow diagram of the Cat-Ox process, which is of the reheat type and has been installed between the existing induced-draft fans and the stack. The electrostatic precipitator is regarded as part of the Cat-Ox process because it was installed with the Cat-Ox equipment and is required by the process to minimize contamination of the catalyst in the converter.

Flue gas from the boiler passes through the economizer and air heater and then enters the mechanical collectors, where particulates are initially removed. Particulates are further reduced to a very low level by the electrostatic precipitator. During the course of this flow the gas temperature has dropped to approximately 400° F., and therefore it must be reheated prior to entering the converter. The SO_2 in the flue is then converted to SO_3 and combined with water vapor in the absorbing tower to formulate sulfuric acid. The mist eliminator removes any sulfuric acid mist that may escape from the absorbing tower with the flue gas. Because of the pressure drop throughout the process, a second I.D. fan is required to make up the losses and restore flow to the stack. Acid from the absorbing tower and mist eliminator is pumped, cooled, and finally stored in a large tank from which it can be periodically removed.

Figure 3.9 shows the points at which measurements are taken and the parameters that are measured at each point, and the reasons for making particular measurements (Table 3.8). The significant parameters that will be measured by continuous recording instrumentation are gaseous concentrations of sulfur dioxide (SO_2), water vapor, oxygen (O_2), carbon dioxide (CO_2), oxides of nitrogen (NO_x), and

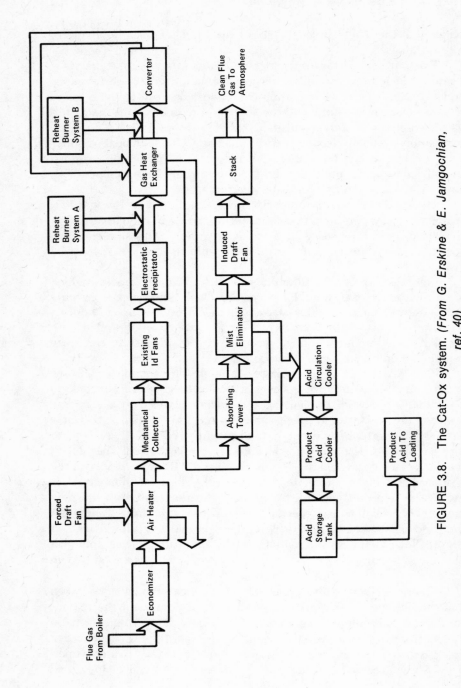

FIGURE 3.8. The Cat-Ox system. (*From G. Erskine & E. Jamgochian, ref. 40*)

58

TABLE 3.8

Measurement Points for One-Year Cat-Ox Demonstration

Point	Location	Parameters Measured	Reasons for Measurement
1′	Prior to economizer	SO_2, O_2, flow, temperature, static pressure	Confirmation of baseline test conditions
2′	Air heater	Mass loading (manual measurement)	Determination of efficiency of mechanical collector
1	Inlet to electrostatic precipitator	Mass loading, flow, temperature, static pressure	Determination of efficiency of electrostatic precipitator, pressure drop across electrostatic precipitator and total Cat-Ox system
3	Outlet from electrostatic precipitator	Mass loading, flow, temperature, static pressure	Determination of efficiency of electrostatic precipitator and pressure drop across electrostatic precipitator
4	Flue gas to gas heat exchanger	SO_2, flow, temperature, static pressure	Determination of efficiency and leakage of heat exchanger as a function of flow rate
5	Flue gas from gas heat exchanger to converter	SO_2, O_2, CO_2, flow, temperature, static pressure	Determination of efficiency and leakage of heat exchanger as a function of flow rate
6	Flue gas to converter	SO_2, O_2, CO_2, flow, temperature, static pressure	Determination of % conversion as a function of flow rate, temperature, and time
8	Flue gas from converter to heat exchanger	SO_2, SO_3, O_2, mass loading (manual measurement)	Determination of % conversion as a function of flow rate, temperature, time; and rate of ash "buildup" as a function of time

59

TABLE 3.8 (Continued)

Measurement Points for One-Year Cat-Ox Demonstration

Point	Location	Parameters Measured	Reasons for Measurement
10	Flue gas entering absorbing tower	SO_2, SO_3, H_2O, flow, temperature, static pressure	Determination of efficiency and leakage of heat exchanger as a function of flow rate and formation of H_2SO_4 in absorbing tower as a function of time
11	Exit from mist eliminator	SO_3 (H_2SO_4 mist), flow, temperature, static pressure	Determination of efficiency of mist eliminator as a function of flow rate
13	Flue gas to stack (downstream of new ID fan)	Temperature, static pressure	Pressure drop across Cat-Ox system
14	Midway in stack	SO_2, CO_2, O_2, NO_x, flow, temperature, static pressure, mass loading (manual measurement)	Determination of power plant emissions

SOURCE: Burton et al, ref. 39.

60

total hydrocarbons (THC). Also differential pressure, static pressure, and temperature will be recorded continuously to obtain gaseous volume flow, system pressure drops, and gas temperatures. In addition, manual measurements will be made of gaseous SO_3, sulfuric acid (H_2SO_4) mist, and particulates.

These measurements will be utilized in subsequent analysis to determine subsystem performance of the power plant and Cat-Ox process as follows:

Efficiency of the mechanical collector
Efficiency of the electrostatic precipitator
Pressure drops across process subsystems and overall system efficiency of the heat exchanger
Percent leakage of heat exchanger
Efficiency of converter
Gas distribution in converter

The data logger and function controller diagrammed in Figure 3.12 are part of an overall measurement system designed to evaluate the performance of the abatement process for the rmoval of sulfur dioxide from power plant emissions. The measurement system determines the concentration of gases, particulates, and mists and the corresponding velocities, temperatures, and pressures from which will be derived mass flow. The output of the instrumentation is recorded simultaneously on strip charts/printers and magnetic tape. All instrumentation is calibrated automatically when possible.

The data-acquisition system is required to record, in digital format, the electrical output of up to 50 devices. The outputs from the devices will be 0–1.000 VDC. A total data-scan operation and the resulting data record is computed within a 2-second time period for 50-channel input. Initiate commands from the computer start the scanning sequence from one second to one scan sequence/hour in integral steps.

Each initiate command, resulting in a scanning operation, constitutes a data record. Each data record is to be preceded by a time label including: Julian days, hour of day, and minute of hour.

The data are recorded on nine-track incremental magnetic tape with a packing density of at least 800 bpi. The data format is compatible with an IBM 360/50 (EBCDIC) used in subsequent data reduction.

An analog scanner is used for polling the individual measurement devices. The scan has a minimum input capability of 50 channels. The input voltage is 0–1.000 VDC; however, the scanner will withstand an overvoltage of up to 50 VDC. It can perform in a single-scan mode of operation, continuous-scan mode, remote-control-scan

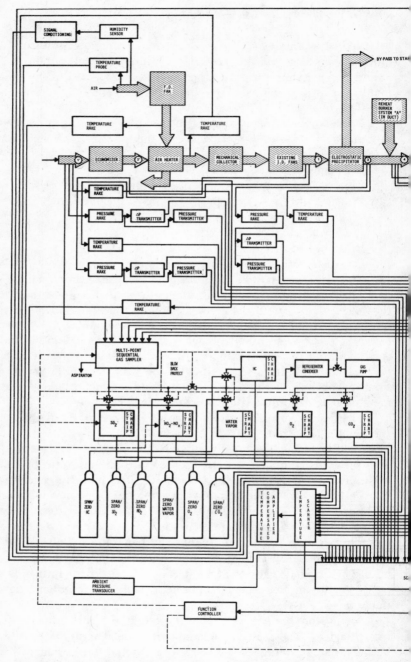

FIGURE 3.9   Cat-Ox instrumentation system. *(From J. S. Burton,* et al, *ref. 39)*

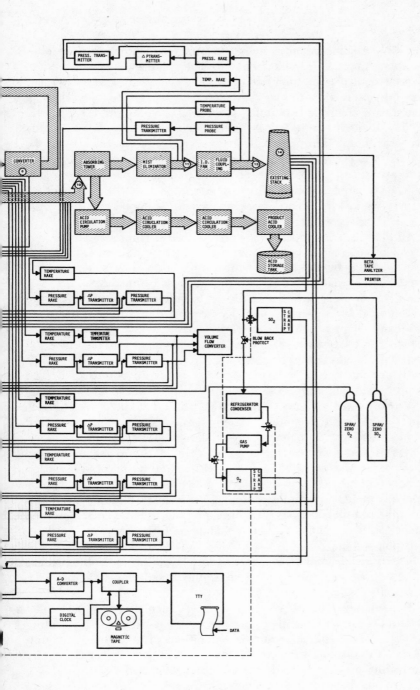

mode, and channel-monitor mode. Scanner synchronizing signal is selectable: internal, external, manual. There are run, advance, stop, and reset controls for manual operation. The scanner also supplies channel identification to the data coupler. In remote operation all functions are controlled digitally, including channel address.

The analog-to-digital converter is used for converting analog signals to digital information. The A/D converter operates over the range of 0–1.000 VDC with a 100 percent overrange capability, with overall accuracy of ±0.02 percent. It can withstand overvoltage of up to 50 VDC without damage. Conversion rate is 2×10^{-2} seconds. A time-of-day clock is incorporated to provide time-label information for each data record.

All data-acquisition functions are controlled from a single source. The clock and timing control functions operate synchronously. Functions controlled by the timing control are: initiate scan, enable A/D converter, clock data, and initiate time output command.

A data-coupling device is employed to buffer and format data from the scanner, A/D converter, and clock and to output the data to an incremental magnetic tape recorder. The data coupler provides an I/O interface for teletypewriter and incorporates manual data entry via thumb wheel switches.

An incremental magnetic tape unit records all output data. The tape is a nine-track unit, 800-bpi packing density, and IBM compatible.

A teletypewriter (TTY) is employed as an input/output device to the data-acquisition system. When enabled, the TTY prints out all data (in parallel with magnetic tape) and produces a punched paper tape. As an input device the TTY writes directly onto magnetic tape via keyboard. Additionally paper tape is read on the TTY and recorded on magnetic tape.

The function controller initiates various start-stop commands to perform control functions wtihin remotely located devices. The time sequence is synchronous with the timing control system of the data-acquisition system.

The function controller system consists of four subsystems: the time-base unit, the time-control unit, the line-driver unit, and the switch unit.

The function-controller system operates such that up to six time-control units are capable of driving a single line-driver unit, resulting in up to six independent sequential operations of that line-driver unit per hour. In addition, each time-control unit has the driver capability of activating up to six line-driver units simultaneously.

The time-base unit is synchronized and slaved to the system

timing control of the data-acquisition system. It is a one-hour time reference (59 minutes, 59 seconds full count), recycling at the end of the hour. The time-control unit initiates time-selectable start/stop commands.

The line-driver unit accepts input from up to six separate time-control units. This is to allow two or more remote functions to be performed sequentially. Each switch unit accepts the output of one line-driver unit. It, in turn, makes or breaks a 110 vac, 60 Hz circuit at a 300 watts maximum.

The Coke Oven Emission-Control and -Monitoring System

The American Iron and Steel Institute (AISI) and the Environmental Protection Agency (EPA) are cosponsoring a production-prototype coke-oven-charging pollution-control program at the Jones & Laughlin Pittsburgh Works.[41, 42] During coal-charging operations, there are considerable emissions to the atmosphere. The program is concerned with substantially reducing these emissions. AISI's major area of effort is with the construction of the prototype charging car and its proper operation, and EPA's major area of effort is the evaluation of the system's emission control function.

COKE PLANT EMISSIONS. The process of converting coal into coke may be divided into six areas of operation. These operations, associated with the generation of emissions, are shown in Figure 3.10. They may be outlined as follows:

OPERATION	EMISSIONS
Coal Preparation—coal is pulverized ⅛ inch top size, blended, and oiled.	Coal dust
Charging—coal is loaded on larry car, carried to oven, discharged into hot oven.	Coal dust, smoke, gas
Coking Cycle—pulverized coal is destructively distilled at 2000°F. for 17 hours.	Smoke, gas
Pushing—at the end of the coking cycle, coke is pushed out of oven into hot-coke car.	Coke dust, smoke
Quenching—hot-coke car goes to quenching station, where coke is water sprayed to cool.	Coke dust, contaminated water
Coke Preparation—coke is crushed and screened to yield furnace coke (1″), nut coke (¼″), and breeze (fine coke).	Coke dust

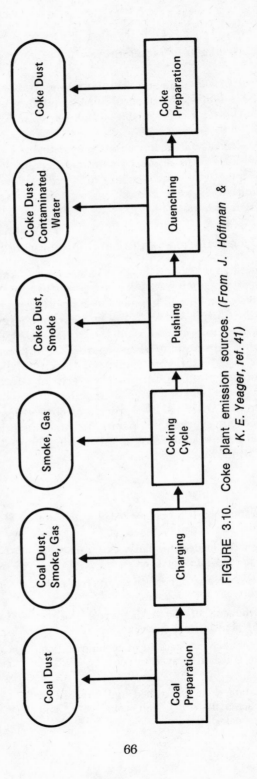

FIGURE 3.10. Coke plant emission sources. *(From J. Hoffman & K. E. Yeager, ref. 41)*

66

THE OBJECTIVES OF THE PROGRAM. The purpose of the program is to evaluate the efficiency of the proposed abatement system involving switching the coal-charging larry car from the Wilputte car to the improved Koppers car with seal. The new charging car has an environmentally controlled operations cab, an automatic charging system, an automatic lid lifter, and a hopper coal seal. Additionally, the doors on the coke oven battery have an improved seal and the emissions are redirected into a by-product recovery system.

THE CONTINUOUS-MEASUREMENT SYSTEM. The environment of a typical coke oven facility is depicted in Figure 3.11. In order to measure the effectiveness of a new control system during the charging process, a complex and automatic instrumentation array was developed.

In order to capture pollutants released during charging, an annulus was designed to fit over the larry car drop sleeve in order to capture and channel the emission. During the charging process emissions are monitored at three points: within the annulus, in the stack of the charging car, and in the outside atmosphere generally surrounding the coke oven.

The overall measurement system for continuously measuring gases, particulates, and physical parameters of the pollutants is shown in Figures 3.11 and 3.12. A gas probe inserted into the annulus draws a portion of the gas through a heated particulate filter assembly from whence it is conducted by means of a heated sampling line to the gas analyzers located in the instrumentation van. The gases are kept hot to prevent condensation of the water vapor which would otherwise cause erroneous readings of the SO_2 and H_2S concentrations. Also, the hydrocarbons must be maintained at high temperature to prevent condensation. Subsequent to the measurement of SO_2, H_2S, and hydrocarbons, the water vapor is removed to prevent corrosion of the analyzers which follow. The system for measurement of gases in the ascension pipe (stack) is identical to the system just described except that fewer gases are measured.

Particulates are measured at both the annulus and ascension pipe. Particulates are normally sampled isokinetically. In order to minimize particulate losses the particulate sampling probe must be short and aerodynamic. As a result the particulate sampler is located outside the instrumentation van in close proximity to the annulus and stack.

The gas-measurement system provides the percentage concentation of the gases. In order to obtain the mass concentration it is necessary to measure the volume flow of the gases. At present this is accomplished by measurement of differential pressure, static pressure,

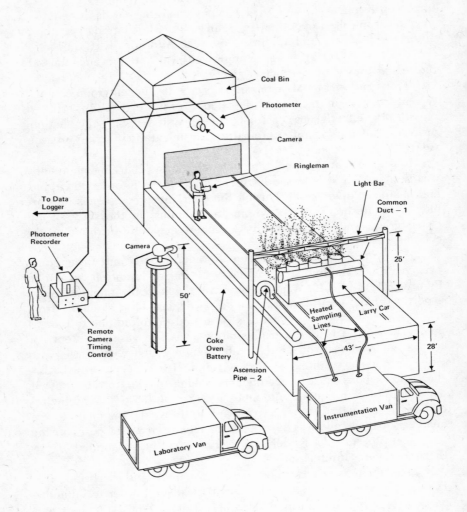

FIGURE 3.11. Schematic coke oven measurement program. *(From J. Hoffman & K. E. Yeager, ref. 41)*

68

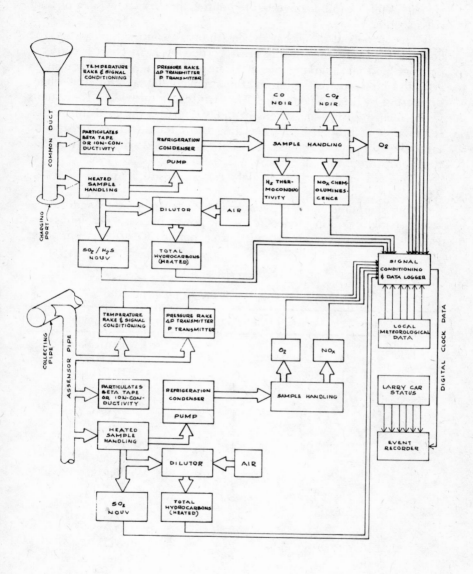

FIGURE 3.12.   *(From A. J. Epstein,* et al, *ref. 42)*

and temperature. This combination of measurements provides the gas velocity, which can be converted to volume flow by knowledge of duct cross section.

The outputs of the gas analyzers, the particulate samplers, and the flow-measurement transducers are recorded on strip chart recorders/ printers and are simultaneously transmitted to a data-acquisition system, which records the information on magnetic tape for subsequent processing by a large computer. The strip charts provide a continuous visual record during measurement indicating that the instrumentation is functioning properly. By recording the data directly on magnetic tape, the subsequent reduction of data is speeded while, at the same time, costs are reduced.

The gas analyzers, particulate samplers, are itemized in Table 3.9.

The sampling of coke oven emissions is different from the relatively steady conditions encountered in power plants, where emissions can be sampled over an extended time period. Coke oven emissions

TABLE 3.9

Analyzers and Associated Equipment

Item	Location	Parameter
1	1	Particulates
2	1	SO_2/H_2S
3	1	HC (total)
4	1	O_2
5	1	H_2
6	1	CO
7	1	CO_2
8	1	NO_x
9	1	Heated S.H.
10	1	Refrig/cond.
11	1	Dry S.H.
12	2	SO_2
13	2	HC (total)
14	2	O_2
15	2	NO_x
16	2	Heated S.H.
17	2	Refrig/cond.
18	2	Dry S.H.
19	2	Particulates

SOURCE: Epstein *et al,* ref. 42.

occur during the short 120-second charging operation. During this time interval emissions rise rapidly in bursts, spurt to some maximum value, and then decay gradually to a lower level. Consequently, an important criterion in the selection of the gas-analyzer instrumentation is the instrument response time. The limited information available indicated that the instrumentation used for coke oven emissions should have a response time of less than five seconds. In most cases the instruments shown in Table 3.9 have response times of approximately one second.

PHYSICAL MEASUREMENTS AND DATA RECORDING. In addition to the gas concentrations, the volume flow of gases must be measured in order to determine the mass flow. This is normally accomplished by measurement of differential pressure, static pressure, and gas temperature. These three measurements are combined to determine gas velocity and then volume flow of the gas from knowledge of the duct cross section. A block diagram of the system for measurement of the physical parameters is shown in Figure 3.13. Measurements of gas flow are made at both locations 1 and 2.

Because the duct cross sections are large at both these locations, multiple point measurements are required for differential pressure and temperature. Pressure and temperature rakes (multiple point source) are utilized to determine the average differential pressure and average temperature at both locations. The outputs of the differential/static pressure sensors and temperature sensors are fed to differential pressure, static pressure, and temperature transmitters. The outputs of the transmitters at the common duct are converted to volume flow by a volume flow computer so that the gas flow can be controlled to the desired level during the charging operation. The outputs of the volume-flow computer and the transmitters at the ascension pipe are simultaneously recorded on strip charts and magnetic tape.

Larry car status is monitored with an event recorder. Significant events that are recorded are initiation of charging, initiation of common duct fan, completion of charging, and replacement of port covers.

Wind direction, wind velocity, barometric pressure, relative humidity, and ambient temperature are recorded for correlation with the optical measurements.

Motor-Vehicle Emission Monitoring

An important and growing area of source testing is the monitoring of vehicular emission, either for research or for certification purpose. Among the interesting systems in operation, we have chosen

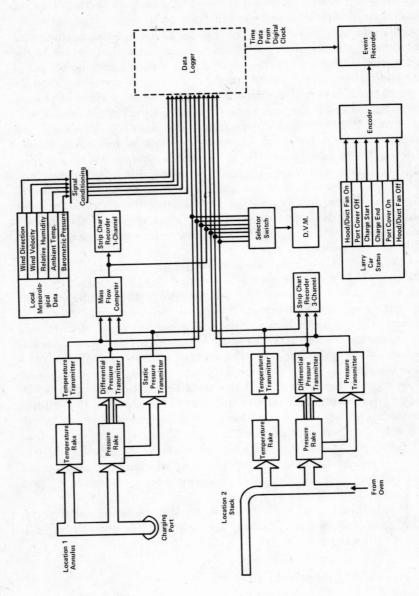

FIGURE 3.13. (*From A. J. Epstein, et al, ref. 42*)

for brief description here the General Motors approach and the EPA Michigan Certification Laboratory.

THE GENERAL MOTORS EMISSION-TESTING FACILITY.[43, 44] The digital-data acquisition and computer-data reduction for the California vehicle-exhaust emission test is part of the much larger research laboratory of General Motors.

The emission test block diagram consisting of 3 test stands and a meteorological station is shown in Figure 3.14. The hub of the system is the IBM 1800 data-acquisition and process-controller computer. The 1800 is a 32K, 16-bit word computer, with two seven-track magnetic

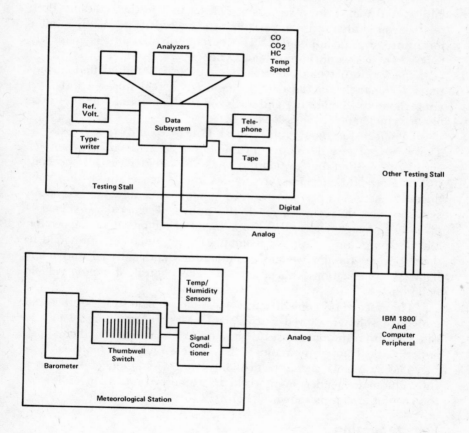

FIGURE 3.14.   Auto-emission monitoring block diagram. *(From R. F. Spain, Y. G. Kim, & R. V. Fisher, ref. 44)*

tape transports, a line printer, a keyboard printer, and a card punch/ reader. Communication between the computer and the test stalls, some 200 feet away, is by dedicated wires using both analog and digital input/output.

More specifically, the remote system (each stall) consists of signal conditioners to adjust the output signal from each gas analyzer to a range comparable with the computer, a circuit to convert speed pulses to DC voltage, a thermocouple reference junction for gas sample and radiator coolant temperature, analog recorders, a manual data-input channel, a display panel, a private telephone, an IBM typewriter, and an audiotape for driver commands. Barometer, humidity, and temperature sensors are all located in the building. Both relative humidity and temperature are recorded in the computer for future data manipulation. The barometric pressure is manually entered by means of thumbwheel switches.

The California mode emission test cycle is initiated under computer command, and the data is acquired in real time (a test lasts approximately 18 minutes) and analyzed to characterize fully both the motor vehicle and its emissions.

EPA DIVISION OF MOTOR VEHICLE POLLUTION CONTROL (DMVPC).[45] The DMVPC of EPA develops and administers a national program for certifying, testing, and evaluating methods and devices for the control of air pollution from automobiles. Surveillance studies are conducted to ascertain performance of automobile manufacturers' control systems once the vehicles reach the public. Technical asisstance is given to state agencies in the development of motor vehicle inspection and test programs. Liaison is maintained and guidance is provided to domestic and foreign vehicle manufacturers and national and international organizations concerned with the control of motor vehicle pollution.

The test data obtained from vehicle emissions testing is processed and the results are stored in two data bases. Information selectively retrieved from the data bases is the input to analytical, mathematical, and statistical programs required for vehicle pollution analyses.

The system is currently evolving from a data-logger basis to a fully automated and computerized real-time system. An overview of the current system is shown in Figure 3.15.

Remote Sensing

Remote sensing, while not a new concept, is only now finding wide application as an integral part of the arsenal of environmental monitoring devices. Remote sensing is easier to define by what it is not.

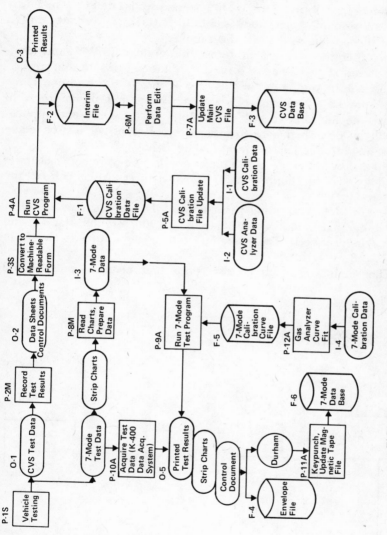

FIGURE 3.15. DMVPC data-base preparation. *(From the MITRE Corp., ref. 45)*

75

It is not in-situ monitoring. Remote sensing is applicable to sources as well as ambient monitoring situations. It can be used to monitor a variety of pollutants in diverse media.

Three types of platforms are in general use: a satellite, typified by the earth resource technology satellite (ERTS); an aircraft; and a ground device removed from the sample.

The literature is vast in terms of applications,[46, 47] and compendium and state-of-the-art surveys [48, 63] are starting to appear.

The role of computers in this area is mostly the traditional one of handling large volumes of data in analog and digital form to facilitate the interpretive task of the investigator. Only one application will be described here to ensure completeness of our coverage and as an introduction to this growing field.

The NASA ERTS program is a major application of remote sensing [58] technology to the improvement of efficient management of the earth's resources.

From a data processing point of use, the system is made up of three integrated components: the satellite, the ground station, and the tracking network. The overall system configuration is shown in Figure 3.16.

The satellite payload consists of a four channel multispectral

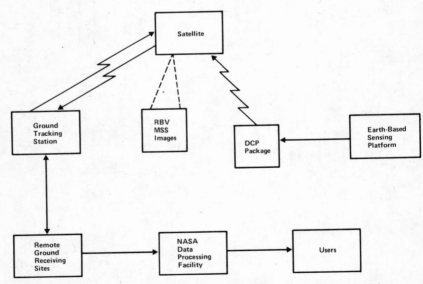

FIGURE 3.16.   The ERTS system. *(From NASA, ref. 58)*

scanner (MSS), a three camera return beam vidicon (RBV), and the space-borne portion of a data collection system (DCS) to collect data from ground-based stations.

The NASA space tracking network consists of three stations: at Fairbanks, Alaska; Goldstone, California; and Greenbelt, Maryland.

The earth-based sites vary greatly in configuration and purpose, but each is connected to the satellite via a data-collection system.

All data collected by the satellite is transmitted to the operation control center via the NASA Communications Systems. The NASA Data Processing facility provides the data-handling compression needs of the program.

Laboratory Automation

Environmental monitoring almost means an impossible mass of samples and raw data. Since most monitoring networks still use basic wet chemistry methods, the bulk of analyses is performed on samples collected in the field and brought to a central laboratory for processing and analysis.

Complex instruments such as gas chromatography, mass spectometer, and optical instruments have all been successfully automated.[64-79]

Instead of compiling an exhaustive list of such applications, we describe in some detail one such application, presenting a before and an after automation picture.

We will now describe the manual operation of a postulated federal or state laboratory handling a great many hi-volume filter paper samples. We will then suggest one among many possible automation approaches.

The Present System

The current operation [80] of the laboratory system for handling and analysis of filters is seen in Figure 3.17. The solid lines represent the main path of flow of the samples and data. The dotted lines indicate second flow and feedback paths.

The first step in the process is the purchase of filters to supply all sites for a substantial period of time (say one year). When the filters are received in the laboratory, each one is screened for holes, numbered, and weighed. The number and weight are recorded on a sample weight sheet. Representative filters are analyzed in the laboratory to determine background levels of the various pollutants.

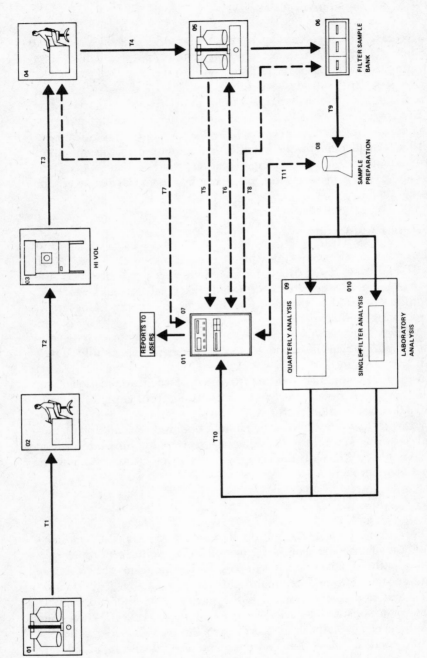

FIGURE 3.17. Filter processing and analysis, present configuration. *(From J. Garrison, et al, ref. 80)*

78

The data on background levels is filed for later use in the analysis of particulates.

One year's supply of filters is boxed with return envelopes and blank Particulate Record Sheets (PRS). Information on the site number, filter number and weight is recorded and filed.

A year's supply of filters is mailed to the operating site. The field operator collects a 24-hour sample on the hi-volume filter. The operator then fills out a Particulate Record Sheet with the following data: site location, date of sample, filter paper number, hi-volume sampler number, flow meter reading, sample time, and remarks on unusual activities.

The filters with the Particulate Record Sheet are then mailed back to the central laboratory.

The sample information is logged into a record book. The filter is then visually inspected for holes or misalignment in the hi-vol. The information on the Particulate Record Sheet is then transcribed to a Particulate Data Card (PDC), which is non-machine-readable. The weight of the filter is then looked up in the file and entered on the PDC. The calibration curve for the hi-vol used is obtained from the file to convert flow meter readings to true flow rate.

Filters are weighed and the weight is recorded on PDC. Samples of weight, air volume, and concentration of total suspended particulates are calculated and recorded on the PDC. A record book is kept in the laboratory of the site of total suspended particulate (TSP) values.

Filters are cut in strips and stored in a sample bank for further analysis. Particulate Data Cards for one quarter are sent to the data processing center. Data is punched on computer cards. The cards are sorted by state, station, site, and date of sample. Tabulations of the data are then printed. Preliminary tabulations are sent to the laboratory for checking and returned with corrections. Corrected quarterly tabulations of TSP are sent to the laboratory.

Appropriate filters are pulled from the file when a predetermined quantity is acquired (between five and seven samples per site in a given quarter). Composite samples are prepared for analysis. Quarterly composites are analyzed for metals, benzene soluble organics, and benzo(a)pyrene, etc.

Data from analysis, after some calculations and calibration corrections, is sent to the data processing center. Final computations of pollutant concentrations are made. All concentration data is punched on cards. Tabulations of concentrations are printed and stored in the data file. Tabulations are sent to the laboratory for checking and returned with corrections. Summaries of data are sent to field operators.

Identification of Points of Automation

The major factors that warrant changes in the future system operation are: projected large increases in number of samples to be analyzed, and increases in types of analysis. These factors will only magnify the present shortcomings of the system. These shortcomings include: (1) long delay between sample analysis and tabulations; (2) long delay between preliminary results and final documentation; (3) need for feedback paths and for data validations; and (4) unnecessary manual transcription of data from one form to another.

In general, an automated laboratory would offer the following major improvements to the current operations: faster turnaround time, more efficient use of manpower, and increased reliability of data.

The design philosophy of the laboratory complex is strongly dependent on the number of samples to be processed and the desired turnaround time. In general, with larger workloads and a greater demand for rapid data analysis, further automation of the process becomes more advantageous in terms of efficiency and accuracy. The workload refers to the total number of samples entering the system and the various analyses required for individual or composite samples. Turnaround time refers to the elapsed time between when a sample enters the system and when the results of the analysis are entered into a data file. If the data is used not as part of an alarm system but as a general/environmental trend measuring function, the following times are typical. For single filter analysis, no longer than one week. Analysis of composites should be completed and entered into the data file no later than one month after the end of the composite period.

The most time-consuming factors in the laboratory analysis are, in general, not due to the operation of analytical instruments but to the time required for sample transportation, sample preparation, sample identification, and calculation of concentrations.

Automation will eliminate the calculations made on raw data and assist in sample identification, but it will not have any impact on the sample preparation for analysis. The requirements for laboratory equipment and procedures for the operation of an upgraded system will not be as sensitive to changes in workload as would be manpower requirements.

A primary purpose for automating the laboratory is to obtain a more efficient operation. Factors such as reduction of the manual transcription of data, instruments on-line to a computer, elimination of hand calculations, data editing software, and improved sample-identification procedures all increase the efficiency of analysis as well as its validity.

Some of the laboratory system procedures would be unaltered by automation of the system. Key points of automation would be recording of filter weights, entry of data recorded at site, computation of total suspended particulates, determination of composite samples, instrument calibration, sample identification, recording of instrument data, and computation of pollutant concentrations.

A major difference in the handling of samples is in the area of record-keeping. The present procedure is to include the data with the filter as it passes through the system. This operation requires transcription of the data from one form to another several times. Much time is spent in manual searching of record books to look up information to be added to the sample record. Each manual data entry offers the possibility of introducing errors into the records. A prime use of any automated system would be to eliminate much of the manual data handling by entering data directly into a suitable computer-compatible form. The entry of data into the record (computer memory for the automated system) would occur at the point the data is first obtained. Additional data entry would contain "filter number" as the basic identifier.

For the computation of total suspended particulates, the parameters of data entry would be initial weight of filter, filter number/site number, data from Particulate Sample Record sheet, and weight of loaded filter. All the information would be stored in a computer memory, and computation of total suspended particulates would then be done on the computer. The response time and the format for the display of results is a function of the type of configuration. Editing subroutines would be included in part of the computation of TSP to check for excessive deviations from expected values.

An interim step to improve the operation of the system would be to record the data directly onto computer cards in the laboratory instead of following the present procedure, which requires the following separate and somewhat redundant documentation:

Sample weight sheet
Particulate Sample Record
Laboratory filter record book

Particulate Data Card
Cumulative work list of suspended particulate values
ADP record books
Computer card
Computer tabulation

The computer cards obtained directly should then be processed on a daily basis at a central computer facility, which would maintain a data file on all filters. The filter number would be sufficient information for identification in the data file.

Proposed Configuration

We now describe one alternative automation scheme using a dedicated minicomputer.[80]

This configuration is characterized by using individual on-line, dedicated minicomputers connected through analog-digital (A/D) interfaces to specific instruments. The system is designed by obtaining from each individual instrument manufacturer his recommended interface between analytical instrument and A/D conversion. The minicomputer selection is made by consulting with instrument manufacturers for their recommendations based on previous experience with instrument/minicomputer systems.

The total system operation with the minicomputer configuration is illustrated in Figure 3.18. The data entry to the minicomputer is through a teletypewriter or directly from a laboratory instrument.

The minicomputer used for recording filter weights would also maintain a file containing all the information on a filter prior to and including the final weight. Computation of total suspended particulates could then be performed on the minicomputer. The data file containing filter and station characteristic information could be maintained on a magnetic tape.

The minicomputers that are connected to the analytical instruments could also perform all the computations required for determination of final chemical concentrations. It would be necessary to enter calibration data and store information on the total volume of the sample. The concentration value could then be displayed at the instrument on the teletypewriter. This would provide an immediate check for validation of the data.

The outputs from the minicomputers would also be magnetic tape, which could then be sent to the central computer facility. The concentration data on tapes would be added to the data bank maintained on the larger computer.

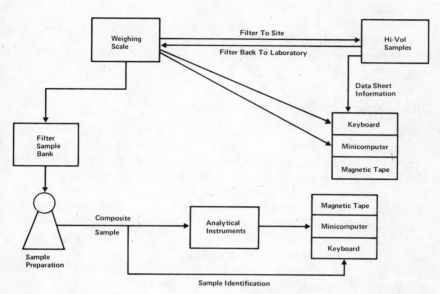

FIGURE 3.18.   Proposed configuration. *(From J. Garrison,* et al, *ref. 80)*

Further Automation

The automation scheme mentioned above is the first step. If the volume of data, the complexity of operation, and the number of analytical steps are very large, additional automation aspects could be included. For instance, a computer could generate machine-readable tags to provide positive sample identification. These tags could contain such items as filter and hi-vol identifiers, the date they should be used, etc. Mark-sense cards could be included for recording necessary additional data at the collection site. An optical scanner would then add this data to the master file.

THE DESIGN OF A MONITORING FACILITY

In this section we will outline the steps and recommendations for the optimal design of a monitoring facility. We will first present general configuration requirements, then analyze alternate data-acquisition and data-analysis schemes.

The need for monitoring the environment has been well documented. Informal and formal lists of priorities exist. Advice concerning the organization of a monitoring facility [81,82] and actual specifications [83,84] abound. While the pertinent literature is vast, the practice is most disappointing. We leave to others the arduous task of organizing this field and move to our immediate interest, the use of computers in a monitoring facility.

Data-Acquisition Systems—General Overview

Data-acquisition systems may be either analog or digital and may or may not include a computer. An analog data-acquisition system without a computer could, for example, be built around a multichannel tape recorder. Or, a data-acquisition system could be built around an analog computer. A digital data-acquisition system without a computer would probably include an input scanner, an analog-to-digital converter, and a digital tape recorder or memory unit. A digital converter would, of course, be the focal point of an computer-directed digital data-acquisition system.

Digital data-acquisition systems are normally categorized as high-speed or low-speed. One manufacturer (Hewlett-Packard Co.) offers low-speed systems, which operate at input scan rates of 40 channels per second, and high-speed systems, which operate inputs at a rate of 100,000 channels per second. Such systems are used, respectively, to gather data on relatively static and on rapidly changing or transient processes.

A typical digital data-acquisition system is shown in Figure 3.19. The transducer and signal conditioner are normally included in the basic measuring equipment, with the signal conditioner providing the power for the transducer and the amplification for the transducer output. The input scanner (or commutator) sequentially samples the multiple inputs, while the signal converter translates the analog signal (from the scanner) into a format acceptable to the analog-to-digital converter. An example of signal conversion would be rectification of an oscillating signal with varying amplitude to obtain a DC voltage equivalent to the original amplitude. The coupler restructures the digital data it receives from the analog-to-digital converter to a format suitable for storage or printout. Manually generated data or any data already in digital form can be entered directly at the coupler, where it can be associated with the analog data entering at the scanner. The coupler, incidentally, may be a relatively simple digital network or it may be a digital computer.

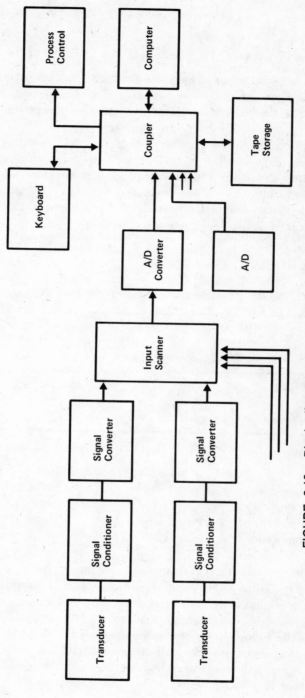

FIGURE 3.19. Block diagram of a digital data-acquisition system. *(From R. P. Ouellette & J. Garrison, ref. 85)*

85

Alternative Systems

The sophistication in hardware and software can cover the entire spectrum from data logger to minicomputer to midi- or maxicomputer. The location of the data-acquisition system can be at the remote site or at a central facility. Of the numerous options that are feasible, we will describe three popular options: single dedicated centralized computer, data-logging system at the site, and automated remote processing and central data recording. To simplify understanding, these three alternatives are further defined in Table 3.10 in terms of the location—remote or central—of the computer, the digitization equipment, and the final storage of the data.

TABLE 3.10

Data-Acquisition and Processing-System Options

Option	COMPUTER LOCATION Central	Remote	DATA STORAGE Central	Remote	DIGITIZATION Central	Remote
1	X		X			X
2		X		X		X
3		X	X			X

These alternative systems are provided as three points on a continuous spectrum of possibilities. The actual selection of a system will depend on the purpose of the monitoring program (alarm, trend, etc.), the number and types of pollutant to be measured, as well as the computations required. This theme will be addressed in detail in Chapter 6.

There exist many points of similarity among the three alternatives considered. In order to limit repetition common subsystems such as analog-to-digital converter, time clock, etc., will be described in detail for only one of the three alternatives.

In the following section reference will be made to mini-, midi-, and maxicomputer systems. For convenience we will characterize these three sizes of computers as shown in the following table, indicating size and expense:

	Mini	*Midi*	*Maxi*
Word length	12 bits	16 bits	32 bits
Primary core (words)	8K	16K	32K
Cost range (dollars)	5-30K	30-150K	150K

Single Dedicated Central Computer [84]

SYSTEM CONCEPT. This configuration is characterized by using one dedicated midicomputer connected through analog-digital (A/D) converter and multiplexers to instruments. Descriptions of remote-station (Figure 3.20) and central-station functions (Figure 3.21) follow.

REMOTE STATION FUNCTIONS.

Signal Conditioners. The main function of the signal conditioners is that of isolating the various sensor output signals and converting their voltage levels so that they fall within a common voltage range for subsequent utilization. Typically, either through the signal conditioners or directly from the sensor devices, an analog signal for each sensor device is available for input to an analog strip chart recorder and on-site visual display.

The signal-conditioning circuit should provide the following features: amplification to the desired voltage levels of the multiplexer, 60 Hz suppression, cross-coupling suppression, high-frequency noise suppression. All signal conditioning can be done with off-the-shelf electronic equipment.

Electronic Calibration. The function of the electronic-calibration component is that of supplying known precision voltage to a specified signal conditioner upon command for checking the operation of the entire system. These substitute voltages may, for example, be equal to 10, 40, or 80 percent of full scale of the output signal for the specified sensor device.

Chemical Calibration. Chemical calibration can be performed either automatically or manually. Here a known concentration of gas is introduced into each specific sensor. If the response is greater than ± 5 percent of the input, the output voltage is adjusted so that it corresponds to the input value.

Analog Strip Chart Recorders. Analog strip chart recorders are used for visual display, historical records, and for sensor trouble-shooting. The produced charts can also be used as backup for the automated system in the event of a system failure.

Multiplexer. A multiplexer is used at each remote station to connect each signal conditioner sequentially to the analog-to-digital

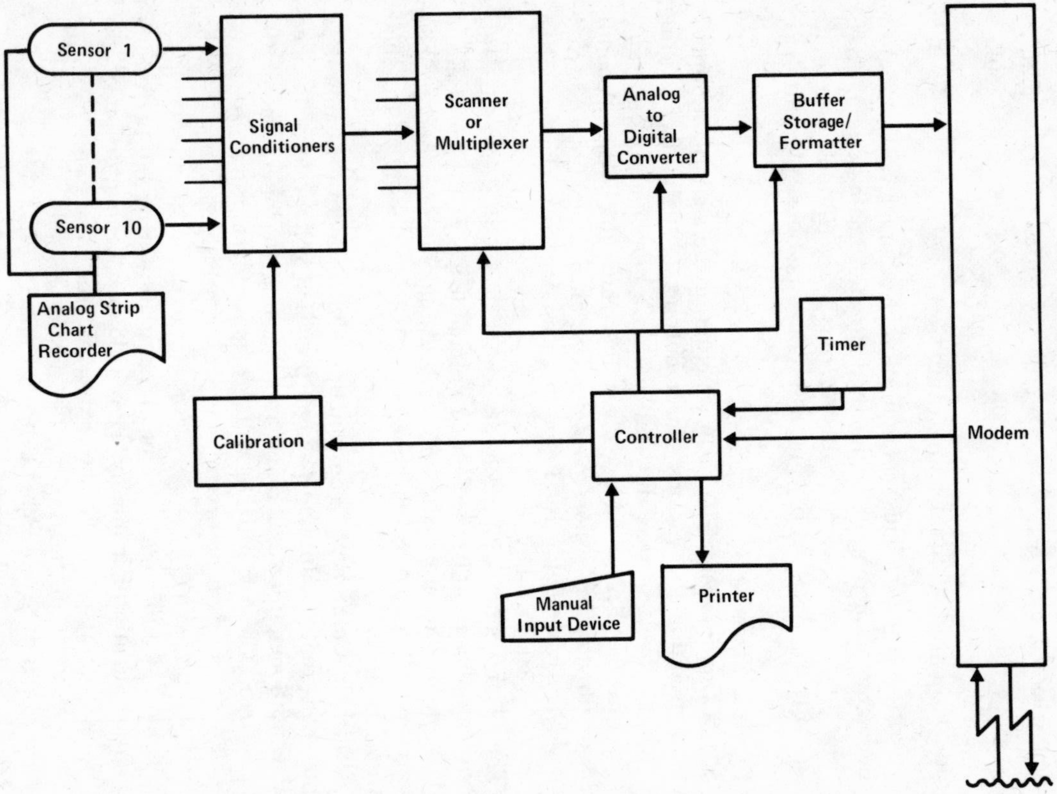

FIGURE 3.20. Remote station.

converter component. The multiplexer begins the signal scanning sequence and subsequently steps through the sequence according to commands received from the remote station controller.

Analog-to-Digital Converter. The analog-to-digital converter will convert the analog signal received from the multiplexer to digital form and pass it to the buffer storage unit.

Buffer Storage/Formatter. The buffer storage/formatter accepts digital sensor data from the analog-to-digital converter and stores it for subsequent reporting to the central control station. The station identifier, date, and time information are held and updated in the buffer storage. In addition, any sensor status data such as that signifying manual or automatic calibration is transmitted through the controller to the buffer storage unit for matching and association with the data for that sensor. Upon command from the central control station, the remote-station controller commands the buffer storage/ formatter to encode and transmit the stored data (station identifier, date, time, sensor status, and sensor digital reading) via the telecommunications modem and link to the central control station.

Modem. The modem converts character serial, digital data from the buffer storage/formatter to a signal compatible for transmission on the telecommunications network to the central control station. At the remote site information is converted to character serial, digital data which is input to the remote station controller. Data transmission at 10 or more characters per second in ASCII code (American Standard Code for Information Interchange) meets most requirements.

Controller. The remote-station controller performs various functions in responding to commands from the central station and manual input devices and in controlling the operations of the other remote-station subsystems and system components. When addressed by the central control station, the controller responds to commands such as turning on and activating the remote-station printer, activating and instructing a specific electronic calibration cycle, and initiating a buffer-storage readout for transmission to the central control station. The controller accepts timing from a real-time clock and subsequently uses it to initiate/terminate the operations of other remote-station components. The controller initiates sampling of the sensor data to assure the availability of new data when requested by the central control station.

Timer. A real-time clock is used to supply timing input to the remote-station controller for determining when to initiate and/or terminate operations.

Manual Input Device. A manual input device is utilized by the remote-station operator to manually set/reset the station identifier, date and time, and to notify the system when it is placing a sensor on-line, taking a sensor off-line, or manually initiating or terminating a calibration cycle. This input is subsequently inserted in the block of data to be transmitted to the central control station.

Printer. The remote-station printer is capable of accepting and printing standard teletype ASCII coded characters transmitted from the central control station. When commanded by the central control station, the remote-station controller initiates the printer operation, passes the received data to the printer, and subsequently terminates the printer operation.

Central Station. The system components required to perform the central control station processes just described are shown in Figure 3.21. Following is a discussion of the functions to be performed by each of the major subsystems of the central control station. Typically, off-the-shelf hardware is utilized for the A/D converter, the multiplexer, and the dedicated computer. The peripherals required by the

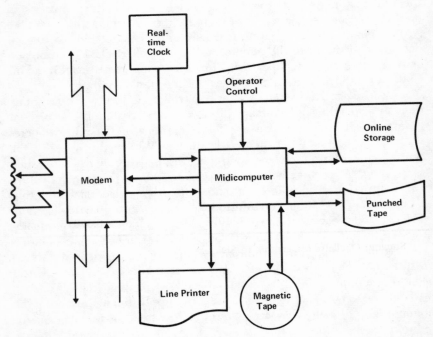

FIGURE 3.21.   Central station. *(From A. F. Mentink, ref. 84)*

computer system are: magnetic tape units, on-line storage, printer, and operator console.

The computer system envisioned should be a 12-to-16 bit word (3 to 4 digits of accuracy are considered sufficient) computer with 16K of expandable primary storage; 128 analog input channels should be provided. This should be expandable. The system will have priority interrupt as part of its architecture. The system should utilize hardware interrupt technique. If software interrupts are used, they must be justified in terms of cost saving, reliability, and effects on programming. The system should drive 3 output devices: a disk storage, a tape transport, and an output terminal. The question of accuracy is examined more in detail in Table 3.11. It is felt that the computer

TABLE 3.11

Accuracy and Word Size

Number of Bits	Decimal Number	Percent Accuracy
2	2	50
3	4	25
4	8	12.5
5	16	6.25
6	32	3.125
7	64	1.562
8	128	0.781
9	256	0.390
10	512	0.195
11	1024	0.098
12	2048	0.049
13	4096	0.024
14	8192	0.012
15	16384	0.006
16	32768	0.003
17	65536	0.0015
18	131072	0.00075

SOURCE: Ouellette & Garrison, ref. 85.

should not add more than one-tenth the error that the sensor is capable of providing. Note, also, that the word length limits the number of instructions that can be assigned as well as the size of the directly addressable memory. Detailed characteristics should be as follows:

Primary Storage. Minimum primary storage capacity should be 16K bytes and must be capable of expansion by the addition of equal speed modules up to 32K bytes. The executive software should be handled within 4K bytes.

The effective cycle time shall be on the order of 2μ sec. Parity checks must be performed on all data transfers to and from primary storage, the main processor, and i/o channels. Arithmetic hardware should provide a capability for fixed-point arithmetic and floating-point arithmetic. One real-time clock shall be provided with a resolution of at least 1/64 second.

The magnetic tape unit should record information on a 9-track tape at 25 ips, 800 bpi, in order to ensure compatibility with most data systems. One single tape unit is required for the entire computer system, as it is backup for disk storage. The teletypewriter should be an asr 33 or asr 35 (the 35 is a more rugged version of the 33, better suited for inclement environment) or its equivalent.

Besides the primary core storage, removable media secondary storage on the order of 0.5 million bytes should be available. A card-read and card-punch unit is required and must have the capability to read and punch 80-column 12-row punch cards and must be fully buffered. Read speed of 200 cards a minute and punch speed of 80 cards a minute are sufficient.

Software Complement. The following software support should be available:

Operating System (Executive Control). The executive system must have priority interrupt and queuing capabilities. Each program must be executed under the control of the operating system with regard to loading, sequence and priority in the queue, i/o and library calls, and program-termination activities under all processing conditions.

Programming Systems. The central facility requires a set of programming languages to satisfy its need for scientific computation, internal development of system software, and on-line applications.

Certainly, fortran iv or equivalent (pl/1-apl–Extended Basic) is required in batch and on-line modes. An assembler or other machine-oriented language is required to facilitate extensions of the operating systems, and the development of special-purpose software with a measure of efficiency not usually found in compilers.

General Utilities. General utility programs that perform the functions of tape-to-printer, card-to-tape, and tape-to-das and das-to-tape are required. A dump routine is required that will output selected areas of core on request. And fortran diagnostic support is required. Standard maintenance and diagnostic programs are also necessary. A sort/merge capability for the magnetic tape and DAS is required.

OTHER CONSIDERATIONS.[85] The following are also important considerations.

Noise. Data-acquisition systems frequently accept signals contaminated with noise. Noise may be generated in the ground system formed by the transducer and signal conditioner, or may be inadvertently picked up by the communications wiring. These two types of noise are called common-mode noise and normal-mode noise, respectively. Normal-mode noise may also be generated within the electronics of the transducer or the signal conditioner.

Common-mode noise can be attenuated by employing various balance techniques. One technique is to utilize a differential amplifier in which the noise is literally subtracted out of the noise-plus-signal combination by the amplifier circuitry. Common-mode noise can also be reduced by using a guarded amplifier or one that protects its input circuits from the effects of circulating ground currents. This is done by electrically isolating the input circuits from the signal ground (usually the chassis) of the amplifier and connecting them to the signal return point associated with the signal source. The effectiveness of a given balance technique is measured by the "common-mode rejection," which is the factor, expressed in decibels, by which the noise voltage seen at the input to the amplifier has been reduced by the balance technique.

There are several techniques available for reducing the effects of normal-mode noise. These include shielding the communications wiring, which tends to be more effective at higher frequencies, and routing the cables away from known sources of noise. Unfortunately, these techniques are often only partially effective in solving a noise problem. One can also filter the desired signal or integrate it prior to converting it to digital form. Filtering cannot be done indiscriminately, however, because it tends to reduce the bandwidth of the communications channel, thus creating a problem in handling rapidly varying signals. Integration (or averaging) of the input signal prior to or after digitizing it also works well for slowly varying signals, though less well for rapidly varying signals. This is because rapidly varying signals must be represented by closely spaced samples (or averages of samples), leaving less time for a given integration and hence limiting the advantages to be gained from signal integration. If signals are recorded either before or after digitizing, averaging can be done at less than real-time speeds, thus allowing this technique to be effectively used even in radar signal detection. Filtering and integrating are, therefore, more attractive when slowly varying signals must be handled, while shielding is more attractive when rapidly varying signals must be handled. Few or no noise problems are expected because of the levels of the signals and the slowness of variation of the signals.

Communications Cabling. Communications cable can be as basic as a single unshielded wire or as sophisticated as a triaxial (doubly-shielded coaxial) cable. When single wires are used, the return path is through the chassis or other conducting structure, while one of the pair of wires making up a two-wire cable serves as the return path.

A pair of wires may be twisted or shielded—or both—to provide interference protection. The outer conductor provides the interference protection in the case of coaxial cable, and the middle and the outer conductors both provide interference protection in the case of triaxial cable. Either shielded pair or triaxial cable (both three-conductor cables) must be used if one is trying to avoid a common-mode noise problem, and a shielded or unshielded pair should be twisted if one is trying to avoid a magnetic (generally low-frequency) field. Of the remaining cable types, shielded parallel and twisted pairs are both suitable to communication circuits that handle only audio frequency signals and that do not require extremes of interference protection. Coaxial or triaxial cable could be used, not for their high-frequency characteristics, but rather to obtain the added shielding they provide. Triaxial cable might be used to obtain high shielding effectiveness and common-mode rejection.

Shielding effectiveness (defined as the ratio, expressed in decibels, of stray pickup without and with the shield) and cost data for the different types of cables that could be used are given in Table 3.12. Considering the cost of triaxial cable, one would not take the option for that type unless it were absolutely necessary.

Because a degree of noise insensitivity can be built into the data-acquisition system, and since by careful routing one can avoid the most probable sources of local interference, it appears that shielded pairs, and in particular twisted shielded pairs, can be used. From an economic point of view one would like to use Type RG-59/U (or similar) coaxial cable, but the risks of creating a common-mode noise problem precludes this choice.

It is recommended that shielded twisted pairs equivalent to Alpha Type 1736 be used for the communications circuits.

Certain precautions should be taken in installing the communica-

TABLE 3.12

Communications Cable Data

Wire Type	Estimated Isolation Relative to Unshielded Pair *	Cost
Parallel pair (Two strands of Alpha Type 1855)	—	$ 2.01/100′
Twisted pair (Belden Type 8481)	10 dB	1.95/100′
Shielded parallel pair (Belden Type 8739)	25 dB	3.85/100′
Shielded twisted pair (Alpha Type 1736)	30 dB	8.00/100′
Coaxial cable (Type RG-59/U)	40 dB	5.45/100′
Triaxial cable (Type RG-6A/U)	60 dB	29.85/100′

* 20dB is equivalent to a reduction in noise voltage by a factor of ten, 40dB is equivalent to a reduction by a factor of 100, etc.

SOURCE: Ouellette & Garrison, ref. 85.

tions cable. The shields should be continuous throughout the cable runs and should be carried through the connectors at the test stations on separate pins for eventual grounding inside the test device case. The shields can be trimmed and left floating outside of (but close to) the connectors at the computer room end of the circuits. The cables should be insulated on the outside to prevent unintentional grounding.

Data Logging System [85]

System Concept

This configuration consists of a multiplexer for each station in addition to A/D converters connected directly to compatible magnetic tape. The concept here is to log all the data from the analytical instrument directly into tapes that will then be processed at a central computer facility. Figure 3.22 shows the overall system design. Manual

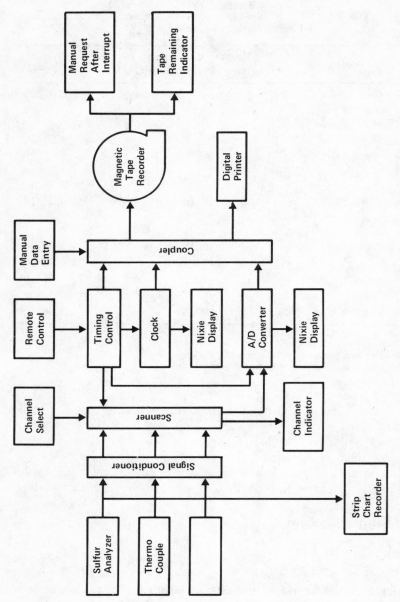

FIGURE 3.22. Data logging system. *(From R. P. Ouellette & J. Garrison, ref. 85)*

96

keyboard-to-tape or other automatic data-entry devices at each experimental station will be necessary for positive sample identification, calibration cycle, etc. All calculations will be made in a batch mode at the central computer facility. There will be no real-time feedback of the results or interactive control in this configuration.

This data-logger system is engineered by using the same techniques as for the dedicated midi- or minicomputer, except that no computer is utilized.

The data-acquisition system consists of a number of off-the-shelf subsystems (see Figure 3.22), most of which are capable of "stand-alone" operation. The individual subsystems are: signal conditioning amplifiers, analog scanner, analog-to-digital converter, time-of-day clock, system timing control, data coupler, incremental tape recorder, and digital printer. Each subsystem will be described in some detail below under the headings of signal conditioning and interfacing and hardware configuration.

Signal Conditioning and Interfacing

The interfaces for each instrument will be the same as mentioned in earlier sections. Careful consideration should be given to making the A/D converters compatible with the magnetic tape units. Owing to the fact that pollutant analyzer outputs, in general, differ from one analyzer to the next, and because in many cases the dynamic range of particular analyzers is broad it is necessary to precondition the input signals to the data-acquisition system. A majority of the available sensors presently in use incorporate a front panel meter or a strip chart recorder as an output display. In many cases the output is in the form of a current that drives a taut, band-type meter or galvanometer on a strip chart recorder. The output current must be converted to a voltage for recording by the data-acquisition system. During this process the output may be scaled so as to present the output in engineering terms, but this is not necessary. The data-acquisition system should be selected for 1.0000 volt full scale. Therefore, it is necessary that all sensor outputs be adjusted to fall within this range.

Each sensor output shall be handled as an individual case. As an example, assume that the output of a particular sensor is 0–8.0 ppm for a current range of 0–1.0 milliamp. The full-scale output of the analyzer is initially adjusted to match the full-scale input of the data-acquisition system. This is accomplished by passing the output current through a 1,000-ohm resistor, producing a potential drop of 1.0000 volt. The voltage across the 1,000-ohm load resistor is measured with a high-input impedance instrumentation amplifier adjusted to unity gain. An amplifier input impedance of 10^8 ohms is typical. The effective loading error introduced by the instrumentation amplifier is calculated as follows:

$$\frac{Z_{load}}{Z_{amp} + Z_{load}} \times 100 = \% \text{ error}$$

which becomes, for the values assumed:

$$\frac{10^3}{10^8} \times 100 = 0.001\% \text{ error}$$

This error is well below the required system accuracy of 0.05 percent full scale.

It is usually desirable to scale the output signal so that 8 ppm corresponds to 0.8 volt. This can be accomplished simply by attenuation of the amplifier output by a factor of 0.8 using a voltage divider.

The full-scale range of the data-acquisition system can be readily adjusted to 0.8 ppm by stepping the amplifier gain by a decade.

Hardware Configuration

Off-the-shelf hardware can be utilized for A/D converters and tape units.

The magnetic tape unit will record information on 9-track tape at 25 IPS, 800 BPI, and ensure compatibility with the typical standard central computer system. One write-only tape unit is required for each experimental station.

The detailed description of the pertinent subsystems, analog scanner, analog-to-digital converter, system timing control, data coupler, time-of-day clock, magnetic tape, and digital printer, follows:

ANALOG SCANNER. For economy reasons data-acquisition systems will employ a single A/D converter. Therefore, its input must be switched to the various sensor outputs by means of an analog scanner or analog multiplexer. An initial capacity of 16-channel inputs is considered adequate for most limited environmental-monitoring facilities. However, provisions for expansion to 32 channels or greater should be available.

Each channel must switch a minimum of three lines. This is required to provide a three-wire guarded differential input to the A/D converter in an attempt to reduce the effects to ground loop currents and common-mode voltages.

In the process of switching low-level analog signals, potential sources of error are the switching contact resistance and the switching thermal offset. A typical contact resistance for a reed-relay type switch is on the order of 0.05 ohms. Other types of switching techniques, such as solid-state switching, introduced a much higher series resistance.

To determine whether a series resistance of this magnitude will introduce an error into the system, assume that the least significant bit of the A/D converter is 10^{-4} volts—then 10^{-4} volts is the smallest detectable error in the system. For an error of this magnitude to be detected, a current large enough to produce a voltage drop of 10^{-4} volts across the series resistor must flow. This is calculated in the following manner:

$$\text{Current} = \frac{\text{minimum voltage error}}{\text{series resistance}} = 2.0 \text{ milliamps}$$

Therefore, it is required that a current no greater than 2.0 milliamps be allowed to flow through the scanner. The scanner current flow is determined by the resistance load at its output, which is, in fact, the input impedance of the A/D converter. Therefore, a minimum input impedance of the A/D converter may be calculated:

$$\text{Analog input impedance} = \frac{\text{full-scale voltage}}{\text{maximum allowable current}} = 500 \text{ ohms}$$

Typical A/D converter input impedances are on the order of 10^5 to 10^7 ohms. Therefore, assuming no low-impedance leakage paths, the contact resistance will introduce no measurable error.

A thermal offset is generated by switch contacts when they are closed due to the absence of a molecular bond between the two similar metals. This offset is affected by temperature. To determine the maximum allowable thermal offset, assume an ambient temperature of 20°C. and an operating range of ±10°C. Assume, also, the worst case condition of a two-wire differential input with the thermal offset voltages being of equal magnitude and opposite polarity so that the offsets add. The offset voltages at ambient temperature are adjusted to zero within the data-acquisition system.

Again, the least significant bit of the A/D converter is 10^{-4} volts. Therefore, for a change of 10°C., the voltage offset must be less than $10^{-4}/2$ volts, and the maximum allowable thermal offset must be 5 μvolts/°C.

In addition to the above, the scanner must be capable of stand-alone operation to permit subsystem checkout, and it should also incorporate some type of visual indication of the active channel. Internal and remote operation should be provided, and channel dwell time should be adjustable.

In summary, the specifications of the analog scanner should be as follows: inputs—16-channel, expandable to 32 or more; four-wire input/channel—reed relay (plug-in type for easy maintenance); input voltage—10^{-4} to 10^{0} vdc; over-voltage—100 vdc without damage; thermal offset—5×10^{-6} V/°C or better; controls—all located on front panel; manual—auto—and remote functions; all i/o connectors in rear of chassis; visual indication of active channel.

ANALOG-TO-DIGITAL CONVERTER. The heart of the data acquisition system is the analog-to-digital converter. It is the function of this subsystem to measure the analog voltage and convert it to an equivalent digital value. There are four conversion techniques that are used in this class of analog-to-digital conversion: the direct-comparison type, the voltage-to-time or ramp type, the voltage-to-frequency integration type, and the dual slope integration type. The following paragraphs discuss the advantages and disadvantages of these classes and identify the optimum approach for the proposed system.

The direct-comparison technique, also known as successive-approximation or continuous-balance, offers a high degree of accuracy. However, it is incapable of rapid conversion because the input incorporates a long-time constant filter required for noise rejection. Also, this is one of the earlier techniques developed for analog-to-digital conversion.

The voltage-to-time technique, or ramp, measures the period of time for a linear ramp to charge from zero to a level coincident with the input voltage. Although this technique offers simplicity, the accuracy and stability are generally poor because of the difficulty of producing a linear repeatable ramp. This technique is also sensitive to noise.

The voltage-to-frequency integration technique produces an output frequency that is proportional to input voltage by the use of a fixed integrator and a level detector. Basically, the higher the input voltage, the more rapidly the integrator reaches its peak value and is reset, starting the cycle over again. The output is proportional to the number of cycles counted in a unit time interval. This technique provides filtering action without the actual use of a filter to slow down the measurement time. However, accuracy and stability are relatively poor because of the drift and nonlinearity associated with the integrator.

The most recent technique developed for analog-to-digital conversion is known as dual-slope integration, which is a two-step technique. The voltage to be measured is applied to the input of a high-impedance operational amplifier that has its output connected to a reset integrator. The output of the integrator is a ramp with slope and direction proportional to the instantaneous amplitude and polarity of the input sample. Once started, the integrator continues to operate until a count of 10,000 has been accumulated by a register (assuming a clock rate of 600 KHz). At this point the second step of the measurement technique begins. The input to the integrator is switched to an internal reference of the opposite polarity from the input sample. The counter is reset to zero and begins counting as the reference voltage drives the integrator back to zero. The slope of the decreasing integrator voltage is proportional to the reference voltage, and the time required to drive the integrator back to zero is proportional to the unknown input. The counter is stopped when the integrator reaches zero and the accumulated count is numerically equal to the input voltage.

This approach offers a number of important advantages over the previously mentioned techniques. Component aging and drift in the integrator are essentially eliminated, as the same circuitry is used in both halves of the operation. It is only necessary for the integrator to maintain the same characteristics for the first and second halves of the cycle, which is 33 milliseconds. The same clock is used for both halves of the cycle. Consequently, long-term stability is not a factor. The oscillator frequency is derived from the 60-cycle power line, providing a high degree of normal mode rejection at 60 cycles and harmonics thereof, which are the major factors in common-mode noise.

The dual-slope technique also provides a relatively rapid conversion rate, slightly less than 30 conversions per second with a 600 KHz clock. Quantization is on the order of 2,000–5,000 bits. It should be pointed out that the types of A/D converters under consideration are not the high-speed aerospace type, but the more common digital voltmeter type or panel meter type.

Normal input impedances for dual-slope technique are on the order of one megohm or greater, satisfying the scanner load requirement.

Of all the techniques discussed, dual-slope integration has the most to offer. Therefore, this technique was selected as the one to be incorporated into the data-acquisition system.

As previously stated, full scale has been selected to be 1.0000 volt. However, a 50 percent overrange is specified. This is common in most available A/D converters of the type under consideration. As a result, a value of 1.5000 volts may be computed with an accuracy equal to that of the 1.0000 volt specified.

The overall accuracy is arrived at in the following manner. It was previously stated that full scale shall be 1.0000 volt. The least significant bit is 100 microvolts. Therefore, resolution becomes 100 microvolts, or 0.01 percent of full scale. However, in an asynchronous digital system the least significant bit cannot be controlled and must always be assigned as ± 1 count, which turns out to be 0.01 percent of full scale. Therefore, it is seen that ± 0.02 percent of full scale is the best overall accuracy possible for an A/D converter of this type, assuming a constant temperature.

The sensors used in air-pollution monitoring are, at best, 1 percent instruments. It is desirable to specify the data-acquisition system to at least one order of magnitude greater accuracy than that of the sensor input. As was seen previously, a four-digit A/D converter more than satisfies this requirement. Because the state-of-the-art easily provides a greater accuracy than required at no increased cost. an accuracy of 0.05 percent of full scale was specified.

The conversion rate is specified at 25 conversions/second, which will allow for expansion of up to 25 channels for a one-second full scan. Additional channels may be added for a slower scan rate, such as 50 channels for a two-second full scan. From the previous discussion of dual-slope integration, it is seen that this technique will meet our conversion requirements.

The information output of the A/D converter is specified to be 8421 binary coded decimal and to be basically compatible with the IBM 360/50 format. In addition, the output may be read directly off the digital display that is to be provided. Again, this type of output is common practice for the types of A/D converter under consideration.

In summary, the specifications of the analog-to-digital converter should be as follows:

1. Range—10^{-4} to 10^0 VDC
2. Accuracy—overall, better than 0.05 percent F.S.
3. Overrange—50 percent
4. Overvoltage—100 VDC without damage

5. Visual readout—Nixie-type or equivalent
6. Minimum of 25 conversions/second
7. CMR—80 db at 60 Hz
8. Utilize dual-slope technique
9. BDC output, 8421 format
10. External-control capability
11. All I/O on rear of chassis

SYSTEM TIMING CONTROL. The timing control subsystem is responsible for controlling the sequence of events and sampling rates. The timing control unit should be as flexible as possible. The scan rate will have the capability of being adjusted from one scan/second to at least one scan/hour. In addition, a series of timing-sequence pulses will be provided to drive external circuitry that will be used for control and calibration functions.

In summary, the specifications of the system timing control should be as follows:

1. Will control the scanner within the following limits:
   a. Scan rate 1.0/sec. to 1 hr./scan,
   b. Measurement time per channel
      Adjustable 100 ms to 10 sec
2. Will control all data-transfer functions:
   a. A/D converter
   b. Clock data
   c. Data converter
3. Will provide time reference output pulses

DATA COUPLER. The data coupler accepts digital information from the clock, the A/D converter, and any other source of digital input that may be used, and formats the data for recording on magnetic tape. In addition, the coupler provides manual data entry for identification and labeling, groups data characters into data blocks, constructs data headers, and simultaneously drives an incremental tape recorder and a digital printer.

In summary, the specifications of the data coupler should be as follows:

1. Will accept BCD from A/D converter and format for incremental recorder
2. Accept time data (BCD) and format for incremental recorder
3. Will construct data header and record upon command
4. Will group data in 100 character/block

5. Will include thumbwheel switches for manual data entry in header
6. Will provide simultaneous buffered BCD output to drive digital printer
7. Provide "Data Transferred" command to timing control unit

TIME-OF-DAY CLOCK. As a means of identifying the data, a time-of-day clock will be employed. The clock will display the day of year, the hour of day, and the minute of hour. The clock digital output will be 8421 binary coded decimals and will incorporate a visual display.

The clock time base will utilize the 60-cycle power line, which provides excellent long-term stability, barring any power failure.

Provision for starting, stopping, and resetting the digital clock will also be made.

In summary, the specifications of the time-of-day clock should be as follows:

1. Shall display day of year, hour of day, minute of hour
2. Output—8421 BCD
3. 60-Hz time base
4. Data storage and display

MAGNETIC TAPE. The magnetic tape recorder records the data incrementally on command from the coupler. The coupler formats the data so that it is compatible with a larger computer for subsequent data reduction.

In summary, the specifications of the incremental recorder should be as follows:

1. Write-only mode
2. 0–500 characters/second
3. 800 BPI packing density
4. Nine-track compatible with central facility computer
5. Echo parity check
6. Erase head
7. Generate vertical parity
8. Interrecord gap time 500 ms minimum
9. End of File—generate upon command
10. Input—compatible with data converter specified

DIGITAL PRINTER. The digital printer should be a standard tele-printer of the ASR 33 type. The major characteristics are 10–15 characters/second print speed and 120 print position. It should be noted that due to the wide variety of equipment available it is possible

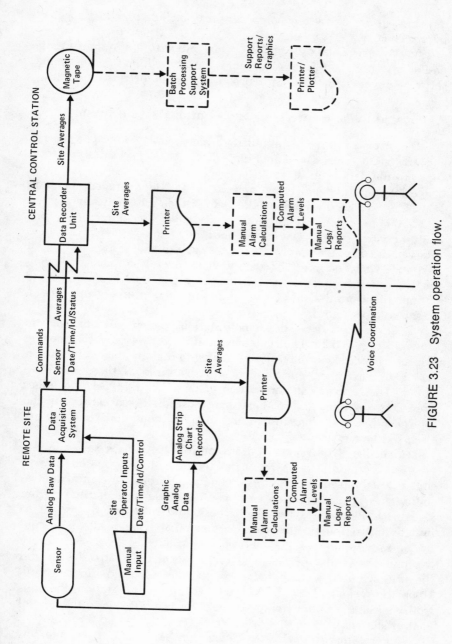

FIGURE 3.23 System operation flow.

105

that one selected subsystem component may include functions specified by a second.

SOFTWARE COMPLEMENT. No special software is required for the on-line system since the entire system is hard-wired; on the other hand, software development for batch processing of the data is required.

Automated Remote Processing and Central Data Recording

SYSTEM CONCEPT. The "automated remote and central data recording" [84] system is presented in Figure 3.23. Analog sensor signals are input to the data-acquisition system (at the remote site), where they are converted to engineering units, stored, and averaged for each hour. The averaged environmental data is then automatically printed on a remote-station printer and is available for sampling by the central control station. Once each hour, or at some other preset time interval, the central control station dials each remote station utilizing a telephone line and requests the previous averaged data. Following the transmission and receipt of the averaged data from a remote station, the central control station produces a printed copy and a magnetic tape record.

REMOTE STATION. The remote-station system components are shown in Figure 3.24. The functions performed by the sensors, analog strip chart recorders, multiplexer, analog-to-digital converter, printer, manual input, timer, and modem are the same as those discussed earlier. Those remote-station system components that perform either more, less, or different functions than those discussed earlier are the controller buffer storage/formatter and signal conditioners. These are discussed below.

Controller. The remote-station controller performs several functions in controlling the operations of the other remote-station systems components and in responding to commands from the central control station and manual input device. The controller accepts timing from a real-time clock on a continuous basis and subsequently uses it to initiate and terminate the operations of other components. The controller initiates a sampling of the sensor data at least once every five minutes. It also initiates the averaging of the sampled data and the printing of the computed averages at some fixed time interval. Upon the receipt of a call from the central control station, the controller initiates a buffer storage readout for transmission to the central control station.

Buffer Storage/Formatter/Calculator. The buffer storage/formatter/calculator accepts digital sensor data from the analog-to-

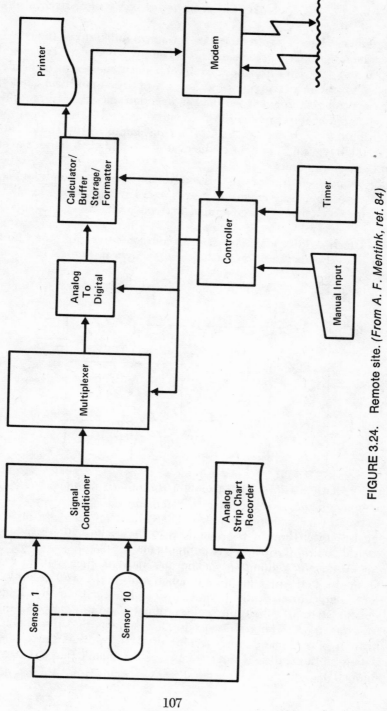

FIGURE 3.24. Remote site. *(From A. F. Mentink, ref. 84)*

digital converter, converts the data to known units, stores the data, and averages the data for each interval. The averaged data (in meaning-ful units, e.g. PPM) are then printed on the remote station printer in order to obtain hard copy reports. In addition, upon command from the controller, the averaged data is encoded and transmitted via the telecommunications modem to the central control station. Each record transmitted to the central control station contains the station identi-fier; the day, year, and hour of the averaging; and each sensor's average in engineering units.

Signal Conditioners. The remote station signal conditioners iso-late the various sensor output signals, convert the voltage levels to be within a common voltage range, and pass the converted signals to a multiplexer.

CENTRAL STATION. The system components required to perform the central control station processes are shown in Figure 3.25. Follow-

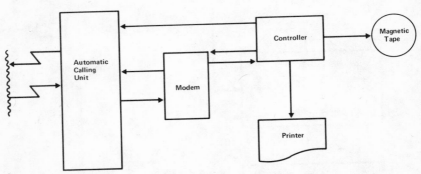

FIGURE 3.25.   Central station. *(From A. F. Mentink, ref. 84)*

ing is a discussion of the functions to be performed by each of the central control station system components.

Automatic Calling Unit. The automatic calling unit, in response to a command and telephone number from the central control station controller, automatically initiates a telephone call to the designated remote station. When the called remote station answers, the ACU transfers the telephone circuit to the modem for subsequent trans-mission of commands and receipt of data. At the completion of a data-sampling call and upon controller command, the ACU terminates the call.

Modem. The modem converts character serial and digital command data received from the central control station controller to an analog signal compatible for transmission on the telecommunications network to the called remote station. In reverse, analog telecommunications signals received from a remote station are converted to character, serial and digtal data, which is input to the controller.

Controller. At fixed time intervals the central control station controller initiates a call to each of the remote stations, commands it to transmit data averages, receives the data, causes a printout of the data on a central station printer, and records the data on magnetic tape.

Printer. A printer is utilized to obtain a hard copy of the data averages obtained by the central control station from the remote stations.

Magnetic Tape. A magnetic tape device is utilized to record averages of the data as received from the remote stations.

REFERENCES

1. C. A. Bisselle, *et al,* "An Integrated Nationwide Environmental Monitoring System." The MITRE Corp., M72-196, December 1972.

2. J. W. Overbey and R. P. Ouellette, 'The Use of the National Aerometric Data Bank for Decision Making." The MITRE Corp., M72-19, October 1971.

3. S. M. Blacker and J. S. Burton, "Environmental Protection Agency's Monitoring Program." The MITRE Corp., M73-34, April 1973.

4. C. A. Bisselle, *et al,* "Monitoring the Environment of the Nation," The MITRE Corp., MTR-1660, April 1971.

5. "Four-Year Summary of Data From the Continuous Air Monitoring Program Operated by Laboratory of Engineering and Physical Sciences." Division of Air Pollution, HEW, August 1966.

6. David A. Lynn and Thomas B. McMullen, "Air Pollution in Six Major U.S. Cities as Measured by the Continuous Air Monitoring Program." *J. APCA* 16(4):186-190, 1966.

7. Elbert C. Tabor and Catherine C. Golden, "Results of Five Years Operation of the National Gas Sampling Network." *J. APCA* 15(1):7-11, 1965.

8. James H. McDermott and William T. Sayers, "The Role of Water Quality Monitoring in Water Pollution Control." 158th National Meeting, ACS, New York, Sept. 11, 1969.

9. William T. Sayers, "The State-Federal Water Quality Surveillance Network for Water Pollution Control." American Chem. Soc. Meeting, Chicago, Sept. 3-18, 1970.

10. *1969 Inventory of Air Pollution Monitoring Equipment Operated by State and Local Agencies.* EPA, Washington, D.C., 1971.

11. *Index to Water Quality Data.* U. S. Department of Interior, Washington, D. C., 1970.

12. L. P. White, "Air Survey Methods for Water Monitoring." *Effluent Water Treat. J.* 12:413-465, 1972.

13. W. E. Jacobsen, "Operational Requirements for a Subsidence Monitoring System." The MITRE Corp., WP-7827, June 22, 1971.

14. W. E. Jacobsen and R. W. Bee, "Preliminary Evaluation of Subsidence Measurement Techniques." The MITRE Corp., WP-8501, October 1971.

15. R. P. Ouellette, J. Golden and R. S. Greeley, "The National Aerometric Data Information Service Concept." The MITRE Corp., M71-11, March 1971.

16. J. Golden, *et al,* "Initial Design of the National Aerometric Data Information Service—Preliminary Report." The MITRE Corp., MTR-1651, June 1971.

17. J. Burton, *et al,* "Guidelines for the Acquisition of Validated Air Quality Data." The MITRE Corp., MTR-6000, April 1971.

18. J. Golden, *et al,* "Storage and Retrieval of Aerometric Data Users Manual." The MITRE Corp., M71-46, July 1971.

19. J. Golden and L. Duncan, "Classification of Existing Air Quality Surveillance Systems." The MITRE Corp., MTR-1662, February 1971.

20. J. Golden, R. P. Ouellette and R. S. Greeley, "National Aerometric Data Information Source." The MITRE Corp., M71-3, February 1971.

21. J. Overbey and R. P. Ouellette, "The Design and Operation of the National Aerometric Data Bank." The MITRE Corp., M71-67, September 1971.

22. R. J. Chleboski, "Air Pollution Control in the Computer Age." *Pollution Engineering* 3(4):20-23, 1971.

23. Edward L. Stockton, "Experience With a Computer Oriented Air Monitoring Program." *J. APCA* 20(7):456-460, 1970.

24. Edward L. Stockton and Winthrop C. Shook, "Automatic Air Monitoring and Telemetering to Central Points in Allegheny County." *J. APCA* 18(3):162-163, 1968.

25. Edward J. Cleary, *The ORSANCO Story.* Johns Hopkins Press, Baltimore, 1967.

26. *ORSANCO Quality Monitoring.* Ohio River Valley Water Sanitation Commission, January 1970.

27. William L. Klein, David A. Bunsmore, and Robert K. Horton, "An Integrated Monitoring System for Water Quality Management in the Ohio Valley." *Env. Sci. Technol.* 2(10):764-771, 1968.

28. Ronald E. Maylath, "Automatic Surveillance of New York's Waters." New York Department of Environmental Conservation, 1971.

29. "Telemetering System Puts Pollution Monitoring Online." *Chem. Engn.* 16:58-59, 1969.

30. Samuel G. Booras, "City of Chicago Air Quality Telemetering System." Proceedings IBM Scientific Computing Symposium Water and Air Resource Management, pp. 11-29, 1968.

31. William P. Stanley and Austin N. Heller, "Air Resource Management in the Chicago Metropolitan Area." *J. APCA* 16(10):536-540, 1966.

32. Austin N. Heller and Samuel G. Booras, "Telemetered Air Quality Network Helps Chicago." *Env. Sci. Technol.* 1(12):984-990, 1967.

33. Donald J. Ogner, "Experience with Ontario's Computer Controlled Air Monitoring System." 65th Annual Meeting, APCA, 1972 (p. 72).

34. Clive Lawrence, "This is the Computer Calling, About Oxygen in the Water." *Christian Science Monitor,* September 23, 1971.

35. J. J. Wilting and H. Van Den Berge, "Air Pollution Monitoring in the Netherlands." *Computer,* 22-27, July/August, 1971.

36. F. Cabot, "SO Goes SO₂." *Ind. Resh.* 12(9):70-72, 1970.

37. B. A. Brodovicz, George B. Murdock and Victor H. Sussman, "Pennsylvania's Computerized Air Monitoring System." 1968 APCA Meeting.

38. B. A. Brodovicz, V. H. Sussman and G. B. Murdock, "Pennsylvania's Computerized Air Monitoring System." *J. APCA* 19(7):484-485, 1969.

39. J. S. Burton, *et al,* "Baseline Measurement Test Results for the Cat-Ox Demonstration Program." The MITRE Corp., M73-42, April 1973.

40. G. Erskine and E. Jamgochian, "MITRE Test Support for the Cat-Ox Demonstration Program." The MITRE Corp., M73-50, May 1973.

41. J. Hoffman and K. E. Yeager, "Management Plan for Coke Oven Charging Emissions Control Test Program." The MITRE Corp. MTR-6055, November 1971.

42. A. J. Epstein, *et al,* "Continuous Monitoring System Coke Oven Charging Emission Test Program." The MITRE Corp., MTR-6215, July 1972.

43. R. F. Stebar, M. J. Ciancinlo and F. M. Ward, "Digital Data Acquisition and Computer Data Reduction for the California Exhaust Emissions Test." Society of Automotive Engineers, Progress in Technology, Vol. 12.

44. Robert F. Spain, Y. George Kim, and Russell V. Fisher, "Central Data Collection and Processing with Emphasis on Emission Data Reduction." Society of Automotive Engineers, Paper 700172, 1970.

45. "Functional Requirements for an Automatic Data Processing System for the National Air Pollution Control Administration." The MITRE Corp., MTR-4150, Vol. II, August 1970.

46. C. U. Peterson, W. V. Dailey and W. G. Amrhein, "Applying Non-Dispersive Infrared to Analyze Polluted Stack Gases." *Inst. Technol.* 45-48, August 1972.

47. D. T. Hudder, "Multispectral Photography in Earth Resources Research." *Optical Spectra* 71-75, July/August 1970.

48. T. Hirschfeld and S. Klainer, "Remote Raman Spectroscopy as a Pollution Radar." *Optical Spectra* 63-66, July/August, 1970.

49. Freeman F. Hall, "Laser Measurements of Turbidity in the Atmosphere." *Optical Spectra* 67-70, July/August 1970.

50. Solomon Zaromb, "Remote Sensing of Invisible Air Pollutants by Lidar Absorption Spectroscopy." 1969.

51. J. J. O. Palgen, "Applicability of Pattern Recognition Techniques to the Analysis of Urban Quality from Satellites." *Pattern Recognition* 2:255-260, 1970.

52. R. A. Naden, "The Use of Long-Path Averaging Sensors for Source Surveillance and Ambient Measurements." 65th Annual Meeting, APCA, 1972 (#72-9).

53. L. R. Snowman, M. L. Nobel and R. J. Gillmeister, "Infrared Laser System for Air Pollution Monitoring." 65th Annual Meeting, APCA, 1972 (#72-10).

54. H. Tannenbaum, D. Tannenbaum and H. Delong, "Remote Raman Field Measurements of Atmospheric Contaminants." 65th Annual Meeting, APCA, 1972 (#72-11).

55. Carl O. Thomas, "Airborne Sensing for Landfill Site Evaluation." *Pollution Engineering*, 3(6):32-33, 1972.

56. L. P. White, "Air Survey Methods for Water Monitoring." *Effluent Water Treat. J.*, 12:459-465, 1972.

57. P. E. Laviolette, L. Stuart and C. Vermillion, "New Satellites Offer Great Potential for Clean Data Collection." *UST* 23-31, November, 1972.

58. *NASA Data Users Handbook.* Doc. No. 715D4249, November 1972.

59. "Remote Sensing of Earth Resources." Committee on Science and Astronautics, U. S. House of Representatives, 1972.

60. "Earth Resources Technology Satellite-1." Symposium Proceedings, September 29, 1972, NASA.

61. "4th Annual Earth Resources Program Review." Houston, Texas, January 17-21, 1971, MSC 05937, 6 vol.

62. "Remote Sensing of Pollution." NASA SP-25, 1971.

63. P. L. Johnson, ed., *Remote Sensing in Ecology.* University of Georgia Press, Athens, 1969.

64. *Instrumentation for Environmental Monitoring.* Vol. I, *Air Parameters;* Vol. 2, *Water Parameters;* Vol. 3, *Radiation Monitoring;* Vol. 4, *Biomodeling.* LBL-1, Vol. 1–Vol. 4, Lawrence Berkeley Laboratory, University of California, Berkeley, 1972.

65. M. V. Mathews, "Choosing a Scientific Computer for Service." *Science* (161):23-27, 1968.

66. Peter B. Denes, and M. V. Mathews, "Laboratory Computers: Their Capabilities and How to Make Them Work for You." *Proc. IEEE* 58(4):520-529, 1970.

67. F. J. Rici, "Survey and Cost Effective Analysis of Digital Computers to be Utilized in an Analytical Instrumentation Laboratory." The MITRE Corp., WP-7295, Aug. 1970.

68. R. J. Spinrad, "Automation in the Laboratory." *Science* 158(3797): 55-60, 1967.

69. W. E. Reynolds, "Instrumentation in a Time-Shared Environment." *Research/Development* 20-26, April 1970.

70. Dell Glover, "Lab Automation at Low Cost." *Research/Development* 22-25, May 1973.

71. D. Schuetzle, A. L. Crittenden and R. J. Charlson, "Application of Computer Controlled High Resolution Mass Spectrometry to the Analysis of Air Pollutants." 65th Annual Meeting, APCA (#72-15), 1972.

72. Marvin Margoshies, "Computerized Optical Instruments." *Optical Spectra* 4(11):26-28, 1970.

73. Ronald A. Hites and K. Biemann, "Computer Evaluation of Continuously Scanned Mass Spectra of Gas Chromatographic Effluents." *Analytical Chemistry* 42(8):855-860, 1970.

74. O. E. Schupp, III and S. S. Lewis, "A System For Storage and Retrieval of Gas Chromatographic Data." *Research/Development* 24-29, May 1970.

75. R. G. Thurman, K. A. Mueller, and M. F. Burke, "Real-Time Computer Control of a Gas Chromatograph." *J. Chromatog. Sci.* 9:77-83, 1971.

76. J. F. Hickerson, "Laboratory Computer Analyzes Samples." *Oil and Gas J.*, 41-44, January 1971.

77. "Computer Controlled Mass Spectrometer for On-Line Gas Analysis." JPL 30-1675/NPO-11427, 1971.

78. Robert C. Ewing, "Chromatographic and Computer = Automatic Control." *Oil and Gas J.* 77-78, October 18, 1971.

79. Stuart P. Cram, "Dedicated Computers in Chemistry." *Research/Development* 30-35, April 1972.

80. J. Garrison, *et al*, "Analysis of Automated Data Acquisition and Processing Systems for the National Air Surveillance Networks Laboratory Automation." The MITRE Corporation, MTR-1661, January 1971.

81. J. Golden and T. R. Mongan, "Designing an Air Monitoring Facility." *Mechanical Engineering* 24-30, August 1971.

82. Frederic C. Hamburg, "Some Basic Considerations in the Design of an Air Pollution Monitoring System." *J. APCA* 21(10):609-613, 1971.

83. Sheldon Turner, *et al*, "State Of Kentucky Air Monitoring Network Design." The MITRE Corporaton, MTR-6106, November 1971.

84. A. F. Mentink, "Specifications for an Integrated Water Quality Data Acquisition System." Federal Water Pollution Control Administration, January 1968.

85. R. P. Ouellette and J. Garrison, "Systems Analysis, Requirements Study, and Functional Specifications for the Automation of the Research Laboratory Branch of the Division of Control Systems." The MITRE Corporation, M71-61, September 1971.

CHAPTER 4

THE USE OF COMPUTERS IN ENVIRONMENTAL CONTROLS

In this chapter we will review the use of computers in environmental control. We will proceed, first, to review in detail the concept of computer-controlled operations; second, to document successful applications in the environment; and third, to develop an example model of computer control in the environment. Environmental control is used here in the sense of controlling sources of pollution, not in the sense of weather modifications, land use, or maintenance of a building's air conditioning.

CONTROL

Control is defined as the set of hardware, software, and procedures trying to keep a process operating under acceptable conditions despite internal and external factors influencing the behavior of the process. Hence the three essential components of a process control are the operator, the control, and the process (Figure 4.1).

It is possible for the human operator to control a simple process. However, on the criteria of speed, reliability, repeatability, and freedom of internal and external influences, the human operator does not compare well with his machine counterpart.

The control hardware may be based on either an analog, a digital, or a hybrid computer system. The analog is fast and inexpensive but not very accurate; the programmable system is slow and expensive but very accurate and flexible. This partially explains the popularity and success of digital control.

While a computer is not essential to process control, it is usually included in a sophisticated process-control system (Figure 4.2). In

115

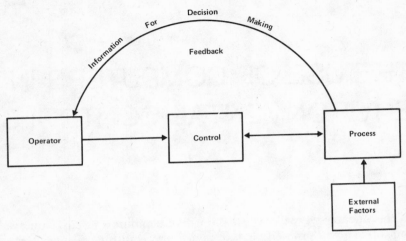

FIGURE 4.1.   The process-control system.

the last few years hybrid computers have become fashionable. The success of remote-access and time-sharing computers is now a most popular topic for future applications. Finally, multiaccess, multi-processing, and multiprogramming have recently made possible more complex and multiple simultaneous process controls.

Some of the ever-present problems are in the areas of signal conditioning, noise prevention, grounding, multiplexing, analog-to-digital conversion, and input/output technologies.

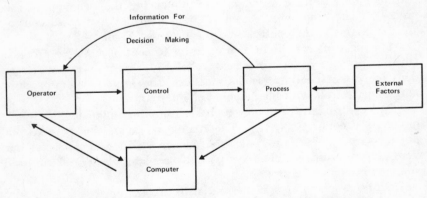

FIGURE 4.2.   The computerized process-control system.

A variety of computer-control methodologies is available. For instance, stochastic control versus deterministic, or multivariate control as opposed to cascade control. We can further distinguish between stabilizing control, or control aimed at maintaining a present level, and optimizing control, which is a technique seeking a general or local optimum. The criteria to separate among stabilizing-control techniques are to identify if the specific control uses observed or measured variables (diagnostic control) as against derived or computed variable (numerical control). The diagnostic control then breaks down into analog, digital, or hybrid, according to the type of control hardware in use. Numerical control is divided into feedback control and feedforward control.

Optimizing control is divided according to the knowledge that optimization is applied to a steady-state condition or based on a transient response. Steady-state controls are further divided in adaptive control or learning control, based on a model or predictive control aimed at forecasting future events.

Applications of Computers to Process Control

Process-control computer applications are numerous and can be found in a variety of areas of human endeavor both in discrete-part processing and continuous processing. Extensive use of process-control computers exists in the petroleum industry,[1] the cement industry,[2, 3] and most chemical industries.[4]

These applications cover the entire spectrum from simple to sophisticated exercises.[5] All techniques of control are represented. However, direct-digital control represents the most frequently encountered usage. The experience, knowledge, and models developed in industry will be useful in helping to solve problems in environmental control.

Computer Control

Computers and process control are intimately associated. Several books, specialized symposia, and review papers [5, 6, 7, 8] have discussed the theoretical derivation, the pilot application, and the full-scale implementation.

Several factors are responsible for the current maturity in this field, but the advent of small, low-cost, versatile, and powerful minicomputers is probably the single most important factor. The dedication of a processor to a single control task and the exchange of knowledge, experience, solutions, and software rank next among the contributary factors. The advent of specialized process-control languages and the promises of a standard language are other intangible advantages.

ENVIRONMENTAL CONTROL

Computers may be utilized in many ways for controlling environmental pollution. Almost all water-distribution systems and municipal wastewater-treatment processes can be automated to some degree, in the sense that mechanical and electronic monitoring and control devices may be used to perform certain routine analytical, maintenance, alarm and control functions normally entrusted to human operators.[9-16] The success of such automation methods is measured by the degree of accuracy and reliability attained and the amount of time and skill of personnel still required after automation.[17]

The field of municipal wastewater treatment is complex, faced with increasing demand for improvement and efficiency and a simultaneous decrease in the availability of qualified personnel.[18] Instrumentation with associated automatic controls is an obvious substitute to partially solve these problems.

An automated control system should perform at least three functions: (1) detect alarm conditions; (2) provide control of variables which are tedious, difficult, or dangerous to deal with; and (3) provide a storage for historical data. The majority of the systems in existence today provide only alarm detection and status recording. A few examples of full-fledged automated control systems can be found, however.[19-24]

The above discussion refers to hardwired process control without the full advantages of modern computers. We will now describe a number of examples of successful applications of computer process control to environmental problems.

Metropolitan Seattle [25, 26, 27]

In many metropolitan areas it is economically feasible to solve the problem of sewage overflow by the construction of independent or separate storm sewers. In many populated and congested areas this is not possible. One workable solution is the use of storage capacity in trunk and interceptor sewers for the regulation of the combined sewage and storm water runoff flows within the limits of the capacity of the interceptor.

Metropolitan Seattle has installed a computer-augmented treatment and disposal (CATAD) system. Its purpose is the utilization of maximum storage within the existing combined sewers in order to minimize the overflow of combined sewage into Puget Sound. This system serves 18 cities and 14 sewer districts. Included in the system are 4 treatment plants, 22 pumping stations, and over 100 miles of trunkline sewers. Remote monitoring is conducted at 36 remote stations and regulator stations. A total of 23 control units have been installed at pumping and regulator stations on the system of trunk and interceptor sewers serving the West Point Sewage Treatment Plant. Stations have also been installed at nine points along the sewer line serving the Renton Treatment Plant.

The immediate result of this direct-digital control system is that it is possible to utilize the maximum storage capacity of combined sewer trunk lines and interceptors for combined storm and sanitary flows in unseparated areas by utilizing the storage capacity of trunk and interceptor sewers in separated areas under storm conditions, controlling necessary overflows at selected locations so as to minimize harmful effects on the environment.

The Central Station

A block diagram of the central station's equipment is shown in Figure 4.3. The central computer is a small-scale, high-speed, 16-bit word computer (Scientific Data System Sigma 2) with 45,000 words of core memory. The bulk memory consists of a 1.5-million-word, high-speed disk unit and two magnetic tape units.

Communications between the computer and field devices are established by virtue of a dedicated-program-controlled input-output channel. Devices and facilities using the channel include central station telemetry equipment, operator's console inputs and outputs, logging and events printers, and satellite terminals. All communication between the computer and external devices utilizes hardware priority interrupts.

Operating equipment at the control center includes the following principal items: (1) desk-type console; (2) map display board; and (3) logging and events printers. The design of the operator's console reflects current space-age technology.

Remote Stations

Regulators and pumping remote stations may be operated under three modes of control—local automatic, remote slave, and remote automatic. Under local automatic control each station is operated by

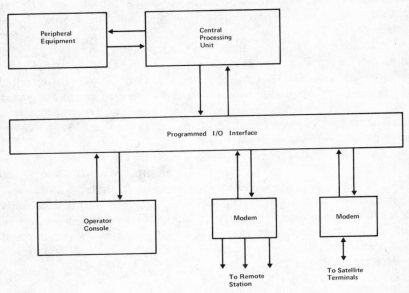

FIGURE 4.3.   Central station block diagram. *(From C. V. Gibbs, S. M. Alexander, & C. A. Leiser, ref. 25)*

an automatic controller within the station itself in response to signals from local sensors. Under remote slave control, the stations are remotely controlled by operator-initiated commands from the central station. With remote automatic control, the stations are operated from the central station under program control by the central computer. Each remote station includes a telementry control unit, a data-communications link, and remote-station control circuits.

The telemetry control unit at each remote station provides for signal conditioning, multiplexing and conversion, coding and transmitting data, and receiving and decoding control commands.

The communication line between the central station and the remote-control units is a leased multistation telephone line.

All commands to remote stations from the control station are achieved by transmitting commands to open or close contacts, which cause relays to be activated in controlling circuits.

Additionally, a water-quality-monitoring data system acquires data from five automatic water-quality-monitoring stations. The data characterizing the waste streams is transmitted to the central computer for storage, data logging, and analysis.

Further, devices for detecting the presence of volatile or explosive wastes in combined sewers are planned or have been installed at 24 sites within or upstream of regulator stations and at pumping stations in the collection network.

An unusual fail-safe capability has been provided to allow the detection of either an equipment failure at the central station or the failure of a communications link. A steady tone signal is continuously transmitted from the central station to each remote station. A detector senses the receiver at the remote station, and any break in the signal opens a relay that interrupts the automatic control circuits at the station.

Procedures and Computation

The time interval for parameter scanning and data computation depends upon storm-water flow conditions. At each time interval the following computations are made for each remote station: (1) inputs are calibrated. (2) Analog sensors are read and checked against stored limits and, if out of limits, an alarm condition is identified. (3) Analog values are digitally filtered to eliminate wave action, surges, and electrical noise that might have been superimposed on the signals. (4) Status conditions are checked for change, and if an abnormal condition exists, an alarm is sounded and a message is transmitted to an events printer.

The computer provides real-time computations of the amount of rainfall, runoff regulator, and pump-station flow rates, storage amounts, and flow routing.

Precipitation is monitored at six remote stations located so that they are representative of the drainage basin. These stations are not permanent, so that their site can be changed to reflect changes in the drainage basin. Rainfall gauges cause closure of a contact for a small increment of measured precipitation. Each contact closure is identified and recorded by a digital pulse counter at the remote station, which is scanned periodically by the central station computer.

Based on the above information a series of critical computations is performed, including a projection of inflow in the combined sewers, routing flows through trunks and interceptors, the volumes through the regulator and outfall gates, and storage information. The raw and the processed data allow the computer to control the sewage flow effectively.

San Antonio

San Antonio currently depends solely on 65 wells to produce water for the demands of its citizens and industries. The total storage capacity is 43,601,000 gallons at 13 elevated tanks and eight reservoirs.[28, 29]

An IBM 1800 data-acquisition-and-control system monitors all domestic water production, distribution, and storage variables at two major pumping stations, six other primary pumping stations, 13 elevated storage tanks, 32 secondary pumping stations, and eight booster stations. The IBM 1800 that performs the monitoring and control functions is a 16-bit midicomputer with 32K of primary storage and up to 2,560,000 digits of storage on two magnetic disk packs. Communication equipment includes an IBM 2260 visual-display terminal and two IBM 1053 typewriterlike printers.

The computer monitors more than 600 points and over 350 variables, including all pumping stations, storage units, and more than 50 pressure-sensing points on water mains. Data collected at these points includes water levels, pressure, flow, on-off status of pumps, battery voltage, and discharge pressures.

Chicago Central District Filtration Plant

The Chicago Central District Filtration Plant serves over three million people in Chicago and 36 suburban communities.[30] The plant has been designed for a maximum capacity of 1.7 billion gallons per day. A plant of the size of Chicago's Central District Filtration Plant (CDFP), with its multiplicity of operations and need for centralized control, literally demands computer control. Originally an IBM 1710 and currently an IBM 1800 Process Control and Data Acquisition Computer is used for monitoring and controlling four large filtration plants operated in concert from one control center.

Two hundred and five analog signals and 106 contact-type signals are input into the computer. The number of measurements at control points include 234 observations on water flows, 19 on water level, and 192 on loss of head. The operator's console is organized so that the desired dosage at the 81 chemical-application points can be easily entered into the computer program along with the time that the change in dosage is required by the filtration engineer. The results of approximately 80 laboratory analyses are also entered into the computer's memory from the console.

All incoming measurements are read, and dosages, averages,

maxima, minima, deviations, and times are computed and logged. At present time intervals filter performances are computed and the results are compared to predetermined guidance values.

San Jose

The San Jose Waterworks, an investor-owned company, averages daily pumpage slightly above 78 million gallons, and at least two-thirds of this comes from 158 wells located within the service area. The balance is obtained from 13 stream intakes and five impounding reservoirs.

In order to better foresee emergencies and maintain a balanced system, San Jose moved to a monitoring and control operation.[31, 32] A Westinghouse Prodac-50 computer performs these functions. Normally the computer checks status once every nine minutes at each of 116 stations. Telephone lines carry the interrogation, status, alarm, and control messages, and the computer processes the information obtained, recording it for the daily log. If conditions require a change in pump settings, the computer automatically issues a control message to put the change into effect.

San Jose can now project accurate water-procurement figures, keep reservoirs filled to an optimum degree, and plan pump operating time so that it can take advantage of the most economical electric power rates.

Minneapolis–St. Paul Sanitary District (MSSD)

In the Minneapolis-St. Paul District (MSSD) [33, 34, 35, 36] storm and sanitary sewers empty into the main treatment plant through the same collecting mains. When heavy rainfall causes the sewers to overflow, the overflow is diverted into the river through gates in the sewers. The job of the computer is to see that the most polluted water goes to the treatment plant and the cleaner water to the river. The Minneapolis–St. Paul sewer system serves approximately 1.5 million people and handles an average annual flow of 230 million gallons per day. The total length of main and interceptor sewers exceeds 30 miles.

One of the main objectives of the current automation program is to obtain continuous measurement of water quality in the river and in the sewer at strategic points in the system. Using this data together with rainfall information, the control system can then route the most polluted water flow into the waste-treatment plant and divert relatively cleaner waters into the river.

Measurements of rainfall, sewer levels, position of gates, and water quality are collected at 28 locations and telemetered via leased phone line links back to the control computer. The control part of the system uses inflatable rubber dams and cylinder-operated gates at 15 locations throughout the sewer. A Digital Equipment Corporation PDP-9 computer interrogates various points in the system, receives data, analyzes it, and relays corrective messages. This computer is a 24K, 18-bit word computer with an additional storage of 1.5 million words on a magnetic disk. Two magnetic tapes, a line printer, and other devices provide access to the central computer. Five quality-monitoring stations measure six chemical and physical parameters on the Mississippi River, and control gates are installed at 18 key locations.

When rain is detected at rain gauges, the operator is alerted and the computer calculates the impact of the storm water on the system and determines the best gate settings to minimize pollution of the river.

Monroe County Water Authority

The Monroe County Authority serves a population of 300,000 people in 13 towns and two villages.[37] Daily water demand averages 35 million gallons per day. Water distribution is provided through 18 booster stations and 22 elevated tanks.

The county uses an IBM 1800 computer for water monitoring and control. The data-acquisition-and-processing system has a 2 μsec, 32K storage capacity; three disk drives provide additional access storage capacity; a card reader, a line printer, and input/output terminals provide peripheral support. The computer operates in a multiprogramming mode under an executive system.

A network of 360 relays collects information on flows, pump status, discharge pressures, and reservoir levels. Readings are collected every 5 minutes, alarm conditions are recorded, and corrective actions are taken as required to effectuate changes in pump status.

Denver

The city of Denver has automated its water-distribution system of 26 pumping stations and 23 pressure zones to move the necessary water out of the Platte Valley and to the users.[38, 39]

The system is built around a Digital Equipment Corporation PDP-8 computer with 8K of core memory and 32K of disk storage.

Communication devices include a teletype terminal and two type-writers and a paper read-and-punch device.

Every 15 minutes data on pressure flows, valve positions, operating pump status, reservoir elevations, and alarm conditions is telemetered to the central facility. The computer closes the loop, remotely controlling pumping units and valves as required.

Survey of Computer Applications

The major characteristics of the examples described above are summarized in Table 4.1 for comparison purposes.

The experience in "hard-wired" or "soft-wired" water distribution and sewage distribution control systems is growing daily. Some of the most interesting examples, not documented here, include:

Metropolitan Toronto Central Pumping[40]
Philadelphia Water Distribution[41, 42]
City of Sunnyvale, California[43]
City of Riverside, California[43]
Helix Distribution District, California[43]
Los Angeles County, California[43]
Santa Clara County, California[44]

Some of the interesting observations derived from these attempts at automation include the universal use of dedicated minicomputers, the delays and problems associated with software development, the lack of standardized software, and the requirements for customized designs.

On the other hand, many of the standard problems associated with water distribution and sewage water control have been solved elegantly, and much can be learned from the recorded trials and errors of the specific systems mentioned. The financial and intangible benefits associated with such automation projects outweigh the initial cost of these systems.[45, 46]

AUTOMATION OF A MUNICIPAL WASTEWATER-TREATMENT PLANT

A Primer on Municipal Wastewater Treatment

There are two kinds of sewer systems: combined and separate. Combined sewers carry away both water polluted by human use (domestic and industrial) and storm waters as it drains off streets

TABLE 4.1

Summary of Automated Water Systems

Jurisdiction	Characteristics	Variables Monitored	Computer	Reference
Monroe County Water Authority	300,000 people served; 13 towns, 2 villages. Av. water demand is 35 million gallons/day; 18 booster stations; 22 elevated tanks	Flow Pump status Pressure Levels	IBM 1800	37
City of Denver	26 pump stations; 53 pressure zones	Pressure Flow Valve position Pump status Reservoir levels	PDP-8	38, 39
Metropolitan Seattle (CATAD)	18 cities; 14 sewer districts; 4 treatment plants; 22 pumping stations; 36 remote stations; 23 control units	Flow Precipitation Pump status Storage level	SDS Sigma-3	25, 26, 27
San Antonio	65 wells; 13 elevated tanks; 8 storage reservoirs; 38 pumping stations; 8 booster stations	Water level Flow On-Off status of Pumps Discharge pressure Battery voltage	IBM 1800	28, 29
Chicago Central District Filtration Plant	36 communities; 1.7 BG/D; 4 filtration plants		IBM 1800	30
San Jose	78 MGD; 158 wells; 13 stream intakes; 116 stations	Status of pump-setting alarm	Prodac-50	31, 32
Minneapolis–St. Paul Sanitary District	5 quality monitoring points; 18 gates; 15 control gates	Rainfall Sewer level Gate position	PDP-9	33, 34, 35, 36

and land. In a separate system one set of pipes (sanitary) carries only sewage while another set (storm) takes care of the large volume of water generated by rains or melting snow.

At present there are three basic methods of treating waste: primary, secondary, and tertiary. In primary treatment solids are allowed to settle and are removed from the water. Secondary treatments essentially use bacteria to remove up to 90 percent of the biological oxygen demand (BOD). Tertiary treatment covers a wide range of techniques, such as coagulation-sedimentation, absorption, electrolysis, distillation, reverse osmosis, and are applied to removing nitrogen and phosphorous nutrients and extending the work started by the biological treatment.

In the simplest case of a treatment plant (Figure 4.4) the polluted water entering the plant first flows through a screen where floating solids are removed. The debris is raked off manually or automatically. Many plants use a comminutor, which combines the function of screening and grinding solids that remain in suspension in the water. After the sewage has been screened, it passes into a grit chamber where sand, grit, cinders, and stones are allowed to settle. The sewage then goes to the sedimentation tank, where the flow is reduced so that solids sink to the bottom of the tank.

This material is called sludge. The supernatant is usually further digested and the solid sedimented again. Chlorination of the supernatant completes the primary treatment. Sludge is handled either by trickling filters or by the activated sludge process. Trickling is a process by which bacteria are fed sludge until they disintegrate most of the organic matter in the sewage. The activated sludge process is an alternative wherein bacteria are mixed with the sludge. The liquor is generously aerated, and the bacteria are allowed to digest the organic material for several hours. The sludge is finally removed and disposed of. At several points in the system chemicals are added to favor specific chemical reactions.

A large part of the U. S. population (some 30 percent) is unsewered. Septic tanks and lagoons are used. A septic tank is a tank buried in the soil where bacteria digest the sewage and the clean water trickles through the soil and is returned to groundwater. Lagoons are ponds where algae feed on the organic material and purify the water.

The above is a simplified, step-by-step description in a nutshell of the typical wastewater-handling process. We will now show how this process could be automated.

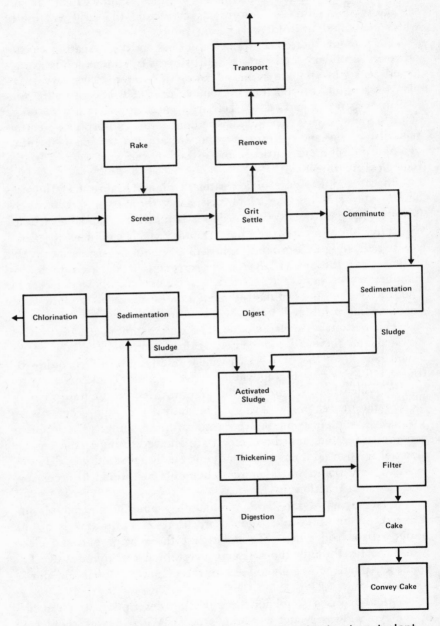

FIGURE 4.4. Simplified diagram of a wastewater treatment plant.

Steps Toward Automation [47]

No two wastewater-treatment facilities are completely alike, and their distinctive characteristics must be taken into account in the system design and in the control hardware and software.[48]

Waste-treatment plants vary mostly in terms of waste loading (i.e., source and type of waste, whether commercial, residential, industrial); in terms of the treatment processes in use; and in terms of the hardware in use in implementing the selected processes. Hence, no two automation programs can be identical even though the general approach should be consistent.

In a typical municipal wastewater-treatment system a number of parameters are manually or mechanically monitored and controlled. These include flow, volume, pressure, temperature, density, time, viscosity, pH, dissolved oxygen (DO), carbon dioxide (CO_2), methane (CH_4), total organic carbon (TOC), suspended solids (VSS), mixed liquor suspended solids (MLVSS), and added chemicals. All of these can be measured accurately, but a number of parameters cannot easily be measured. These include bacterial activity, scum production, oil, etc.

Computer automation of wastewater facilities appears to be a partial answer to combating rising costs and disappearing qualified manpower; to optimizing integrated systems; to achieving stringent regulatory standards; and to generating the information required to operate and manage such a complex facility.

An added advantage of automation is the possibility of maximizing the operation of the plant within design capacity, promoting effective primary settling and maximum aerobic decomposition by making programmed adjustments to take into account diurnal peaks. It should also be possible to avoid gross overload of the capacity and hence flushing of the activated sludge.

A recent survey[49] concluded that the state-of-the-art of sensors and the ability to close the loop between monitored variables and plant-control functions are the limiting factors to widespread automation.

Many chemical processes are controlled by computers; we will now try to apply this knowledge to the control of specific wastewater-treatment steps.

Returning to the broader issue, a potential scheme for the total monitoring and control of a municipal waste handling plant is shown in Figure 4.5. This analysis must obviously be pursued several steps further before automation is possible.

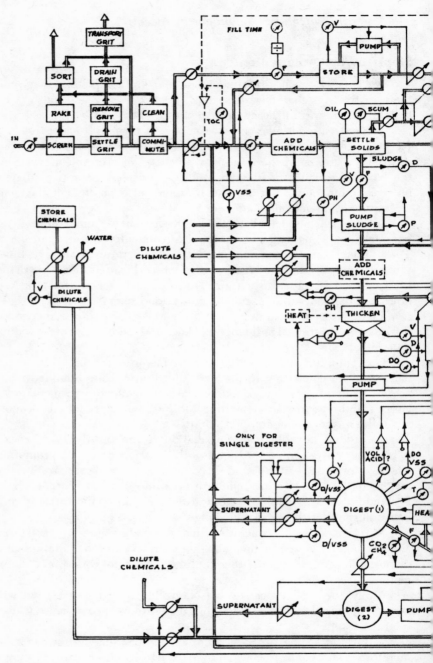

FIGURE 4.5.   Waste-treatment plant automation. *(From the MITRE Corp., ref. 47)*

130

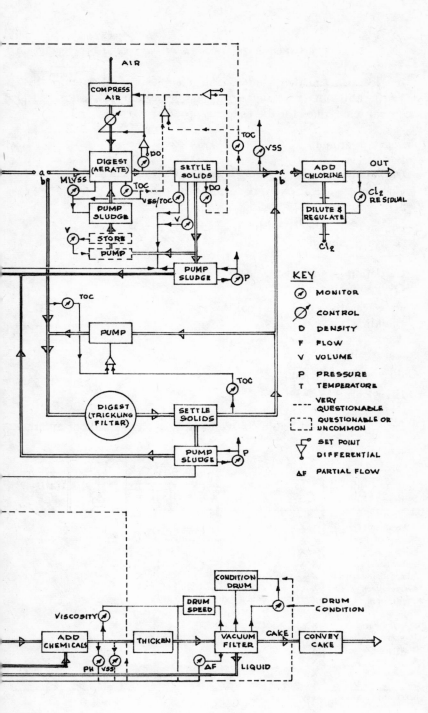

KEY

- ⊘ MONITOR
- ⊘ CONTROL
- D DENSITY
- F FLOW
- V VOLUME
- P PRESSURE
- T TEMPERATURE
- --- VERY QUESTIONABLE
- [---] QUESTIONABLE OR UNCOMMON
- SET POINT
- DIFFERENTIAL
- ΔF PARTIAL FLOW

131

A recent exhaustive study[50] and comparison of specific studies[51-59] describe in great detail alternative automation and control conceptual techniques for the following processes:

Primary treatment
  Bar Screen [52]
  Comminution
  Grit removal, collection, concentration, disposal
  Sedimentation

Secondary Biological Treatment
  Activated sludge
  Trickling filters
  Oxidation ponds
  Oxygen aeration

Sludge Handling and Disposal [53]
  Blending
  Anaerobic digestion
  Thickening

Chlorine Disinfection

  pH Control [57, 58, 59]

In Figure 4.6 and Table 4.2 we identify typical points of automa-

MONITORING POINTS	FLOW	DEPTH	POWER	TEMP	PH	COD	TOC	PHOS	NITR	ORP	DO	SS	TOX	BOD	DENS	MLSS	CHLOR	TURB	PVM	CO2	METH	TOT. SOL.	WEIGHT
Influent gates	X	X																					
Mechanical screen	X	X																					
Pump	X	X	X	X																			
Grit channel	X	X			X	X	X	X	X	X	X	X	X	X									
Prim. sedimentation	X					X	X	X						X		X	X						
Aeration tank	X					X	X	X					X	X		X		X					
Clarification	X					X	X	X			X	X	X	X	X	X							
Trickling filter	X					X	X									X							
Chlorination	X							X	X	X	X		X					X	X				
Thickener	X												X		X	X			X			X	
Digester	X	X				X	X			X									X	X	X	X	
Regulator	X	X				X	X																
Dewatering	X						X												X				X

NOTE: BOD can be replaced by COD or TOC.

FIGURE 4.6.   Monitoring points. *(From EPA, ref. 60)*

TABLE 4.2

List of Symbols

FLOW	Flow of liquid
DEPTH	Depth of liquid
POWER	Power to operate pumps
TEMP	Temperature
PH	Potential hydrogen
COD	Chemical oxygen demand
TOC	Total organic carbon
PHOS	Phosphates
NITR	Nitrogen
ORP	Oxidation-reduction potential
DO	Dissolved oxygen
SS	Suspended solids
TOX	Toxicity
BOD	Biological oxygen demand
DENS	Sludge density
MLSS	Mixed liquor suspended solids
CHLOR	Chlorine
TURB	Turbidity
PVM	Percent volatile matter
CO_2	Carbon dioxide
METH	Methane
TOT SOL	Total solids
WEIGHT	Sludge weight

tion and monitoring. The devices and the variables identified should be measured for several reasons: estimation of plant efficiency, logging, alarm, historical records, process control, etc. In no case would all variables and all points be measured. They represent the maximum diversity in sampling points and variables.[60] Figure 4.6 summarizes the key automation points in a wastewater treatment system and the variables that could be measured and subsequently used to control the process.

The next question that arises concerns our ability to measure the variable in such a way that an analog or digital signal would indicate the value of the parameter of interest. Table 4.3 is the result of a rapid state-of-the-art survey in detection characteristic, output signal, and commercial availability of the necessary devices. This is a very dynamic field, and while we pointed out earlier that sensors were a limiting factor to automation, we are expecting rapid progress in that very same area.[61]

TABLE 4.3

State-of-the-Art Survey

	Variable	Function	Real Time Detection/ Continuous	Analog or Digital Signal	Detection Technique	Automated Device Commercially Available
1.	pH	Indicate acid-base composition	Yes	A/D	Electrical	Yes
2.	BOD	Oxygent requirements of organic matter and chemicals	No	–	Biological	No
3.	Temperature	Temperature of process	Yes	A/D	Electrical	Yes
4.	COD	Total oxygen consumption	No	A	Wet-Chem	Yes
5.	TOC	Total organic carbon	No	A	Wet-Chem	Yes
6.	DO	Dissolved oxygen	Yes	A	Electrical	Yes
7.	SS	Suspended solid	Yes	A	Electrical	Yes
8.	PVM	Percent volatile matter, measure organic contents	No	A	Ignition	No
9.	Phosphates	Measure phosphates nutrient	No	A	Wet-Chem	Yes
10.	Nitrogen	Nitrogenous compounds	No	A	Wet-Chem	Yes
11.	ORP	Potential required to transfer electrons from oxydant to reductant	Yes	A	Electrical	Yes
12.	Toxic Compounds & Metals	Levels of variety of compounds	No	–	Wet-Chem	No
13.	Depth	Detect outfall sewer overflows	Yes	A	Electrical	Yes
14.	Flow	Flow of liquid	Yes	A	Electrical	Yes
15.	Density	Sludge density	No	–	Chemistry	No
16.	Turbidity	SS < 500 mg/L	Yes	A	Electrical	Yes
17.	MLSS	Mixed liquid suspended solid indicates return sludge needs	Yes	A	Electrical	Yes

Throughout the nation plans are being developed for automating waste-treatment facilities including Nassau County, Long Island,[62, 63] Dallas, San Jose, and Philadelphia.[64]

Some of the best-documented cases include the Philadelphia Waste Water System,[64, 65] the Japanese Plan in the Saitama Prefecture,[66, 67] and the Iowa City Chemical Addition Process.[68]

REFERENCES

1. Wallace E. Block and James A. Bodine, "Computer-Controlled Petroleum Production Systems." *IEEE Trans.* IGA-5(4):403-410, 1969.

2. Ronald E. Evans and Joseph H. Herz, "Seven Years of Process Control at California Portland Cement Company." *IEEE Trans.* IGA-6(5): 472-475, 1970.

3. Donald L. Grammes, "Direct Digital Control at Lone Star's Greencastle, Indiana, Plant." *IEEE Trans.* IGA-6(5):480-487, 1971.

4. T. E. Fluringer and G. Revere Smith, "Liquid Pipeline Scheduling and Control with an On-line Multiprogramming Process Computer." *IEEE Trans.* IGA-5(4):389-402, 1969.

5. Theodore J. Wlliams, "Computers and Process Control." *Ind. Eng. Chem.* 61(1):76-89, 1969.

6. Second U.K.N.C. Convention on Advances in Computer Control. IEEE Conf. Publication N. 29, 1967.

7. W. E. Miller, ed., *Digital Computer Applications to Process Control.* Plenum Press, New York, 1965.

8. Proc. IBM Scientific Computing Symposium on Control Theory and Its Applications. IBM, 1966.

9. J. F. Andrews, "Control Systems for Wastewater Treatment Plants." *Water Research* 6:575-582, 1972.

10. J. F. Andrews, "Design-Operation Interaction for Waste Water Treatment Plants." *Water Research* 6:319-322, 1972.

11. Crisis in Megalopolis Demands New Electronics. *Electronic Design* 1:66-84, 1968.

12. Robert C. Freeston, "Controls for a Small Water Utility." *J. Am. Water Works Assoc.* 63(7):523-525, 1971.

13. "How to Automate Your Water Treatment." *Control* 11(106):182–186, 1967.

14. W. V. Iacina and S. D. Heden, "Automatic Control of Water Softening." *J. Am. Water Works Assoc.* 63(7):530-531, 1971.

15. Robert H. Jones, "Instrument for Water Pollution Control." *Pollution Engineering* (November/December) 22-23, 1971.

16. Richard G. Green, "Sensing and Controlling Liquid Level." *Automation* 15(2):61-71, 1968.

17. H. M. Rivers and G. W. Schweitzer, "Practical Automation of

Water Treatment Monitoring and Control Systems." Am. Water Works Assoc., 1970 Annual Conf., Washington, D. C.

18. Russel H. Babcock, "Evaluation of Instrumentation and Control." *J. Water Poll. Control*, Fed, 44(7):1416-1424, 1971.

19. Dan A. Brock, "Closed-Loop Autmatic Control of Water Systems Operations." *J. Am. Water Works Assoc.* 467-479, April 1962.

20. Harry D. Harman, "A Remote Controlled Filtration Plant." *The American City* 81(5):100-102, 1966.

21. Richard Wood, "Automatic Control Systems." *Water Research* 6:583-585, 1972.

22. W. Paul Winn, "Supervisory and Remote Control of Pressure Structures on Large Pipelines." *J. Am. Water Works Assoc.* 61:585-591, 1969.

23. "Telemetering: Five Utilities Experiences." *J. Am. Water Works Assoc.* 62(8):491-507, 1971.

24. Robert A. Ryder, "Automatic Control for Smaller Water and Waste-Water Facilities." 9th Sanitary Engineering Conf., University of Illinois, February 1967.

25. Charles V. Gibbs, Stuart M. Alexander and Curtis A. Leiser, "A Computer Directed System for Regulation of Combined Sewage Flows." ASCE National Water Resources Engineering Meeting, Atlanta, Georgia, January 24-28, 1972.

26. C. V. Gibbs and S. M. Alexander, "CATAD System Controls for Regulation of Combined Sewage Flows." *Water and Wastes Engineering*, pp. 46-49, August 1969.

27. "Maximizing Storage in Combined Sewer Systems." U.S. Environmental Protection Agency, Water Pollution Control Research Series 11122 ELK, December 1971.

28. Robert P. Van Dyke, "Computer Completely Controls Water Utility." *Water and Sewage Works*, pp. 76-79; September 1968.

29. Paul C. Nail and Leo F. Campos, "Automation of San Antonio's Water System." *Public Works*, pp. 76-79, September 1968.

30. Delbert M. Leppke, "Computer Goes to Work in Chicago." *Water and Wastes Engineering*, pp. 82-84, May 1966.

31. N. J. Kendall, "A Computerized Water System." *The American City*, pp. 99-100, September 1967.

32. N. J. Kendall and L. F. Dunton, "Computer Control at San Jose." *J. Am. Water Works Assoc.* 65(2):92-98, 1973.

33. "Computer to Regulate Water Pollution." *Control Engineering*, p. 20, December 1967.

34. J. J. Anderson, "'Sewer Control and Plant Automation." *Water Research* 6:611-615, 1972.

35. "Computer to Regulate Water Pollution." *Control Eng.* p. 20, December 1967.

36. James L. Anderson, R. L. Callery and D. J. Anderson, "How to Control Sewer Overflows." *Water Wastes Eng.*, September 1972.

37. Charles M. Frenz, "Automated System Control." *J. Am Water Works Assoc.* (218):508-512, 1971.

38. Carl E. C. Carlson, "The Denver System of Water Works Control." *J. Am. Water Works Assoc.* 63(8):513-516, 1971.

39. M. E. Barber, "Experience in Denver, Colorado." *J. Am. Water Works Assoc.* 138-139, February, 1973.

40. P. M. Emery, "Metropolitan Toronto Central Pumping Control." *J. Am. Water Works Assoc.*, 128-133, February 1973.

41. V. A. Pagnotto, "Experience in Philadelphia, Pa." *J. Am. Water Works Assoc.* 134-137, February 1973.

42. C. F. Guarino, "The Use of Computers in Philadelphia's Water Pollution Control Activities." *Water Research* 6:597-600, 1972.

43. "Telemetering: Five Utilities' Experience." *J. Am. Water Works Assoc.* 63(8):491-507, 1971.

44. J. W. Garrett, "Experience in Santa Clara County, Calif." *J. Am. Water Works Assoc.* 140-143, February 1973.

45. R. C. Neel, "Computer Applications in Distribution." *J. Am. Water Works Assoc.* 63(8):485-489, 1970.

46. J. Sheldon Tart, "Value of Telemetering and Recording." *J. Am. Water Works Assoc.*, 124-127, February 1973.

47. "Application of Automation Techniques to Sewage Treatment Plants." The MITRE Corporation, M70-63, March 1970.

48. William B. Field, "Design of a pH Control System by Analog Simulation." *ISA Journal* 6(1):42-50, 1969.

49. "'Instrumentation, Control, and Automation for Water Supply and Wastewater Treatment Systems." Proceedings, 9th Sanitary Engineering Conference, University of Illinois, 1967.

50. Joseph L. Pavoni and Peter R. Spinney, "Automation of Wastewater Treatment Systems." *AD* 753-926, December 1972.

51. "Industrial Environmental Control Systems." Bulletin B-36, Foxboro Company.

52. "Continuous Measurement and Control of Fluoride in Public Water Supplies." *Application Engineering Data* 434-442, Foxboro, June 1969.

53. "Sludge Digester Control." *Application Engineering Data* 435-450, Foxboro, April 1968.

54. "Digester Level Measurement, Pneumatic." *Application Engineering Data* 435-453, Foxboro, March 1966.

55. "Digester Level Measurement, Electronic." *Application Engineering Data* 435-454, Foxboro, February 1970.

56. "Raw Sewage Measurement at Pumping Stations." *Application Engineering Data* 435-15, Foxboro, May 1968.

57. "pH Measurement and Control." Bulletin K-15A, Foxboro.

58. "pH Control of Waste Stream Neutralization." Foxboro.

59. William B. Field, "Design of a pH Control System by Analog Simulation." *ISA Journal* 6(1):42-50: 1959.

60. "Feasibility of Computer Control of Wastewater Treatment." EPA, 1709000Y 12/70, Washington, D.C., December 1970.

61. Robert Patton, "Automation in Industrial Water Management." *Env. Control & Safety Management* 3:14-17, 1971.

62. "Public Works Computer Applications Guidelines for Installation and Operation of Computerized Process Control Systems." Am. Public Works Assoc., Spec. Report No. 38, August 1970.

63. Dexter J. Olsen, "Programming the War Against Water Pollution." *AFIPS Conf. Proceed.* 39:115-121, 1971.

64. C. F. Guarino and G. W. Carpenter, "Philadelphia's Plans Toward Instrumentation and Automation of the Wastewater Treatment Process." *Advances in Water Pollution Research*, Vol. 1, S. H. Jenkins, ed., Pergamon Press, New York, 1971.

65. C. F. Guarino, H. D. Gilman, M. D. Nelson and C. M. Koch, "Computer Control of Wastewater Treatment." *Water Pollution Control Fed.* 44(9):1718-1728, 1972.

66. S. Tohyama, "Computer Control—Arakawa Treatment Plant." *Water Resh.* 6:591-595, 1972.

67. S. Tohyama, "Basic Problems in the Design of Large Treatment Plants—Arakawa Treatment Plant." *Water Resh.* 6:347-350, 1972.

68. A. W. Manning, "Computer Control of Chemical Addition at a Water Treatment Plant. *J. Am. Water Works Assoc.* 498-503, July 1973.

CHAPTER 5

THE USES OF COMPUTERS IN SCIENTIFIC AND ADMINISTRATIVE FUNCTIONS

The impact of using computers on the business of protecting the environment has been long in coming despite the ubiquitous use of computers for such trivial functions as account processing and sophisticated applications such as mathematical modeling. General review papers [1, 2, 3] and surveys [4, 5] on the use of computers by agencies concerned with the environment are available.

In this chapter we will review the use of computers in administrative applications.

ADMINISTRATIVE USES

State, county, and city water- and air-pollution departments have the same accounting problems as small- to medium-sized commercial firms. A recent survey[5] among public works agencies showed that some 58 percent of the municipalities in the 250,000–500,000 population group and some 40 percent in the 100,000–250,000 class use computers.

Most uses of computers in this category are for the business type of applications, including payroll, accounting[4, 6] and budgeting, inventory control, project records, permits, etc. These standard procedures have been modified to apply to such environmental problems as incinerator operations [7] and sanitary landfill.[6] In addition to these normal accounting uses of computers, governmental environmental agencies have developed procedures to assist in the bookkeeping and clerical tasks of compiling and maintaining inventories of emission sources and of industrial and commercial production capacities and schedules, determining the status of control device implementation schedules or environmental impact statements, and the development of bibliographies of applicable environmental techniques or directions of experts conducting research.

An example of the above types of procedures is the National Emission Data System developed by the U. S. Environmental Protection Agency (EPA).

The National Emission Data System

The Federal EPA has developed the National Emission Data System (NEDS), which is a system for the coding, storage, retrieval, and analysis of nationwide air emission data.

NEDS is essentially an inventory that provides information concerning source emissions and that defines location, magnitude, frequency, duration, and relative contribution of these emissions.

When coupled with local meteorological air-quality-and-effects data, NEDS provides the basis for a plan of action for improving air quality. The overall concept of NEDS is diagrammed in Figure 5.1, where the relevant files are identified on the left and the supporting ADP functions are on the right.

Files Descriptions. The following files are integral parts of the system:

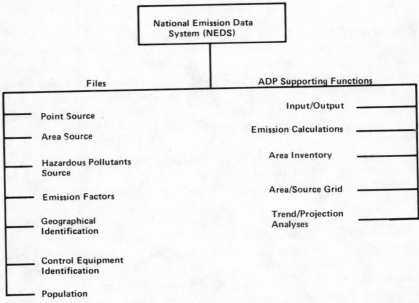

FIGURE 5.1. Demonstration of the national emission data concept.

1. Point source—information on sources emitting more than 100 tons per day
2. Area source—nonpoint source information
3. Hazardous pollutants—informations on each source of hazardous or potentially toxic trace elements or other compounds
4. Emission factor—quantitative estimates of emission rate of pollutant released to the atmosphere by industrial activity
5. Geographical identification—concerns EPA regional offices, AQCR, and county names, plus coordinate identifiers
6. Control equipment—contains air pollution control equipment names and codes
7. Population—population data from various sources including Bureau of Census

ADP *Supporting Functions of* NEDS. The necessary software to store, maintain, and manipulate the data is performed through a series of computer programs, including:

1. Input/output—all data is put on coding forms for storage in the computer. Representative card images are shown in Figures 5.2 and 5.3
2. Emission calculations—apply the emission factors to the source data to obtain total emission
3. Area Source Gridding Program—for apportioning the area source emissions to grids
4. Trend/projection Analysis Programs—utilize available data to estimate trends and forecast emissions by source categories and and geographical activities

Status of NEDS. The files are currently being designed and data are being submitted from each state and EPA region. The software is under development for installation in the EPA computer at Research Triangle Park in North Carolina.

SCIENTIFIC FUNCTIONS

In this section we describe computer applications in simulation, mathematical modeling, statistical analysis, and mathematical data treatment such as linear programming.

Simulation

A simulation is an imitation of a process that is under study. A simulation can be either a physical model of the process or a mathematical representation of the events of the process. Physical simula-

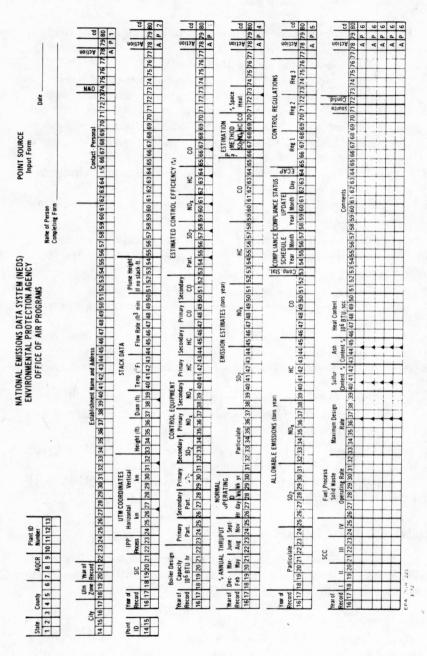

FIGURE 5.2.   NEDS point source input coding form. *(From EPA, ref. 8)*

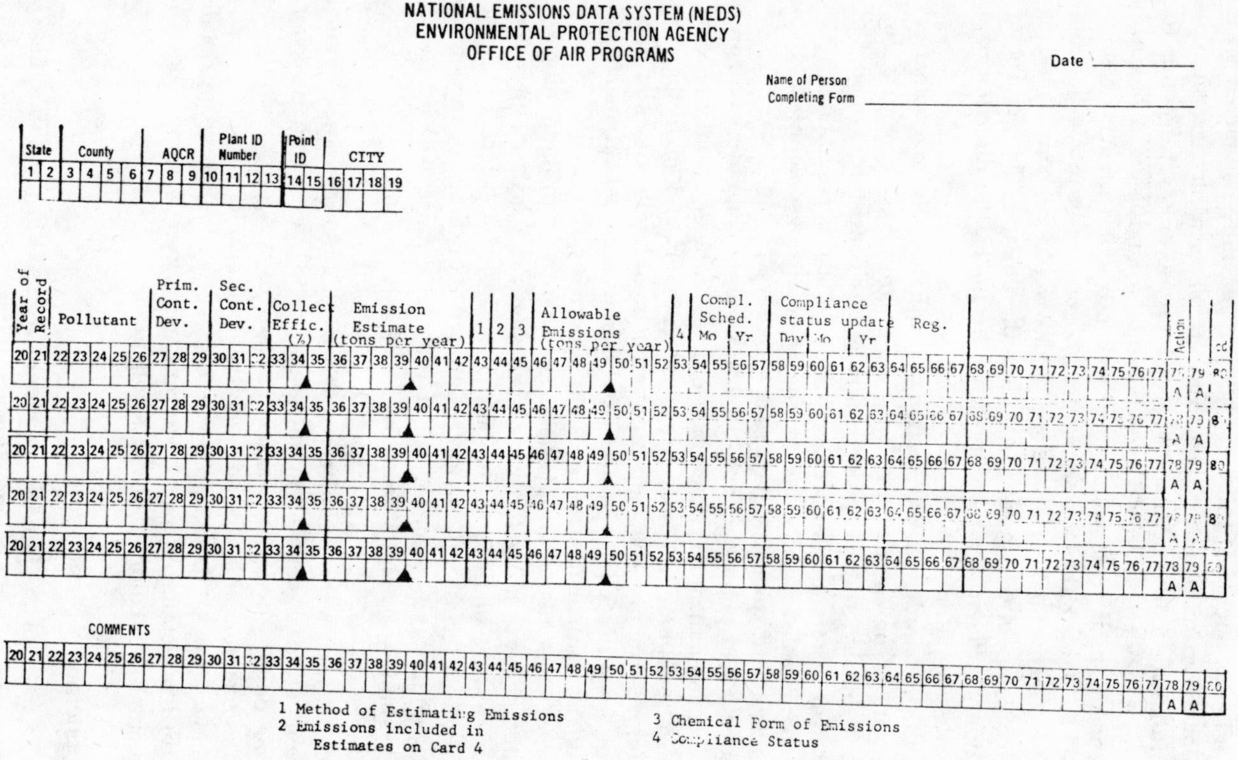

Name of Person _____
Completing Form

Date _____

State	County	AQCR	Plant ID Number	Point ID	CITY
1 2	3 4 5	6 7 8 9	10 11 12	13 14 15	16 17 18 19

Year of Record | Pollutant | Prim. Cont. Dev. | Sec. Cont. Dev. | Collect Effic. (%) | Emission Estimate (tons per year) | 1 2 3 | Allowable Emissions (tons per year) | Compl. Sched. 4 | Compliance status update Mo Yr. | Reg. | Action

| 20 21 | 22 23 24 25 26 | 27 28 29 | 30 31 32 | 33 34 35 | 36 37 38 39 40 41 | 42 43 44 45 | 46 47 48 49 50 51 52 | 53 54 55 | 56 57 58 59 60 61 62 63 | 64 65 66 67 68 69 70 71 72 73 74 75 76 77 | 78 79 80 |

COMMENTS

1 Method of Estimating Emissions
2 Emissions Included in Estimates on Card 4
3 Chemical Form of Emissions
4 Compliance Status

FIGURE 5.3. NEDS trace materials/hazardous pollutant input coding form. (From EPA, ref. 8)

tions can be conducted at full scale but are generally conducted on a scaled-down version of the system. An example of a physical simulation at full scale is the addition of dye into one of several ponds to determine if they are interconnected by underground flows. A physical simulation at small scale would be the construction of a laboratory model of an industrial plant discharging heated water into a flowing, turbulent stream. Such a laboratory model would be constructed to determine temperature gradients within the stream. The control of turbidity and effluent temperature could be under the direction of a small-scale computer.

In the remainder of this section we will describe mathematical representations or simulations, since these are more generally employed. Typically, these computer simulations consist of a model of the physical system and an abstract mathematical representation programmed for solution on either a digital or analog computer.[9] Both deterministic and stochastic models are used.

Three broad phases are seen in developing a computerized simulation: conceptualization, execution, and results evaluation. The conceptualization phase is concerned with defining and analyzing the problem, determining the data requirements and collecting the data, adopting hypotheses to be tested, establishing a model rationale, and deriving the mathematical expressions describing the model. The execution, or implementation, phase consists mostly of programming the computer and executing the prescribed runs. The last phase is centered around the analysis of the outputs and the interpretation of the results both in terms of the model and in terms of the phenomenon we wish to understand. Some or all of the above steps will be recognized in the few examples described below.

Simulation using both analog and digital computers has been applied to such varied subjects as thermal addition, BOD, regional development, pest control, urban water runoff, estuarine behavior, reservoir design, hydrology, activated sludge, waste-treatment plant design, sewer network, and air-pollution microchemistry.

Below, two of these applications are described in some detail. Then, in less detail, a general description is given of some other environmental simulations that are available.

Microchemistry Simulation

The study of the fate of compounds released in the atmosphere [10] has proceeded along two complementary lines: a study of the ecological cycles (water, CO, nitrogen, phosphorus, etc.) starting as far back as Lotka [11] and studies in microchemistry. [12, 13, 14, 15, 16]

Examples of cycle and first-order-associated microchemistry equations are presented for the CO_x and SO_x subsystems in Figures 5.4 and 5.5.

The complexity of the model [18] and the tediousness of the computations call for computer simulation.[19, 20] These models use a large number of chemical reactions with associated reaction rate and can be simulated over any portion of time, usually until equilibrium is achieved. In most cases a set of differential equations is solved by the Runge-Kutta method for numerical integration. A description of this, as well as many other numerical methods, can be found in many texts.[21, 22, 23]

Waste-Treatment Systems Simulation

Computer simulation is being applied to simulating the design and operation of wastewater-treatment systems from the traditional primary and secondary treatments to the sophisticated and advanced tertiary treatments.

A waste-treatment facility is a complex system. Subroutines are now available [24, 25, 26] to simulate the operation of most components. The individual involved in the research of an existing system or the analysis of a proposed system can quickly model a specific configuration. The process of developing a simulation employing these subroutines can be most easily developed by constructing a schematic of the process flow with key sets of symbols. Figure 5.6 summarizes the key sets of symbols, and Figure 5.7 shows a typical formulation of a waste-treatment plant.

The following processes already have been programmed in FORTRAN:

Process Name	Subroutine Name
Preliminary Treatment	PREL
Primary Settler	PRSET
Aerator—Final Settler	AERFS
Mixer	MIX
Splitter	SPLIT
Digester	DIG
Vacuum Filter	VACF
Sludge Thickener	THICK
Sludge Elutriation	ELUT
Sludge Dryng Beds	SBEDS

Additional processes being programmed are trickling filter, final clarifier for activated sludge process, fluidized-bed incineration of

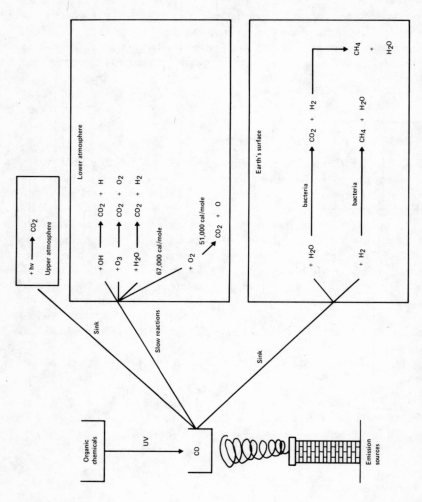

FIGURE 5.4. Example of a CO_x subsystem simulation.

146

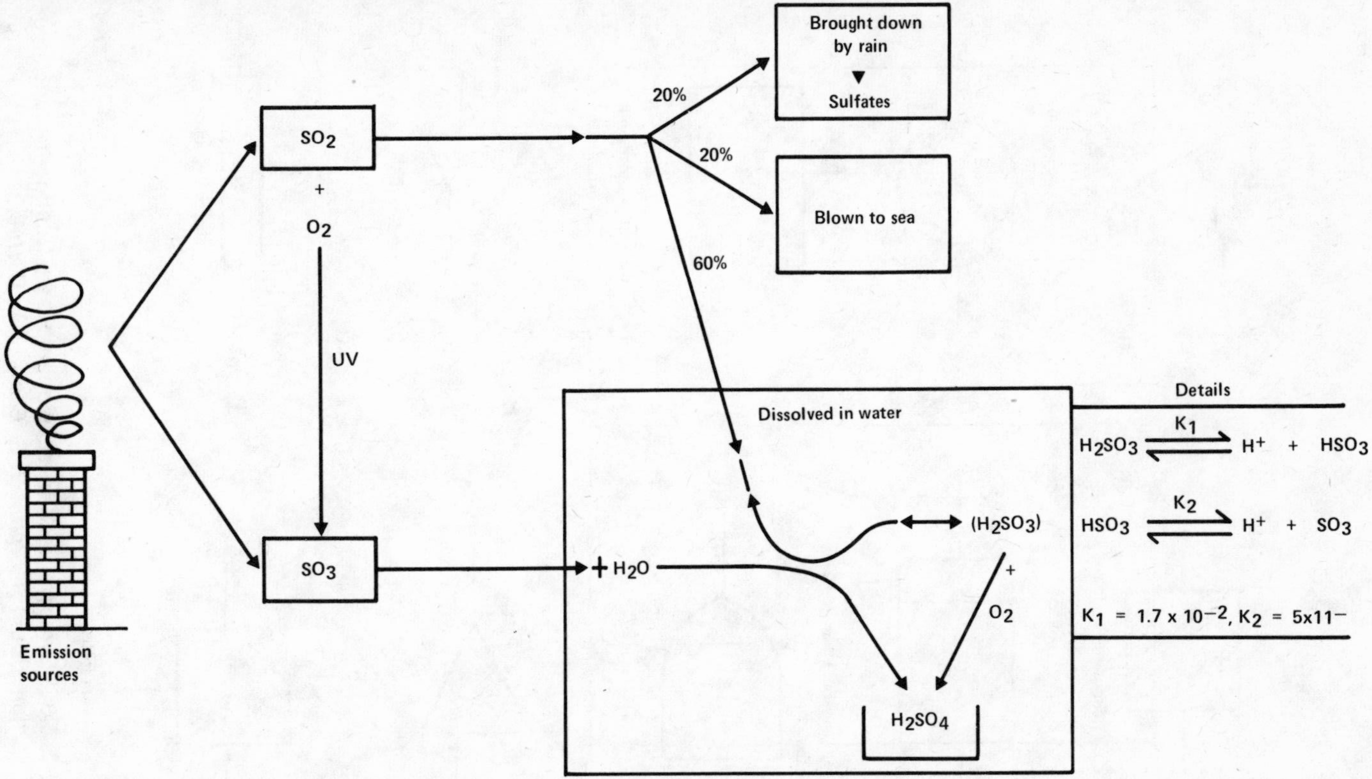

FIGURE 5.5. Example of a SO_x subsystem simulation.

Emission sources

SO_2 + O_2 → UV → SO_3

20%

20% Brought down by rain → Sulfates

20% Blown to sea

60%

Dissolved in water

+ H_2O

(H_2SO_3)

+ O_2

H_2SO_4

Details

H_2SO_3 ⇌ K_1 ⇌ H^+ + HSO_3

HSO_3 ⇌ K_2 ⇌ H^+ + SO_3

$K_1 = 1.7 \times 10^{-2}$, $K_2 = 5 \times 11 -$

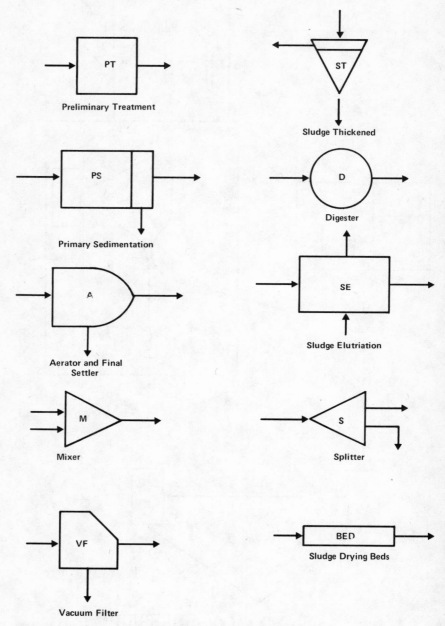

PT
Preliminary Treatment

ST
Sludge Thickened

PS
Primary Sedimentation

D
Digester

A
Aerator and Final
Settler

SE
Sludge Elutriation

M
Mixer

S
Splitter

VF
Vacuum Filter

BED
Sludge Drying Beds

FIGURE 5.6.   Symbols used in developing waste-treatment plant solution. *(From R. Smith, R. G. Eilers, & E. D. Hall, ref. 25)*

148

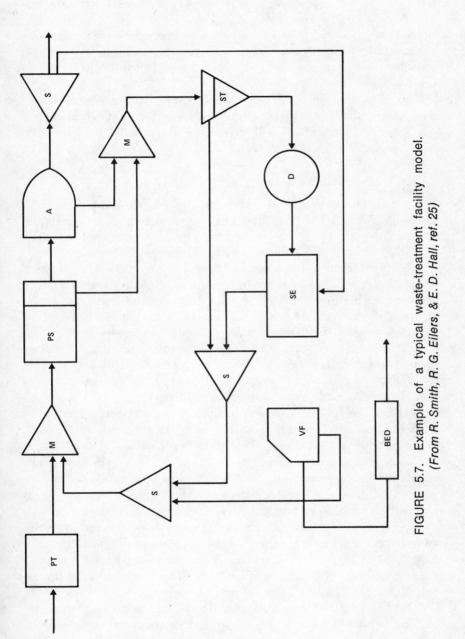

FIGURE 5.7. Example of a typical waste-treatment facility model. (*From R. Smith, R. G. Eilers, & E. D. Hall, ref. 25*)

149

sludges, coagulation and sedimentation of secondary effluent follow-ing addition of lime or alum, ammonia stripping of secondary effluent, granular carbon absorption, ion exchange, electrodialysis, and re-verse osmosis.

An important effort is the accumulation of construction costs and operating and maintenance costs. It is suggested that within a few years detailed simulations will have been completed for all primary, secondary, and tertiary treatments.

Other Environmental Simulations

Simulation methodology has been applied to a wide variety of problems in the fields of air and water environment. A few examples will be discussed to provide the reader with an overview of this field.

One, HYDRO,[26] is a content-oriented language designed to provide simple input/output formats consisting only of data and content-oriented command; the ability to string a long chain of commands; a standard for writing computer programs in the water-resources-man-agement area; modularity; and the possibility of extending the list of primitive commands. A number of operational segments of HYDRO in-clude frequency analysis, precipitation analysis, hydrograph analysis, open-channel hydraulics, flood routing, and piping-network analysis.

Other procedures in progress or planned include groundwater flow, hydraulic modeling and water quality segment.

The entire system is written in HYDRALGOL, which is a mixture of HYDRO commands (written in ALGOL) and the basic ALGOL language. A FORTRAN IV version has also been developed.

The standard watershed Model V (SWM-V) [27] is a streamflow simulation program written in PL/I for the IBM System 360 series com-puter. In this model hydrologic simulation is applied to the process of creating and operating a mathematical model of the hydrologic cycle. The model data inputs are the time profile of demand for water and the description of existing physical water-supply facilities. The model determines a solution to meet the current demand optimally (as allowed by input and facilities), and develops a plan for the ex-tension of facilities based on demand forecast.

Numerous other simulations have appeared in the literature, in-cluding one of biological oxygen demand in streams [28] and of pollu-tion in air masses over Connecticut [29] and other areas.[30] To extend the list would be mere cataloging and would not further our purpose.

Network Analysis

Network analysis is a technique based on the abstract mathematical concept of graph theory.[31] It has been successfully applied to solving large-scale transportation problems, as in the case of commodity flow. A typical application is the optimal design of off-shore natural gas piping.[32, 33]

The use of network analysis and graph theory concepts is new in the environment.[34, 35, 36] The problem of designing a sewage collection system to minimize pipeline use or to more efficiently size the workload is reminiscent of transportation commodity flow problems.

A minimum amount of information is necessary for applying network technology to optimum waste-distribution systems, such as a knowledge of the topography and the locations of outlets, i.e., treatment plants or main sewer trunks. Limitations such as right-of-way, location of buildings and streets, and the hydraulic nature of the network are added constraints often included in models.

A practical application [37] to the Merrick Harbor collection district in Nassau County has shown in a relatively complex real-world

it is possible to estimate design flows, design sewers,

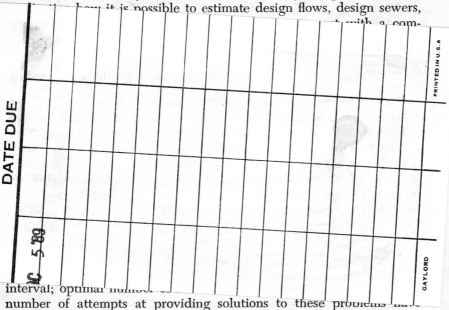

interval; optimal number of

number of attempts at providing solutions to these problems have been undertaken, typically based on sound statistical premises. Because of the complexity of the situations encountered, the computer is a necessary tool.

Two basic approaches to developing solutions to the station-location problem have been used thus far. The first approach is basically a regression technique based on the concept that observations at different stations are correlated as a result of being under the influence of similar environmental phenomena. Based on the study of the variance and information content in the parameters studied, it is possible to develop siting strategies within budgetary constraints.[38] The second approach uses power-spectrum analysis and attempts to solve especially the problem of optimum sampling interval.[39, 40, 41]

The third problem of the number of sites can be solved easily by elementary statistical techniques if both the desired precision of the data and the variability of the parameters measured are known.

The last problem has been solved conceptually by requesting that averaging time should be identical to the averaging time stipulated in the standards. The integration time-conversion problem has been solved technically by Larsen.[42]

Statistical Analysis

The whole spectrum of statistical tools from stochastic models of pollutant behavior [43, 44] to hypothesis testing in the univariate, bivariate, and multivariate fields has been brought to bear on environmental problems. Most attempts at summarizing environmental data have taken the form of simple statistical descriptors. Measures of central tendency (arithmetic mean, geometric mean) and measures of scatter (arithmetic standard deviation, geometric standard deviation) are usually supplemented with percentile distribution. Recently an attempt has been initiated in developing aggregate indices of several measures of derived parameters.[45, 46]

The number of studies using a computer as a computational aid are too numerous to be repeated or even summarized here. As an alternative we will describe some of the analyses being currently applied to the National Aerometric Data Bank.

As Figure 5.8 indicates, two broad types of analyses are being directed to the National Aerometric Data Bank. The first is involved with defining a siting rationale for air-pollution sensors and a statistical definition of the methodology and instrument complement in use. The first findings from this study indicate that the instruments in use are nonsophisticated and mostly of the integration type. It further indicates that only a handful of sites measure the six primary air pollutants.[48] The left side of the figure, and the most important aspect of the analysis, is termed pollutant analysis. This is broken

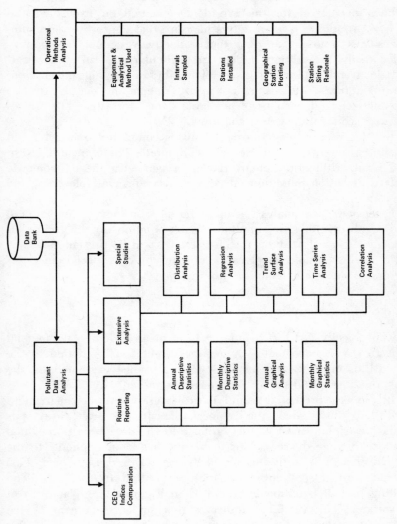

FIGURE 5.8. Approach of data analysis applied to the NADB. *(From J. W. Overbey & R. P. Ouellette, ref. 47)*

153

down into indices computation, routine reporting, extensive analysis, and special studies. Each will be generally described below.

The concept of developing indices to monitor trend and status has been developed for the President's Council on Environmental Quality. An index is a quantitative measure that aggregates and summarizes vast amounts of data that collectively cannot be comprehended easily. In addition, indices are particularly useful for illustrating major trends and can be used for highlighting significant environmental conditions. Indices are not measurements and may be formed from only selected portions of available data. More than 110 indices have been conceptualized at this time.[45, 46]

Routine reporting of the data bank is completed quarterly, and elementary descriptor statistics are computed. These include arithmetic mean, arithmetic standard deviation, geometric mean, geometric standard deviation, minimum, maximum, percent available data, and percentiles.

Extensive data analysis usually requires a long, uninterrupted series of observations or simultaneous observation on diverse pollutants. Some typical analyses in this category will be presented below. Special analysis usually involves the preparation of a special computer program to answer a technical question.

Trend Surface Analysis

The objective of this technique is to fit an n-degree polynomial to a set of XYZ coordinates. A goodness-to-fit test is applied to the surface thus created, and an analysis of variance explained by the linear, quadratic, and cubic components is presented.[49]

In the case presented X and Y are geographical coordinates and the Z's are observed-air-quality measurements. In most cases it is possible to explain most of the variance in the data by a polynomial of less than three degrees. This technique has been applied[47] to the Chicago area air-quality measurements for SO_2 and TSP. Using 1965 SO_2 measurements, a cubic equation was fitted to the data. The resulting best fit equation is presented in Figure 5.9. An analysis of the variance (Figure 5.10) indicates that some 68 percent of the variance is explained by the cubic surface. The contour lines of this cubic surface are shown in Figure 5.11. An overlay of the Cook County outline provides some orientation. Further, it shows that there is generally good agreement between the trend surface analysis fit and a fit developed by the more sophisticated and time consuming air-quality diffusion model.

COEFFICIENTS OF LINEAR EQUATION

$$Z = -11.65632 + 0.96637\ X + 0.41745\ Y$$

COEFFICIENTS OF QUADRIC EQUATION

$$Z = 34.67349 + -2.72514\ X + 4.88660\ Y + 0.02614\ X2 + 0.01319\ XY + -0.04277\ Y2$$

COEFFICIENTS OF CUBIC EQUATION

$$Z = -242.04608 + -37.73093\ X + 47.82057\ Y + 1.14570\ X2 + -1.26355\ XY + -0.02497\ Y2 +$$
$$-0.00702\ X3 + 0.00362\ X2Y + 0.00790\ XY2 + -0.00335Y3$$

FIGURE 5.9.   Trend surface analysis. *(From J. W. Overbey & R. P. Ouellette, ref. 47)*

SURFACE	LINEAR	QUADRIC	CUBIC
STANDARD DEVIATION	34.59	30.32	21.46
VARIATION EXPLAINED BY SURFACE	0.50540977E 04	0.10880953E 05	0.20510852E 05
VARIATION NOT EXPLAINED BY SURFACE	0.25130277E 05	0.19303422E 05	0.96735234E 04
TOTAL VARIATION	0.30184375E 05	0.30184375E 05	0.30184375E 05
COEFFICIENT OF DETERMINATION	0.16744083	0.36048293	0.67951882
COEFFICIENT OF CORRELATION	0.40919536	0.60040230	0.82432932

FIGURE 5.10.   Analysis of variance. *(From J. W. Overbey & R. P. Ouellette, ref. 47)*

155

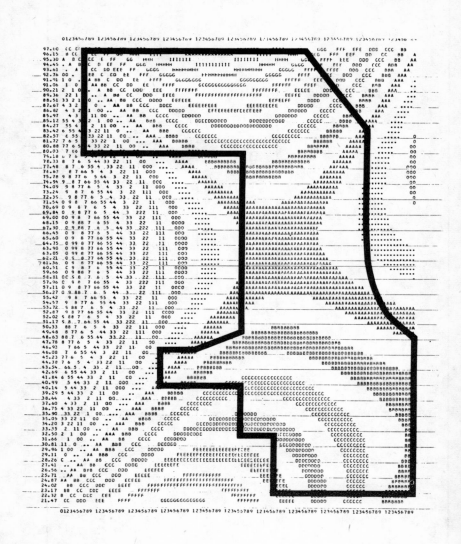

FIGURE 5.11. Trend surface. *(From J. W. Overbey & R. P. Ouellette, ref. 47)*

156

Principal Components Analysis

Principal components analysis is a technique for reducing the dimensionality of the observed space to a limited number of orthogonal components explaining a major part of the variance in the data. Specifically, the following determinental equation is solved:

$$(R - \lambda I) \; x = O,$$

where R is traditionally a correlation matrix, λ is the eigenvalue, or characteristic root of the polynomial expansion, I is the unit matrix, and x is the eigenvector associated with the eigenvalue.

Traditionally, this technique has been applied to explaining the latent structure of a correlation matrix, but there is no reason why this technique cannot be applied to other matrices. In fact, other matrices should be of great interest. An example of one such matrix is the matrix of observed concentrations of various pollutants versus station identification. In this case it is possible to plot the eigenvectors obtained over a map of a particular area. A second form is the matrix of observed concentrations at various sampling dates versus station locations. Peterson [50] has examined patterns of sulfur dioxide concentrations at St. Louis using this technique of analysis.

The authors have also used this technique when the matrix R is the correlation matrix of pollutant concentrations.[47] Using 22 separate sets of observations at a single site in the Chicago area on 20 variables (Dust, Br, Mn, V, Al, Cl, Na, Hg, Cr, Zn, Fe, Sb, Sc, Co, La, Cs, Eu, Ce, Ag, Se), it is possible to explain 64 percent of the variance with the first eigenvalue and 90 percent of the variance with the first 5 roots. Table 5.1 shows the results. The first eigenvector is unipolar, and the elements of the vector are about equal. All other vectors are bipolar, with high loadings for specific elements.

Averaging Time

Larsen [42] has studied the relationship among air-pollutant concentration, averaging time, and frequency. His model assumes the universal occurrence of a log-normal distribution. Based on this assumption, he proceeds to develop the necessary mathematics to compute pollutant parameters of interest at varying averaging times. Larsen and others have computerized the tedious problems of these computations and graphical presentations.

Statistical Distribution

Knowledge of underlying statistical distribution of aerosol systems is sought to aid in the understanding of the phenomenon or in order to satisfy assumption requirements of more complex analyses. Some of the distributions frequently encountered are the Poisson, negative binomial, exponential, normal, log normal, Weibull, Maxwell.[51] A computer program has been developed [52] for calculating parameters associated with the Pearson generalized-statistical distribution, which can be used to accurately approximate all forms of unimodal statistical distribution.

TABLE 5.1

Results of Principal Components Analysis

Eigenvalues	Cumulative % Variance
12.75	64
1.88	73
1.55	81
0.97	86
0.63	87
0.58	92

SOURCE: Overbey & Ouellette, ref. 47.

Regression Analysis

Regression is probably the statistical technique most often used analysis of the environment. The aim in regression analysis is to estimate parameters in a functional representation of a dependent variable based on observations of other independent variables. Simple linear and nonlinear functional forms having single or multiple independent variables have been used. Among these applications we can list estimation of mortality levels based on sulfur dioxide, and suspended particulate levels,[53] an estimation of precipitation temperature and runoff,[54] and ranking of cities on the "dirty" scales.

Other Mathematical Techniques

Mathematical modeling is used for analyzing all aspects of the environment. The separate stage of development and techniques used are different enough to warrant separate treatment.

Modeling in the Air Environment

Extensive literature is available on mathematical modeling in the environment.[55-80]

We will describe in detail the following models: Air Quality Diffusion Model (AQDM), Implementation Program Planning Model (IPP), Air Quality Monitoring Network Cost Approximation Model, Fuel Availability Model, and Economic Impact of Environmental Control Model. A preliminary taxonomy of models Figure 5.12) brings to light the complexity, variety, and difficulty of using mathematical models to describe specific aspects of the environment.

AIR QUALITY DIFFUSION MODEL (AQDM). Numerous variants of an atmospheric diffusion model are in general use. Most are very similar, and the Tikvart/Martin bivariate diffusion model [81] will be described as an example. The purpose of the model is to calculate long-term average pollutant concentration at ground level. The model has been applied solely to describing the behavior of SO_x and suspended particulates. The model starts from a series of localized points, line and area emission sources, and estimates downwind concentrations. A typical point source location is described in terms of three coordinates (Figure 5.13).

The pollutant concentration, X, at any position located at (x,y,z) for substances emitted from a source located at $(0,0,h)$ is given by

$$\chi(x,y,z;h) = \frac{10^6 Q}{2\pi\sigma_y\sigma_z u} \exp\left[-\frac{1}{2}\left(\frac{v}{\sigma_y}\right)^a\right]\right\} \exp\left[-\frac{1}{2}\left(\frac{z-h}{\sigma_z}\right)^2\right]$$
$$+ \exp\left[-\frac{1}{2}\left(\frac{z+h}{\sigma_z}\right)^2\right]\right\}$$

where:

$\chi(x,y,z;h)$ = pollutant concentration, micrograms/meter,[3] at point x,y,z for an effective stack height h.

Q = emission rate, grams/sec.

u = mean wind speed, meters/sec.

σ_y,σ_z = standard deviation of the plume concentration distribution in the cross-plume and vertical directions, meters. (σ_y and σ_z are given as functions of downwind distance and atmospheric stability.)

By setting $z = 0$ in the above, ground-level concentrations are represented as

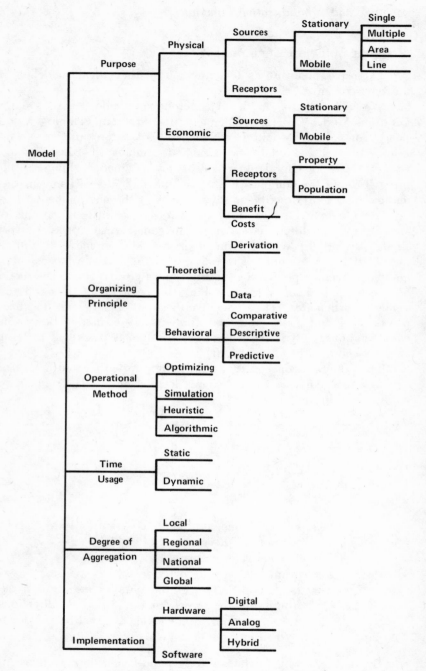

FIGURE 5.12. Taxonomy of models.

160

$$\chi\,(x,y,z;\,h)\,=\,\frac{10^6 Q}{\sigma_y \pi \sigma_z u}\,\exp\left[-\frac{1}{2}\left(\frac{y}{\sigma_y}\right)^2\right]\exp\left[-\frac{1}{2}\left(\frac{h}{\sigma_z}\right)^2\right]$$

This equation can be modified to yield estimates of long-term (annual or seasonal) average concentrations of sources emitting at a constant rate from hour to hour and day to day if applicable stability windrose data is available. A stability windrose contains the frequency of occurrence of windspeed for each period divided according to atmospheric stability classes.

One should not be deceived by the apparent simplicity of the above equations. Numerous difficulties arise in estimating parameters —σ_z, for instance.

This basic equation has been slightly modified for computational purposes and represents the downwind diffusion of pollutant concentrations in a computer program capable of handling 1,000 sources and 225 receptors. To be executed, the program requires extensive input data, sufficient primary storage, and large amounts of time on a medium- to high-speed computer. The first point is documented by a typical list of input requirements (Table 5.2). The typical AQDM

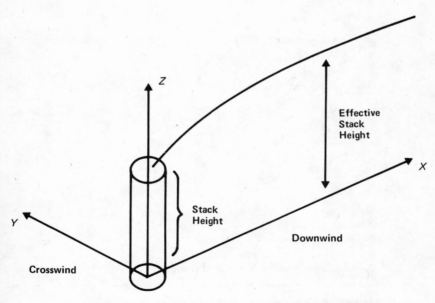

FIGURE 5.13.   Point source coordinate system.

requires some 275K of primary storage, and execution times of ten hours or more on an IBM 360/50 are not uncommon.

TABLE 5.2

Major Input Data for the Execution of the Air Quality Display Model

Emission data—for each source the following data recorded.
> Position; X and Y grid coordinate points
> Source area (0.0 for point source), km^2
> Sulfur dioxide emission (tons/day)
> Particulate emission (tons/day)
> Stack height (m)
> Stack exit velocity* (m/s)
> Stack diameter* (m)
> Stack exit temperature* ($°k$)

Meteorological data
> Stability wind data—one card giving frequency of occurrence for each wind direction (16), wind speed class (6), and stability class (5) combination,
> Mixing depth height (m)
> Ambient temperature ($°k$)
> Ambient pressure (mb)

Sampling station concentration data (to be used for calibration);
> Sulfur dioxide observations, $\mu g/m^3$
> Particulate observations, $\mu g/m^3$
> Background data, $\mu g/m^3$

Program option
> Output deck
> Calibration of model
>> Sulfur dioxide
>> Particulates

Grid receptor data
> Origin
> Number of rows
> Number of columns
> Spacing between rows and columns
> Number and location of nongrid receptors

SOURCE: TRW, ref. 81.
* For point source only.

For display purposes the AQDM is often linked to the SYMAP display package or other isocontour plotting software to supplement tabular output (Table 5.3).

TABLE 5.3

Concentration Data by Census Tract

Census Tract Number	1965 Sulfur Dioxide $\mu g/m^3$	1968 Sulfur Dioxide $\mu g/m^3$	1968 Total Suspended Particulate $\mu g/m^3$
1	139.	73.	126.
2	146.	74.	127.
3	134.	68.	124.
4	114.	62.	121.
6	114.	62.	121.
7	123.	62.	121.
8	123.	62.	121.
9	132.	73.	125.
11	132.	73.	125.
12	132.	73.	125.
13	132.	73.	125.
14	132.	91.	136.
15	123.	73.	125.
16	114.	73.	125.
17	114.	67.	123.
18	178.	62.	120.
19	178.	62.	120.
10	132.	91.	136.
22	178.	91.	136.
23	178.	91.	136.
24	178.	74.	127.
26	146.	91.	136.
27	146.	74.	127.
28	146.	74.	127.
29	178.	91.	136.
20	178.	91.	136.
31	146.	74.	127.
32	146.	74.	127.
33	146.	74.	127.
34	146.	74.	127.
35	146.	74.	127.
36	146.	74.	127.

TABLE 5.3 (*Continued*)

Census Tract Number	1965 Sulfur Dioxide $\mu g/m^3$	1968 Sulfur Dioxide $\mu g/m^3$	1968 Total Suspended Particulate $\mu g/m^3$
37	146.	74.	127.
38	146.	74.	127.
39	146.	74.	127.
30	146.	74.	127.
41	152.	88.	134.
42	152.	88.	134.
43	152.	88.	134.
44	152.	88.	134.
45	152.	88.	134.
46	132.	73.	125.

SOURCE: J. Golden, ref. 82.

The output of the model can be further calibrated with observed data from air-quality-monitoring stations from the area observed. The calibration occurs by calculating parameters of the regression equation

$$X \text{ (calculated)} = a + bY \text{ (observed)}$$

which provides best fit by the least-squares criteria. An example of this calibration regression is shown by Figure 5.14. The data was taken from a study of air quality in Cook County, Illinois.[82]

AQDM Cost Approximation Model. The cost of an air-quality-monitoring network can be easily calculated by a method recently developed.[83] The method enables the user to readily examine the relationship between fixed (investment) and variable (recurring) costs for different degrees of network automation, different network sizes, varying data-collection rates, and different "basis-of-cost" assumptions about the elements that make up any network.

The relationship of the individual cost elements to the fixed, variable, and total costs is shown schematically in Figure 5.15. There are 31 individual cost elements in six different "system configurations." Calculations of system costs by hand is not practical. A FORTRAN program has been developed for use on a time-sharing computer system. The general characteristics of the six system configurations are summarized in Table 5.4. Inherent in the configurations is the possibility

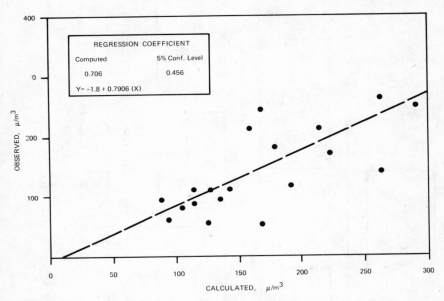

FIGURE 5.14.   AQDM calibration data—1965 sulfur dioxide. *(From J. Golden, ref. 82)*

TABLE 5.4

Characteristics of AQMN System Configurations

System 1 (minimal)—all-manual	(52 samples/yr)
System 2—all manual	(Continuous, but one hour means used for comparisons)
System 3—automatic sensors, all-manual data analysis	(continuous, but one hour means used for comparisons)
System 4—automatic sensors, manual data reduction, computer analysis	(continuous, but one hour means used for comparisons)
System 5—automatic sensors, paper tape, computer analysis	(continuous, but one hour means used for comparisons)
System 6—all automatic	(continued, but one hour means used for comparisons)

SOURCE: Hickey *et al*, ref. 83.

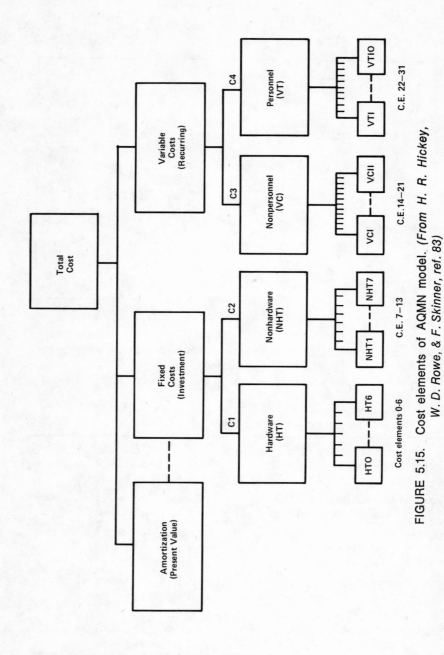

FIGURE 5.15. Cost elements of AQMN model. (*From H. R. Hickey, W. D. Rowe, & F. Skinner, ref. 83*)

166

of an almost unlimited number of combinations of number of site locations, number and kinds of sensor arrays, and life of the equipment. For each system type the 31 cost elements can be examined to select an appropriate cost equation for describing the effect of variations in sensor type, location, etc.

The program output permits cost/benefit comparisons of the six system configurations. Figure 5.16 is a plot of the output showing cumulative system cost versus number of years the network is operational. Each of the configurations contains any combination of number of sites and number of samplers per site whose product is 24. Inherent in the data shown in this figure are assumed values for equipment amortization schedule, "basis-of-cost," and equipment lifetimes. The nonlinearity in the curves at the end of system operation year 4 reflects the cost of equipment replacement. The crossover points on the curves show the point at which the higher initial investment costs of more automated types is overtaken by the continuing labor cost of less automated systems.

IMPLEMENTATION PLANNING PROGRAM. The implementation planning program IPP) [84] is a set of computer programs allowing the user to evaluate the cost of alternative air-pollution-control strategies. An emission-control strategy is generally made up of a selection of emission standards covering all significant source types. Based on the regional emission assessments and projected increase, each strategy is evaluated to determine if it is capable of achieving the desired air-quality standards. Among the strategies used to achieve this goal, the one that minimizes the overall cost is selected.

The IPP contains the following segments (Figure 5.17):

Source data management program
Air pollutant concentration segment
   Air pollutant concentration program
   Source contribution file merge program
Control cost segment
   Control cost program
   Control cost file update program
Control strategies segment
   Emission standards program
   Emission standards file update program
   Region strategies program.

The computer programs are written in FORTRAN IV and COBOL F for execution on the IBM 360 Model 40 computer. The execution time of this model is exceedingly long. Run times of 10 to 15 hours are

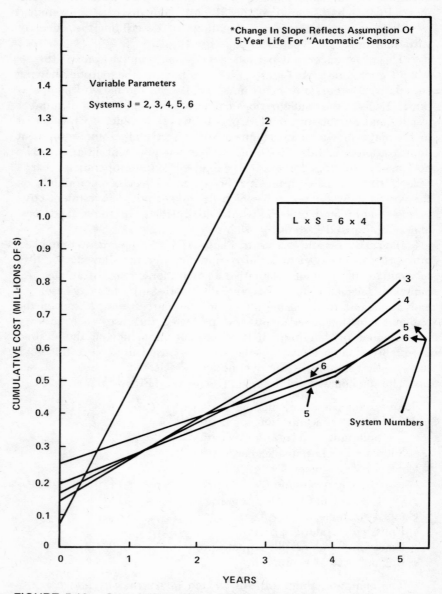

FIGURE 5.16. Cumulative costs of 6x4 network size vs. time for five-system types. *(From H. R. Hickey, W. D. Rowe, & F. Skinner, ref. 83)*

168

not uncommon. Core requirements are of the order of 535K bytes, but this can be reduced by the use of program overlays.

FUEL MODEL. In many areas of the country control technologies for achieving air-quality standards are not readily or economically available for currently employed fuels. Thus the pollution-control engineer often switches to low-sulfur fuels to achieve air-quality standards without modifying his stack gas-cleaning technology. This increased reliance on low-sulfur fuels has increased the price of such commodities and has altered the demand-supply relationship.

Under sponsorship by the Environmental Protection Agency, a computer-based mathematical model has been developed[85] to simulate the interrelationships of supply, demand, and cost of coal, residual and distillate oil, and natural gas at different sulfur contents. In Figure 5.18 the flow of the model is shown. The model employs linear programming to arrive at a least-cost solution for the delivery of ten fuel types to each of up to 157 energy-use regions in the U. S.

From this basic structure two general fuel-supply problems can be formulated. One can be stated as follows: given sulfur restrictions, exogenuous fuel demands, and the cost of alternative techniques by which fuel requirements can be met, determine the quantity of fuel demanded in each region. The second problem can be stated as follows: subject to a minimum acceptable selling price of fuel for each supply district, the quantity each district can supply, the unit transportation cost of fuel, and the fuel demanded in each region, determine the price at which fuel would actually be traded. Each of these questions can be structured as a linear programming formulation having an objective function to be optimized and accompanying constraint equations. The final solution to either formulation has the form of identifying a source and quantity of fuel for each region so that the nationwide cost is least.

A formulation with 23 supply districts for coals, 41 for fuel oils, and 28 for natural gas—using a 1970 data base—has been exercised for a number of regions in the U. S. (10 to 100).

ECONOMIC MODELING OF THE IMPACT OF AIR-POLLUTION CONTROL. The purpose of this computerized economic model[86] is to assess the economic impact of control strategies at the national, regional, and interregional levels.

The model describes the growth patterns of key economic sectors and estimates the regional product, employment, capital stock and investment change, value added by industry, tax receipts, and regional unemployment. These variables, as well as others, are sensitive to a variety of air-quality-control strategies that can be simulated in

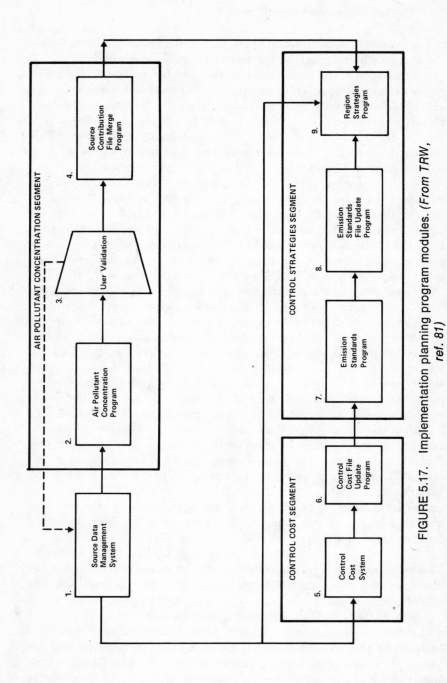

FIGURE 5.17. Implementation planning program modules. *(From TRW, ref. 81)*

the model. The model has two major sequences: one represents the empirical relations of the economic structure within a particular region and one represents the economic relationship of the region with others in the nation. There is provision within the model for representing up to 100 separate regional economies. The relationship among the

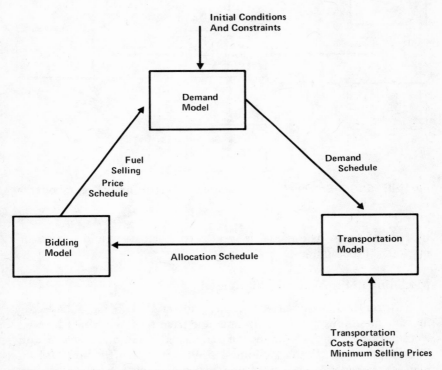

FIGURE 5.18.   Conceptualization of fuel-flow model. *(From C. H. Chilton, et al, ref. 85)*

major economic components is shown schematically in Figure 5.19. The model contains 162 separate equations for the economic relationships of supply, demand, etc., in addition to the 1969 Office of Business Economics input-output matrix.

   The typical output of a run for a specific control strategy is comprised of profit, investment, value added, capital stock, employment, regional consumption, personal income, labor force, government expenditures, government revenues, total electric consumption

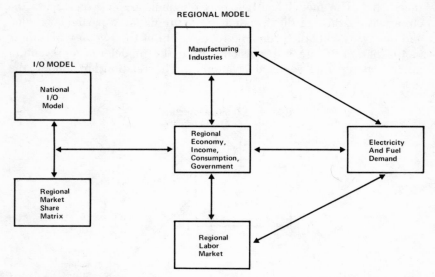

FIGURE 5.19.   Schematic of economic-effects model components.

by type of users. The model is written in FORTRAN IV and run on the IBM 360/50 computer.

Modeling in the Water Environment

Currently a large variety of waste materials is being added daily in vast quantities into the streams and rivers of the United States. These wastes are by-products of our social (economic and institutional) processes. Water pollution results from two fundamental human characteristics: the tendency to remove distasteful items from sight and forget about them; and the tendency to become concerned about correcting an objectionable situation only when personally affected by it. Right now a large number of people is personally affected by water dirty enough to arouse interest in reversing the current misuse of our freshwater sources.

This interest, coupled with the traditional quest for increasing scientific knowledge, has resulted in an extensive amount of research directed toward mathematical modeling of the water environment.

This research can be generally categorized as oriented toward water-quality modeling, water-quantity modeling, and water-resources management.

Water-quantity modeling typically addresses the natural phenomena (such as rainfall-runoff relationships, hydrophysiography, and hydrological forecasting) and the economically oriented phenomena (irrigation and water-supply control, hydroelectric power generation, and flood control).

Water-quality models are generally categorized by the type of waste modeled. These include models for nonbiodegradable wastes (dissolved materials, metal ions, chemicals and radioactivity), models for biodegradable wastes (BOD and DOG), temperature models (both natural variation and thermal plumes resulting from industrial usage of cooling water), and other models for turbidity and flows. The reader can develop an understanding of the inherent assumptions, capabilities/restrictions, and data requirements of a variety of these models by inspection of Table 5.5.

The basis for most models of BOD and DO is the work of Streeter and Phelps [88] in 1925. In 1964 Dobbins [89] expanded and generalized the Streeter and Phelps model by including the additional effects of benthal demand, land runoff, and reaeration upon BOD and DO.

By making the assumptions that the stream flow is steady and uniform, that the process is in a steady-state condition, and that BOD and DO are uniformally distributed over any cross section, the Dobbins formulation showed the rate of change of pollution, L, with respect to time of travel, t, follows the determinate differential equation:

$$\frac{dL}{dt} = La - (K_1 + K_3)\, L,$$

where

La is the uniform rate of addition of pollution,

K_1 is the rate of decrease of pollution due to the action of bacteria, and

$K_3 L$ is the rate of decrease of pollution data to sedimentation and absorption.

Dobbins states the rate of change of the dissolved oxygen, C, with respect to the time of travel, follows the differential equation:

$$\frac{dC}{dt} = K_2\,(C'_N - C) - K, L - D_B,$$

where

C'_N is the maximum oxygen solubility at given temperature and pressure,

$K_2 C$ is the increase in DO due to reaeration by the atmosphere,

K, L is the decrease in DO due to action of bacteria, and

D_B is the DO decrease due to benthal demand and effects of algae.

TABLE 5.5

MODEL	RIVER BASIN SIMULATION MODEL	DYNAMIC ESTUARY MODEL	STEADY-STATE AND TIME-VARYING MODELS	MODEL FO FLOW-AUG BENEFITS
PURPOSE	TO SIMULATE HYDROLOGY AND WATER QUALITY AND ASSESS THE IMPACT OF DIFFERENT WASTE LOADS AND RESERVOIR OPERATING POLICIES ON WATER QUALITY	TO SIMULATE A WIDE VARIETY OF HYDROLOGIC AND WATER QUALITY CONDITIONS	TO SIMULATE HYDROLOGY AND WATER QUALITY ALLOWING FOR TIME VARIATION OF CERTAIN PARAMETERS; TO DETERMINE THE OPTIMUM SOLUTION OF PLANTS AND TREATMENT LEVELS TO MEET WATER QUALITY GOALS.	TO SIMULATE QUALITY AND COMBINATIONS MENT AND LOW
APPLICATION	RIVER BASINS, INCLUDING RESERVOIRS	ANY ESTUARIES WHEREIN VERTICAL STRATIFICATION IS ABSENT OR LIMITED TO A SMALL AREA	A STRETCH OF RIVER WHERE BORDERING POPULATIONS AND INDUSTRIES USE THE RIVER FOR WATER SUPPLY, DISPOSAL OF TREATED SEWAGE AND RECREATION	COMPLEX RIVE ING RESERVOI
SIMULATION TECHNIQUES	STATISTICAL METHODS	A SET OF DIFFERENTIAL EQUATIONS (MOTION, CONTINUITY, ADVECTION, DIFFUSION, DEGRADATION AND REAERATION)	STREETER-PHELPS OXYGEN SAG EQUATIONS AND OTHER MATH-EMATICAL EQUATIONS	STATISTICAL EQUATIONS (S OXYGEN SAG)
WATER QUALITY CONSIDERATIONS	HANDLES UP TO FIVE WASTE CONSTIT-UENTS, ONE OF WHICH MAY BE NON-CONSERVATIVE	HANDLES BOTH CONSERVATIVE AND NON-CONSERVATIVE WASTE CONSTITUENTS, MAXIMUM OF 5	BOD, DO, COLIFORMS AND CHLORIDES	D
OPTIMIZATION AND ECONOMIC ASPECTS	NOT CONSIDERED	NOT CONSIDERED	PATH OF STEEPEST ASCENT TECHNIQUE. COST IS FUNCTION OF FLOW	LINEAR PROG FUNCTIONS P FROM AVAILA COST CURVES FROM COST/V
OUTPUT	HISTORICAL AND SIMULATED FLOW CHARACTERISTICS; STORAGE LEVEL DISTRIBUTIONS FOR RESERVOIRS; STATISTICS OF DEFICIENCIES (FAILURES TO MEET QUALITY STANDARDS FOR FLOW REQUIREMENTS)	HYDROLOGIC CHARACTERISTICS AT EACH JUNCTION AND CHANNEL; AVERAGE CONCENTRATION OF EACH WASTE CONSTITUENT AT EACH JUNCTION FOR EACH TIDAL CYCLE	IF TREATMENT LEVELS ARE SPECIFIED FOR EACH COMMUNITY, PROGRAM EVALUATES QUALITY THROUGHOUT STREAM; IF SINGLE QUALITY CRITERION IS SPECIFIED FOR EACH RIVER SECTION, OPTIMIZING ROUTINE DETERMINES DESIRABLE LEVELS OF TREATMENT.	FLOW STATIST PREDICTIONS OPTIMAL SOL TION OF TRE AUGMENTATIO
DOCUMENTATION	FAIR	EXCELLENT	FAIR	
INCLUDES: PROGRAM LISTING	YES	YES	NO	
SAMPLE OUTPUT	YES	YES	NO	
INSTRUCTIONS FOR USER	YES	YES	NO	
FORMAT OF INPUT	YES	YES	NO	
FLOW CHART	NO	YES	YES	
TIME ESTIMATE FOR EACH RUN	NO	YES	YES	
PROGRAM	FLEXIBLE	VERY FLEXIBLE		IN
MACHINE AND LANGUAGE	IBM 360/65 FORTRAN IV	IBM 7094, CDC 6600, IBM 360/65 FORTRAN IV	CDC 3300 FORTRAN II	IBM 360/65, MPS PACKAGE
DATA REQUIREMENTS	AT LEAST 30 YEARS OF HISTORICAL DATA	NOT EXCESSIVE	NOT EXCESSIVE, BUT INCLUDES ECONOMIC AND ADMINISTRATIVE AS WELL AS HYDROLOGIC AND QUALITY DATA	LARGE AMOU
COMMENTS	VERY STATISTICALLY ORIENTED; ENORMOUS PROGRAM REQUIRING THE FULL COMPUTING POWER OF THE LARGEST COMPUTERS	MODEL VERIFIED ON SAN FRANCISCO BAY AND SUISON BAY NETWORK	FLOW-ROUTING PROCEDURE IN TIME-VARYING MODEL VERIFIED ON SUSQUEHANNA RIVER IN NEW YORK AND PENNSYLVANIA	SIMULATION FARMINGTON CONN. AND MODEL USED REGION; EACH STEP MISSING DA DATA, SELE SYNTHESIZE WATER QUAL OPTIMIZAT SEPARATE I HAS TO SU PROGRAMS T RESULT.
ADVANTAGES	CONSIDERS ENTIRE RIVER BASIN AS A UNIT; GOOD FOR DESIGN AND OPERATION OF RESERVOIR SYSTEMS; FLEXIBLE	DATA REQUIREMENTS NOT EXCESSIVE, INITIAL INPUT CAN BE ESTIMATES; VERY FLEXIBLE	ALLOWS FOR TIME-VARIATION OF DATA BY USE OF TIME INTERVALS IN ADDITION TO PHYSICAL STATIONS; INCLUDES OPTIMIZATION TECHNIQUE; CONSIDERS GENERAL COMMUNITY DATA	CONSIDER INCLUDES TECHNIQU FOR QUAN FLOW AUG
DISADVANTAGES	REQUIRES LARGE AMOUNTS OF HISTORICAL DATA; DOES NOT CONSIDER ECONOMIC ASPECTS	ECONOMIC ASPECTS NOT CONSIDERED	OPTIMIZATION DEPENDS ON COST FUNCTION	LARGE A DATA RE DEPENDE PACKAGE MUST BE FINAL R

(From S. Poh, ref. 87)

	MODEL FOR QUANTIFYING WATER USE BENEFITS	REGIONAL WATER QUALITY MANAGEMENT MODEL	HYDRO-QUALITY SIMULATION MODEL	SIMPLIFIED MATHEMATICAL MODEL OF WATER QUALITY
ATER M ON	TO SIMULATE HYDROLOGY, AND ALLOCATE WATER STORED IN RESERVOIRS TO COMPETING DEMANDS ON THE BASIS OF ECONOMIC EFFICIENCY	TO ESTIMATE THE LEAST COST COMBINATION OF WASTE TREATMENT ALTERNATIVES AND BY-PASS PIPING WHICH WILL ACHIEVE PRE-SPECIFIED WATER QUALITY GOALS	TO SIMULATE HYDROLOGY AND WATER QUALITY CONSIDERING ALL TYPES OF INFLOW AND OUTFLOW	TO GIVE REASONABLE GUIDELINES FOR EVALUATING WATER QUALITY BY MEANS OF DETAILED PRESENTATION OF TABLES NOMOGRAPHS, AND TECHNICAL DATA
TD-	RIVERS AND RESERVOIRS ALLOCATION OF RESOURCES	ESTUARIES OR POSSIBLY OTHER WATER BODIES	RIVER BASINS, INCLUDING RESERVOIRS	WATER BODIES (RIVERS, ESTUARIES, TIDAL RIVERS) WHICH CAN BE DESCRIBED AS APPROXIMATELY 1-DIMENSIONAL AND FOR WHICH SYSTEM GEOMETRY IS RELATIVELY SIMPLE
IAL	STATISTICAL METHODS		DIFFERENTIAL EQUATIONS	DIFFERENTIAL EQUATIONS USED TO PRODUCE TABLES AND NOMOGRAPHS
	DO AND COLIFORMS	DO, BOD	DO, BOD, SALINITY, AND TEMPERATURE	TOTAL DISSOLVED SOLIDS, COLI-FORMS, DO, NUTRIENTS
S	THEORY OF FIRM STEEPEST ASCENT	LINEAR PROGRAMMING - COST IS A FUNCTION OF FLOW	NOT CONSIDERED	NOT CONSIDERED
K A-	RESERVOIR AND CHANNEL STATISTICS; STATISTICS OF BENEFITS RECEIVED AND PERCENT OF TIME WATER QUALITY TARGETS WERE MET	THE SOLUTION (LEASE-COST COM-BINATION OF TREATMENT ALTERNATIVES AND BY-PASS PIPING TO ACHIEVE QUALITY GOALS), COST FOR EACH SITUATION TESTED	MONTHLY AVERAGE VALUES AT BOTH ENDS OF EACH REACH AND ANNUAL TIME PROFILES FOR PREDESIGNATED POINTS FOR FLOW AND QUALITY PARAMETERS; PREDICTED DIURNAL VARIATIONS IN DO AND TEMPERATURE; MONTHLY MASS BALANCE WATER BUDGET	TOTAL FLOW FOR RIVERS; MINIMUM DO FOR RIVERS ASSUMING SINGLE WASTE SOURCE AND MULTIPLE WASTE SOURCES; MINIMUM DO FOR TIDAL RIVERS AND ESTUARIES, ASSUMING SINGLE AND MULTIPLE WASTE SOURCES; DILUTION FLOW FOR TIDAL RIVERS AND ESTUARIES
	FAIR	FAIR	GOOD	EXCELLENT
	YES	NO	YES	NO (NO PROGRAM)
	NO	NO	YES	YES
	NO	NO	YES	YES
	NO	NO	YES	NO
	YES	NO	YES	NO
	NO	YES	YES	NO (NO RUN)
		FLEXIBLE		
ON	CDC 6600 FORTRAN, DYNAMO	IBM 360/65 FORTRAN IV	UNIVAC 1108 FORTRAN V	NONE
	NOT EXCESSIVE	NOT EXCESSIVE; TRANSFER COEFFICIENTS ARE CALCULATED PRIOR TO APPLYING THE MODEL	COEFFICIENTS OF DIFFERENTIAL EQUATIONS ARE DETERMINED BY REGRESSION ANALYSIS OF FIELD DATA PRIOR TO APPLYING THE MODEL	MINIMUM
	MORE WORK NEEDED IN DEVELOP-MENT OF BENEFIT FUNCTIONS FOR VARIOUS WATER USES; MODEL TESTED ON CALAPOOIA RIVER IN OREGON	THE DETERMINATION OF TRANSFER COEFFICIENTS FOR IN-STREAM DO CHANGES DUE TO INPUT BOD NOT INCLUDED IN DOCUMENTATION REPORT. PROGRAM LISTING AND DECK OBTAINABLE FROM SYSTEMS ANALYSIS AND ECONOMICS BRANCH OF OFFICE OF WATER PROGRAMS, ENVIRONMENTAL PROTECTION AGENCY, WASHINGTON, D.C. MODEL APPLIED TO DELAWARE ESTUARY AS AN EXAMPLE	DEVELOPED AND VERIFIED USING DATA FROM LITTLE BEAR RIVER BASIN IN UTAH	A GENERAL SIMPLIFIED METHODOLOGY FOR THE APPLICATION OF MATHEMATICAL MODELS TO THE ANALYSIS OF WATER QUALITY
	CONSIDERS BENEFITS REAPED FROM VARIOUS WATER USES, AND ALLOCATES LIMITED STORED WATER TO COMPETING DEMANDS OR USES ON BASIS OF ECONOMIC EFFICIENCY	CONSIDERS ALL WASTE TREATMENT ALTERNATIVES AND THEIR COSTS; GOOD FOR REGIONAL PLANNING	CONSIDERS ALL TYPES OF INFLOW AND OUTFLOW, INCLUDING RESERVOIRS	LITTLE DATA REQUIRED, NO COMPUTER REQUIRED; COULD BE WIDELY USED FOR DEVELOPING INITIAL ROUGH ESTIMATES OF WATER QUALITY AND NECESSARY TREATMENT LEVELS.
	DEPENDS ON BENEFIT FUNCTIONS WHICH WERE DIFFICULT TO DEFINE AND FOR WHICH THE VALIDITY MAY, IN SOME CASES, BE QUESTIONABLE	DEPENDS ON COST FUNCTIONS	ECONOMIC ASPECTS NOT CONSIDERED	RESULTS MUST BE CONSIDERED AS TREND INDICATIONS ONLY AND NOT AS PRECISE, CERTAIN PREDICTIONS

Thayer and Krutchkoff [44] developed a stochastic model whose mean values were compatible with the values of Dobbins for BOD and DO. In addition they found the marginal distribution for both BOD and DO. They view the problem as a birth and death process wherein BOD and DO are increased and decreased only by small amounts, Δ, in a very short interval of time, h. They define a pollution state, M, as a concentration, L_M, divided by Δ. A dissolved oxygen state, N, is a concentration, C_N, divided by Δ. To facilitate use of their results, a computer program was written in FORTRAN. Initial correlation for $t = 0$ must be known in order to use the program. The program computes the probability distribution for pollution and sums individual probabilities to give a confidence interval for pollution. Finally, the mean and variance functions are evaluated for pollution. A similar process is followed for dissolving oxygen concentrations.

Other Mathematical Techniques

A number of mathematical techniques made popular by the advent of large-scale computers and canned software are in use attempting to solve old environmental problems with new approaches and techniques. Among the most successful attempts are spectral analysis [90, 91], linear programming [74, 92–96], dynamic programming [98–100], queuing theory [101, 102], MARKOV process [103], factor analysis, time series analysis [104], game theory [105], and Monte Carlo. [106, 107]

The aim of spectral analysis is to decompose a time-series set of observations into a set of frequency components that can be recognized and interpreted. The aim of auto-correlation analysis is to examine the product-moment correlation coefficients obtained by correlating the members of a time series among themselves. The superiority of auto-correlation analysis over spectral analyses, in terms of amount of effort and time required, is discussed by Quimpo [90] in a case study of mean daily flows in the drainage area of a river basin. The conclusion drawn from this illustration is that often relatively easily performed analysis can yield sufficient information to resolve the problem under study. One is cautioned against immediately rejecting more sophisticated techniques until consideration is given to their intrinsic assumptions, capability, limitations, and computational demands.

Linear programming is optimization of a linear objective function subject to linear constraint equations. This method has been applied [95] to the management of water quality in a river basin. The objective function reflected the costs of water-treatment plants at various fractional efficiencies. Constraint equations defined plant efficiency at load levels, BOD inventory, water quality as set forth by standards, and permissible plant efficient values. Constraints on plant efficiency values were necessary to linearize the equations.

Another application[92] of the linear program method is in the estimation of parameters of hydrologic models. Various formulations enable the objective function to (1) minimize the sum of squared deviations; (2) minimize the sum of absolute deviations; (3) minimize the maximum deviation; and (4) minimize the sum of absolute deviations without ordering the parameters. The deviations are in the amount of runoff between successive time intervals. Usual statistical analysis cannot cope easily with these formulations of the objective function, particularly when inequality restrictions are involved.

The objective of dynamic programming is to determine, for a given initial state of the system, a set of subsequent decisions that constitute an optimal policy. This method can be applied to non-linear constraint and objective functions that cannot be decomposed into linear components and thus analysed by linear programming methods. The dynamic programming method of analysis was applied[100] for optimizing operations of a reservoir-river system producing hydroelectric power and providing water. Complex constraints such as provisions for mandatory flood control, minimum flows needed for navigation, and interbasin diversions of water can be accommodated.

Queuing theory involves laws governing arrival rates, servicing times, and the order in which arrivals are served. A general assumption is that transition of the process into a steady state has occurred and that the solution for this stable condition is desired. The aim of studying queues is to determine the optimal number of servicing units. This technique has been applied[101] in the selection of optimal reservoir design for average (i.e., expected value) gross benefits of irrigation, hydroelectric power, and flood control. Arrivals are stream inflows, removals are drafts, and the length of the queue is the reservoir size. Costs are divided among reservoir costs and specific user costs.

The aim in factor analysis is to explain the structure of a covariance (or correlation) matrix by a minimum number of hypothetical factors, or varieties. A model is postulated to explain the structure. The objective is to determine if it represents the observed data. This differs from regression analysis because the factors are not viewed as fixed quantities.

The problems to which those methodologies have been applied

are diversified: hydrologic analysis, water-pollution control, water-quality management, resources allocation, reservoir design and operation, water storage, flow regulation, and waste discharge. The practicality of employing any of these techniques without the computational assistance of a high-speed computer is questionable when the number of variables or constraints approaches those actually encountered in even the simplest environmental problem.

Data Banks

Data bases exist in support of most environmental programs in air,[108] water,[109] solid waste, pesticides, radiation, and land use.[110] Data banks also exist in support of monitoring enforcement and control programs. Coordinating efforts are in progress.[111-114] Below, we describe the National Aerometric Data Bank (NADB) and the STORET water-quality-management system.

The National Aerometric Data Bank

The 250 individual nonfederal agencies [47] contributing air-quality data to the NADB span a wide range as to the scope of their activity, the stage of development of their systems, and the completeness or availability of information. Historical data files are being kept in stages of development ranging from handwritten log sheets to well-planned and efficiently organized computerized systems. The only consistency found among the individual contributors is the lack of consistency.

An integral part of the activity of collecting and analyzing air-quality data is the development of a standardized, centralized data-storage and information-retrieval system designed to maintain efficiently the ever-increasing amount of data available. Just as the scope of the data-collection effort has expanded, the system for data storage and information retrieval has evolved from a simple system to the elaborate process necessary to maintain a large multifile data bank.

We describe below the system used for creating, maintaining, inventorying, summarizing, and querying the data files containing pollutant concentrations measured by nonfederal agencies throughout the United States.

SYSTEM OPERATION. The present system consists of six major activities: (1) transformation of data from the form in which it is received into one compatible with the standardized form; (2) maintenance of the master data sets; (3) inventorying the data contained in the master data sets; (4) summarizing the data into simple statistical descriptors; (5) describing the individual sampling sites, and (6) querying the summary data sets to respond to individual and unique requests for information regarding the air quality of specified locations.

PRELIMINARY DATA PREPARATION. Source data can be submitted in three forms: (1) as record images on magnetic tape; (2) as decks of punched cards; and (3) as paper copies of site-reporting forms or log records. Regardless of the data form, sampling site characteristics must be specified and SAROAD site-identification numbers assigned. Cards containing this information are punched so the site-attribute file can be updated. The data is checked to ensure all information necessary to identify the data characteristics is specified and that the SAROAD format is followed.

Generally agencies do not use the information-coding schemes or the data formats used by the national system. Consequently data as received must be transformed prior to its being introduced into the master data files. The data-characteristics-identification coding scheme and data-formatting structure used by each particular agency are inspected to define a transformation algorithm for changing the source data into the system standard coding scheme and formatting structure.

In addition to correcting data-characteristics-identification coding, an equally important function of the transformation algorithm is to separate individual observations into individual records in files segregated according to the interval of observations.

DATA FILE MAINTENANCE. File maintenance is performed by a group of MARK IV* modules designed to incorporate new air-quality measurements into the data files, to correct invalid data characteristics of previously stored data or to replace erroneous concentration values, to perform secondary data editing and validation functions, and to generate files necessary to the update of the inventory and summary files.

Secondary data editing and validation criteria include those of the preliminary criteria, more rigidly specified, and additional criteria to ensure "reasonableness" of the observation values. These additional procedures compare measured values with anticipated values to flag those values consistently falling below or above anticipated values. Outlying values are flagged to indicate editing failure but are not prevented from entering the master file, since an excessive amount of overages or underages often signifies inconsistencies between stated data characteristics and the values.

* Proprietary software of Informatic, Inc.

INVENTORY FILE MAINTENANCE. The addition of, or modification to, data in the master file necessitates changes in the inventory file. The individual inventory-updating subfiles created by the maintenance program for each of the individual master data files are sort/merged to create a single inventory-updating transaction file. This file is processed against the old inventory file to generate a new inventory file. Reports to update previously created inventories are produced as a by-product.

SUMMARY FILE MAINTENANCE. Requests for information regarding the air quality of specified locations typically contain the same information elements. Addressing the large master data files to recompute frequently the same descriptor statistics wastes computer processing time. The data-summary file provides a means of quickly obtaining the required descriptor statistics. Unnecessary recomputation of the information elements is eliminated by storing the statistics in the summary file record. However, the existence of such a file necessitates programs to update the file contents with newly received data, purge unnecessary or outdated information, and generally maintain the integrity of the file.

Maintenance of the summary file is a two-stage process: the first stage is involved with actual computation of the summary statistics, while the second stage is concerned with file maintenance. Computations in the summary program use standard statistical equations to produce annual arithmetic averages and standard deviations, annual geometric means and standard deviations, quarterly means, annual minimum and maximum values, and distribution percentiles.

SITE ATTRIBUTE FILE MAINTENANCE. When data is first substituted for a particular site, the agency must supply information describing the location and surroundings of the site. This information is examined for completeness. As necessary, agencies are contacted to obtain missing characteristics. After all site attributes are available, punched cards are prepared so the site-attribute file may be updated.

REPORTING AND DATA QUERYING. The reporting and data querying capabilities fall into two classes: routine summarizing and inventorying of the data bank, performed quarterly, and nonroutine, individually tailored query-responding, performed on an "as-received" basis.

The quarterly reporting is involved with supplying data summaries and inventories for the data received during the prior quarter. Figures 5.20 through 5.25 are illustrations of the information contained in these quarterly reports.

DATA EDITING AND VALIDATION. An essential part of maintaining

STANDARD REPORT NO. 1
AIR QUALITY DATA REPORT
STATE OF ILLINOIS

LOCATION: CHICAGO ILL   SITE: 03

SAROAD NUMBER: 14122003
SAMPLING ADDR: TAFT HS 5625 N NATOMA AVE
CITY NAME: CHICAGO ILL
SMSA NUMBER: 0690
AQCR NUMBER: 003
LATITUDE: D.   M.   S.
UTM NORTHING:
ECONOMIC ACTIVITY TYPE: UNIDENTIFIED
ELEVATION ABOVE GROUND: 49 FEET
REPORTING AGENCY TYPE: CITY
SMSA POPULATION(1000'S): 6815
COUNTY POPULATION(1000'S): 5399
SUPPORTING AGENCY: CITY OF CHICAGO

STATE NAME: ILLINOIS
COUNTY NAME: COOK
SMSA NAME: CHICAGO,ILL
AQCR NAME: CHICAGO
LONGITUDE: D.   M.   S.
TIME ZONE: CENTRAL
ELEVATION ABOVE SEA LEVEL: FEET
TOPOGRAPHIC CODE: PLAIN
CITY POPULATION(1000'S):
AQCR POPULATION(1000'S): 7539

POLLUTANT METHOD INSTRUMENT INTERVAL & UNITS / YEAR	TOTAL PERCENT OF YEAR COVERED	ARITHMETIC AVERAGE	ARITHMETIC STD DEV	EXTREMES MIN OBS	EXTREMES MAX OBS	FIRST NUM OBS	FIRST ARITH AVG	SECOND QUARTER NUM OBS	SECOND QUARTER ARITH AVG	THIRD QUARTER NUM OBS	THIRD QUARTER ARITH AVG	FOURTH NUM OBS	FOURTH ARITH AVG
66 SULFUR DIOXIDE CONDUCTIVITY BECKMAN 1-HR PPM	92	0.028	0.050	0.000	0.685	2033	0.049	1971	0.026	2013	0.014	2124	0.024
67 SULFUR DIOXIDE CONDUCTIVITY BECKMAN 1-HR PPM	75	0.037	0.064	0.000	0.955	2048	0.043	2053	0.047	1766	0.016	740	0.046
68 SULFUR DIOXIDE CONDUCTIVITY BECKMAN 1-HR PPM	80	0.040	0.074	0.000	1.305	2024	0.063	1633	0.040	1989	0.017	1367	0.036
69 SULFUR DIOXIDE CONDUCTIVITY BECKMAN 1-HR PPM	76	0.035	0.057	0.000	0.715	1050	0.049	1867	0.034	1870	0.021	1877	0.041

FIGURE 5.20. NADB Standard Report No. 1. (From J. W. Overbey & R. P. Ouellette, ref. 47)

05/14/71

STANDARC REPORT NC. 2
AIR QUALITY DATA REPORT
STATE OF ILLINOIS

LOCATION: CHICAGO ILL   SITE: 03

SAROAD NUMBER: 14122003
SAMPLING ADDR: TAFT HS 5625 N NATOMA AVE
CITY NAME: CHICAGO ILL
SMSA NUMBER: 0690
AQCR NUMBER: 003
LATITUDE: D. M. S.
UTM NORTHING:
ECONOMIC ACTIVITY TYPE: UNIDENTIFIED
ELEVATION ABOVE GROUND: 49 FEET
REPORTING AGENCY TYPE: CITY
SMSA POPULATION(1000'S): 6815
COUNTY POPULATION(1000'S): 5399
SUPPORTING AGENCY: CITY OF CHICAGO

STATE NAME: ILLINOIS
COUNTY NAME: COOK
SMSA NAME: CHICAGO,ILL
AQCR NAME: CHICAGO
LONGITUDE: D. M. S.
UTM EASTING:
TIME ZONE: CENTRAL
ELEVATION ABOVE SEA LEVEL: FEET
TOPOGRAPHIC CODE: PLAIN
CITY POPULATION(1000'S):
AQCR POPULATION(1000'S): 7539

YEAR	POLLUTANT METHOD INSTRUMENT INTERVAL & UNITS	NUM OBS	MIN OBS	PERCENTILES 10	30	50	70	90	95	99	MAX OBS	ARITH AVG	GEOMETRIC MEAN	STD DEV
66	SULFUR DIOXIDE CONDUCTIVITY BECKMAN 1-HR PPM	8141	0.000	0.000	0.002	0.010	0.022	0.076	0.127	0.240	0.685	0.028	0.003	24.879
67	SULFUR DIOXIDE CONDUCTIVITY BECKMAN 1-HR PPM	6607	0.000	0.000	0.010	0.015	0.032	0.097	0.145	0.332	0.955	0.037	0.005	24.689
68	SULFUR DIOXIDE CONDUCTIVITY BECKMAN 1-HR PPM	7013	0.000	0.000	0.010	0.017	0.032	0.092	0.155	0.340	1.305	0.040	0.009	16.036
69	SULFUR DIOXIDE CONDUCTIVITY BECKMAN 1-HR PPM	6664	0.003	0.000	0.010	0.015	0.030	0.087	0.137	0.307	0.715	0.035	0.005	28.130

FIGURE 5.21. NADB Standard Report No. 2. (From J. W. Overbey &
R. P. Ouellette, ref. 47)

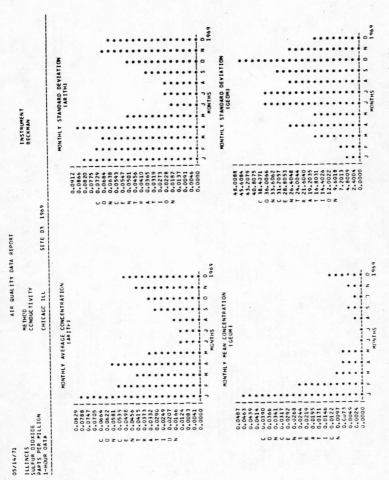

FIGURE 5.22. NADB basic statistics time series display. (*From J. W. Overbey & R. P. Ouellette, ref. 47*)

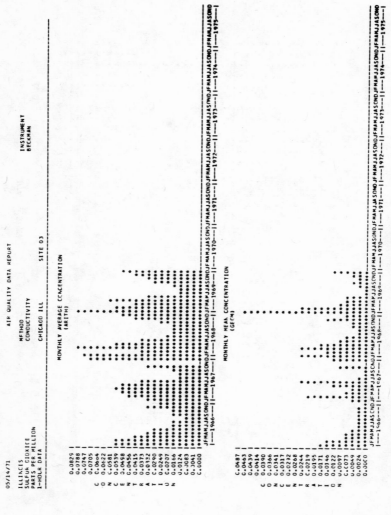

FIGURE 5.23. NADB concentration time series. *(From J. W. Overbey & R. P. Ouellette, ref. 47)*

184

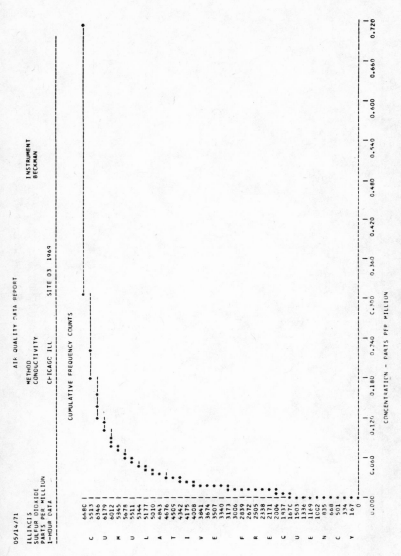

FIGURE 5.24. NADB concentration distribution display. *(From J. W. Overbey & R. P. Ouellette, ref. 47)*

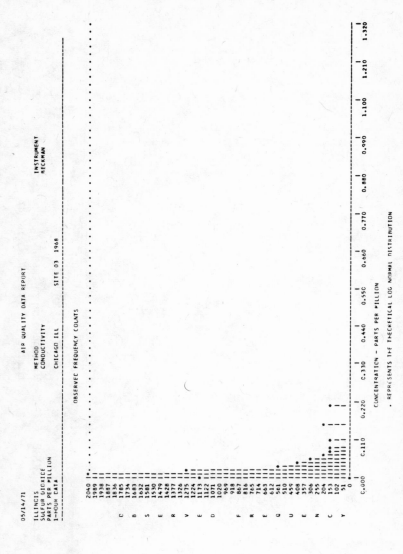

FIGURE 5.25. NADB concentration frequency display. *(From J. W. Overbey & R. P. Ouellette, ref. 47)*

186

the aerometric data bank is data validation and editing to compare observations submitted by individual agencies against logical values set with a prior knowledge of the air quality for the area. Values that consistently fall below an anticipated low value or that consistently fall above an anticipated high value should not be removed from the data bank but should be flagged for a future in-depth examination. This type of editing can identify logical inconsistencies between the stated data characteristics and the reported values. For instance, order-of-magnitude discrepancies might be indicative of incorrectly specified units in which the observations are recorded. Automatic rejection or elimination of such data from the master data file is undesirable since correction of data characteristics is more easily accomplished than reentering the data afresh.

Observations of a given pollutant in a specified set of units and at an indicated interval between observation must fall within certain limits.

In addition to high and low value checks, rate-of-change editing should detect values inconsistent with surrounding sets of time-ordered values. Such editing will identify both outliers of the group and lack of anticipated variation within the group.

Abrupt changes in concentration values typically do not occur within short intervals of time. A single value that is much greater (or much less) than other values obtained at approximately the same time is highly suspect. Such outliers are likely to be the result of data-transcription errors or incorrect specification of the characteristics of the particular data.

Similarly long periods of no-change in concentration values typically do not occur. Perturbations may be minor, but they do occur. A series of constant values is thus highly suspect, and observations should be flagged for future examination. The only exception to this is a long series of values below the sampling instrument's minimum detectable threshold. Automatic rejections of such values should be deferred until it can be determined what circumstances caused such a series.

Data should be examined to ensure that observations are reported frequently enough during, and uniformly distributed within, the long-term interval for which summary statistics are to be calculated, in order that the statistics can be based on observations "representative" of that time interval. Observations not meeting these criteria should be suppressed when summary calculations are being performed rather than culling those values from the master data files.

Water Quality Control Information System (STORET)

The STORET (Storage and Retrieval) [115, 116] computerized water-quality data-handling system was put in operation in 1964. Over the years the system has proven its effectiveness and flexibility in handling a variety of data, including water-quality standards, water-quality measurements, municipal waste inventory, fishkill information, beach and shellfish bed-closing information, municipal waste implementation plans, and municipal waste-treatment plan operation and maintenance information.

STORET is a state/federal cooperative effort that provides regulatory and control agencies with a direct-access system allowing them to: measure compliance of water quality with promulgated standards; define cause/effect relationships of water pollution; check status of waste-treatment plant needs, grants, and implementation plans; and study pollution trends and status.

Data pertinent to the nation's 3.5 million miles of streams, 17,000 miles of coastline, and over 65,000 square miles of inland open waters is assembled in a single data depository. In the first four years of use data from 12,000 point locations has been stored; today there are over 100,000. Along with increases in the number of point locations for which data is available, the amount of water quality parameters in use (e.g., temperature, dissolved oxygen, fecal coliform, DDT) has increased from 200 to over 600. Increases result from an expansion of the number of system users. Currently more than 60 state, interstate, and federal agencies and related groups are utilizing the system to store and retrieve station-location information and water-quality data.

Thus STORET is essentially a complex of computer programs and program elements that are activated by the system user at remote terminal locations by coding parameters on control cards. By judicious use of these parameters, the actual method of storage, retrieval, and analysis can be modified to reduce the amount of preliminary data preparation required or the extent of responses needed to satisfy operational requirements.

DATA INPUT AND STORAGE. Individual system users prepare their own data for input into data-base storage by coding in the STORET data format. A variety of formats is available to facilitate this process.

Data that is machine coded for storage is identified as to a point location: political (city, town, county, state); geographical (latitude-longitude); hydrological (river-mileage and index); and type (e.g., stream, reservoir, well estuary, lake, stream gauge, influent or effluent). Location designation has recently been extended to include congressional districts and standard metropolitan statistical areas.

The river mileage and index coding begins by numbering the terminal streams, i.e., those that terminate at a lake or an ocean. The miles are measured beginning at the mouth of the stream and computed for each stream intersection, along with assigning the level and an arbitrary index. With such coding the station locations and selected data can be retrieved by the computer in hydrological sequence.

Data is submitted on punched cards at remote terminals connected by voice-quality telephone lines to the system control computer. The data is stored on-line in a mass-storage, random-access device in one of five files: water quality, waste facilities, standards, criteria, and special (e.g. fishkills). The stored data is protected against loss, and its availability may be restricted to a single user to ensure privacy and prevent unauthorized retrieval or modification.

Individual users are required to ensure the accuracy of their own data. No editing to detect logical inconsistencies between stated data characters and reported values is performed routinely by STORET. However, a generalized housekeeping routine is available for a user to make appropriate adjustments for deleting errors.

DATA RETRIEVALS. Various types of mileage-index and geographic-coordinate retrievals are possible. These include retrieval above or below a specified point by river-mile index. The latter is useful in identifying locations downstream that might be affected by an accidental spill or large discharge of wastes. To obtain these outputs the system user needs only to supply control cards with appropriate parameter values and is not required to perform any programming. Retrievals can be performed for a single location as well as for all locations within a selected area.

All water-quality data retrieved can be subject to ten statistical functions: average, maximum, and minimum values; number of observations; sum of values and of values squared; variance; standard deviation; standard error and/or coefficient of variance. Also, the statistics can be computed using the values transformed logarithmically. Statistical results are printed in fixed-point notation, but the decimal-point location must be specified for each individual parameter.

The user can determine the availability of stored data at a specific location by requesting an inventory listing. This listing gives the exact location of the point where the data was collected, the parameters available, the period of record, and the number of observations. After examining such an inventory for many point locations, a second retrieval can be made for the specific conditions of interest.

GRAPHIC DISPLAY. Present capabilities permit plotting, on a drum plotter, water-quality data versus time. A generalized plotting routine that employs a plot-control parameter card enables the user to specify the size of graph, to scale for data points, to determine the plot symbol to be used and to indicate if intermediate points are to be connected with a line.

Soon to be added is the capability for plotting multiple stations on the abscissa and statistical results for one or two parameters (e.g., mean, maximum, minimum, confidence interval) on the ordinate.

For better interpretation of output and to facilitate selection of stations for data retrieval, a procedure to plot point locations of stations and show their spatial distribution is being developed.

REFERENCES

1. Charles E. Zimmer and Gerlad J. Nehls, "The Impact of Computers upon Air Pollution Research." *J. APCA* 18(6), 1968.

2. Ralph I. Larsen, "How Computers Aid in Air Management." *J. APCA* 17(7), 1967.

3. "Uses of Computers in Water Utility Work." *J. Am. Water Works Assoc.*, August 1966.

4. "Public Works Information Systems." Spec. Report No. 36, Am. Public Works Assoc., October 1970.

5. "Public Works Computer Applications." Spec. Report No. 38, Am. Public Works Assoc., August 1970.

6. Eric R. Zausner, "An Accounting System for Sanitary Landfill Operations." HEW, BSWM, Washington, D.C., 1967.

7. Eric R. Zausner, "An Accounting System for Incinerator Operations." HEW, BSWM, Washington, D.C., 1970.

8. "Guide for Compiling a Comprehensive Emission Inventory." Applied Technology Division, Office of Administration, EPA Publication No. APTD-1135, June 1972.

9. Francis F. Martin, *Computer Modeling and Simulation.* John Wiley & Sons, Inc., New York, 1968.

10. E. Robinson and R. C. Robbins, "Sources, Abundance, and Fate of Gaseous Atmospheric Pollutants." Stanford Research Institute, February 1968.

11. Alfred J. Lotka, *Elements of Mathematical Biology.* Dover Publications, Inc., New York, 1956.

12. Louis S. Jaffe, "Ambient Carbon Monoxide and Its Fate in the Atmosphere." *J. APCA* 18(8), 1968.

13. Edgar R. Stephens, "Chemistry of Oxidants." 61st Annual Meeting of the Air Pollution Control Assoc., St. Paul, Minn., 1968, Paper #68-57.

14. Lyman R. Ripperton, James J. B. Worth and Lawrence Kornreich, "Nitrogen Dioxide and Nitric Oxide in Non-Urban Air." 61st Annual Meeting of the Air Pollution Control Assoc., St. Paul, Minn., 1968, Paper #68-122.

15. F. E. Flacet, "Photochemistry in the Lower Atmosphere." *Ind. Eng. Chem.* 44, 1952.

16. Frank P. Terragliv and Raymond M. Manganelli, "The Absorption of Atmospheric Sulfur Dioxide by Water Solutions." *J. APCA* 17(6), 1967.

17. R. P. Ouellette, unpublished data, The MITRE Corp., 1970.

18. S. K. Friedlander and J. H. Seinfeld, "A Dynamic Model of Photochemical Smog." *Envir. Sci. and Tech.* 3(11), 1969.

19. E. A. Ulbrich and R. A. Jones, "Simulating Low Concentration Chemical Reactions as in Smog." *Simulation* 12(4), 1969.

20. Lowell G. Wayne and Terry E. Ernest, "Photochemical Smog— Simulated by Computer." Air Pollution Control Assoc., 1967, Paper #69-15.

21. A. Ralston and H. S. Wiff, *Mathematical Methods for Digital Computers,* Vols. 1 & 2. John Wiley & Sons, Inc., New York, 1967.

22. R. W. Southworth and S. L. Deleeuw, *Digital Computation and Numerical Methods.* McGraw-Hill, New York, 1965.

23. R. H. Pennington, *Introduction to Computer Methods and Numerical Analysis,* 2nd ed., Macmillan, New York, 1970.

24. Robert Smith, "Preliminary Design and Simulation of Conventional Wastewater Renovation Systems Using the Digital Computer." Dept. of Interior, UP-20-9, Washington, D.C., 1968.

25. Robert Smith, Richard G. Eilers, and Ella D. Hall, "Executive Digital Computer Program for Preliminary Design of Wastewater Treatment Systems." WP-20-14, Dept. of Interior, Washington, D.C., 1968.

26. George Bugliarello and John T. Onstott, "A Progress Report on HYDRO." Proc. IBM Scientific Computing Symposium on Water and Air Resources Management, 1968.

27. Norman H. Crawford, "Application of Hydrologic Simulation in Management Information Systems for Water Resources." Proc. IBM Scientific Computing Symposium on Water and Air Resources Management, 1968.

28. Robert V. Thomann, "Systems Analysis and Simulation in Water Quality Management." Proc. IBM Scientific Computing Symposium on Water and Air Resources Management, 1968.

29. Glenn R. Hilst, "Air Pollution Model of Connecticut." Proc. IBM Scientific Computing Symposium on Water and Air Resources Management, 1968.

30. E. S. Savas, "Computers in Urban Air Pollution Control Systems." Proc. IBM Scientific Computing Symposium on Water and Air Resources Management, 1968.

31. Robert G. Busacker and Thomas L. Saaty, *Finite Graphs and Net-*

works: An Introduction with Applications. McGraw-Hill, New York, 1965.

32. R. Rothfarb, H. Frank, D. M. Rosenbaum, K. Steiglitz, and D. J. Kleitman, "Optimal Design of Offshore Natural-gas Pipeline Systems." *Operations Research,* 1970.

33. Howard Frank and Ivan T. Frisch, "Network Analysis." *Scientific American* 223(1), 1970.

34. Rolf A. Deininger, "Computer Aided Design of Waste Collection and Treatment Systems." Proc. 2nd Annual American Water Res. Conf., November 1966.

35. Rolf A. Deininger, Robert W. Parrott, Hamdi Akfirat, "Computer Aided Design of Waste Water Treatment Plants." *Water Resources* 3, 1969.

36. John C. Liebman, "A Heuristic Aid for the Design of Sewer Networks." *J. San Eng.,* Div. Proc. ASCE, 1967.

37. H. P. Soehngen and P. R. De Cicco, "Design of a Sanitary Sewage Collection System by Electronic Computers." *Socio-Econ. Plan. Sci.,* 1968.

38. Nicolas C. Matalas, "Optimum Gaging Station Location." Proc. IBM Scientific Computing Symposium on Water and Air Resources Management, 1968.

39. Fiering, M. B., "An Optimization Scheme for Gaging." *Water Resources Research* 1(4), 1965.

40. Charles G. Gunnerson, "Optimizing Sampling Intervals." Proc. IBM Scientific Computing Symposium on Water and Air Resources Management, 1968.

41. Charles G. Gunnerson, "Optimizing Sampling Intervals in Tidal Estuaries," *J. San Eng. Div.* (ASCE) 2, 1966.

42. Ralph I. Larsen, "A New Mathematical Model of Air Pollutant Concentration, Averaging Time, and Frequency." 61st Annual Meeting Air Pollution Control Assoc., St. Paul, Minn., June 1968.

43. Richard H. Moushegian and Richard G. Krutchkoff, "Generalized Initial Conditions for the Stochastic Model for Pollution and Dissolved Oxygen in Streams." Virginia Polytechnic Institute, 1969.

44. Richard P. Thayer and Richard G. Krutchkoff, "A Stochastic Model for Pollution and Dissolved Oxygen in Streams." Virginia Polytechnic Institute, 1966.

45. C. A. Bisselle, S. H. Lubore and R. P. Pikul, *National Environmental Indices: Air Quality and Outdoor Recreation.* The MITRE Corp., MTR-6159, April 1972.

46. W. A. Thomas, L. R. Babcock, Jr., and W. D. Shults, "Oak Ridge Air Quality Index." ORNL-NSF-EP-8, Oak Ridge National Laboratory, Oak Ridge, Tennessee, September 1971.

47. J. W. Overbey, II, and R. P. Ouellette, "The Design and Operation of the National Aerometric Data Bank." The MITRE Corp., M71-67, September 1971.

48. Victor M. Yamada, "Current Practices in Siting and Physical Design of Continuous Air Monitoring Stations." Air Pollution Control Assoc., New York. 1969 (Paper APCA-69-111).

49. Patricia M. Anderson, "The Use and Limitations of Trend Surface Analysis in Studies of Urban Air Pollution." *Atmospheric Envir.* 4, 1970.

50. James T. Peterson, "Distribution of Sulfur Dioxide over Metropolitan St. Louis, as described by Empirical Eigenvectors, and Its Relation to Metropolitan Parameters." *Atmospheric Envir.* 4, 1970.

51. Gerald Van Belle, "Statistical Problems in Aerosol Studies." Paper presented at Symposium in 1971.

52. James A. Chisman, "The Pearson Generalized Statistical Distribution." Engineering Experiment Station Bulletin No. 11, Clemson University, South Carolina, February 1968.

53. Lester B. Lave and Eugene P. Seskin, "Does Air Pollution Cause Ill Health?" *Science* 169, 723, 1970.

54. S. I. Solomon, J. P. Donouvilliez, *et al*, "The Use of a Square Grid System for Computer Estimation of Precipitation, Temperature and Runoff." *Water Resources Research* 4(3):919-929, 1968.

55. Phillip A. Plato, Donald F. Menker and Maxwell Daver, "Computer Model for the Prediction of the Dispersion of Airborne Radioactive Pollutants." *Health Physics* 13, 1967.

56. David H. Slade, "Modelling Air Pollution in the Washington, D. C. to Boston Megalopolis." *Science* 157, 1967.

57. John F. Clarke, "A Simple Diffusion Model for Calculating Point Concentrations from Multiple Sources." *J. APCA* 14(9), 1964.

58. Francis Pooler, Jr., "A Prediction Model of Mean Urban Pollution For Use wth Standard Windrises."

59. Harry Moses, "Mathematicas Urban Air Pollution Models." Annual Meeting of APCA, 1969.

60. Wm. J. Moroz. "Weather and Pollution: A Survey of Modelling Techniques." Annual Meeting of APCA, 1968.

61. N. E. Browne, "A Simulation Model for Air Pollution over Connecticut." *J. APCA* 19(8), 1969.

62. S. K. Friedlander and A. L. Ravimohan, "A Theoretical Model for the Effect of an Acute Air Pollution Episode on a Human Population." *Env. Sci. Technol.* 2(12), 1968.

63. Paul E. Wilkins, "Automatic Real Time Prediction for Control of Maximum Ambient Contamination Concentration from Large Point Sources." Annual Meeting of APCA, 1968.

64. Wayne Ott, John F. Clarke and Guntis Ozolins, "Calculating Future Carbon Monoxide Emissions and Concentrations From Urban Traffic Data." HEW, Washington, D. C., 1967.

65. R. F. Jewett, "A Survey of Air Pollution Models." TRW Inc., Redondo Beach, Calif., 1967.

66. Norman E. Browne, "A Simulation Model for Air Pollution Over Connecticut." Annual Meeting of APCA, 1968.

67. Raymond G. Holmes and William G. MacBeth, "Statistical Model Relating Meteorological and Air Pollution Parameters," 225th Annual Meeting of the Am. Meteorological Soc., 1964.

68. J. B. Kuogler, R. S. Sholtes, A. L. Danis and C. I. Harding, "A Multivariate Model for the Atmospheric Dispersion Predictions." *J. APCA* 17(4), 1967.

69. Irving A. Singler, John A. Faizzula, and Maynard E. Smith, "A Simplified Method of Estimating Atmospheric Diffusion Parameters." *J. APCA* 16(11), 1966.

70. C. Rajasekara Murthy, "Wind Tunnel Modelling of Chimney Plumes." Annual Meeting of APCA, 1968.

71. E. M. Wilkins and T. Johnson, "Transport and Deposition of Contamination From an Instantaneous Source." RTI ORE-11, 1966.

72. Edward J. Kaplin, Rchard L. Reinert, and William T. Ingram, "Meteorological Variables Related to Selected Pollution Parameters." Meeting of APCA, 1968.

73. S. K. Friedlander and J. H. Steinfield, "A Dynamic Model of Photochemical Smog." *Envir. Sci. Tech.* 3(11), 1969.

74. Robert E. Kohn, "Linear Programming Model for Air Pollution Control: A Pilot Study of the St. Louis Air Shed." Annual Meeting of APCA, 1969.

75. Henry W. Herzog, Jr., "Urban Air Quality Planning, A Simulation Approach."

76. E. A. Ulbrich and R. A. Jones, "Simulating Low Concentration Chemical Reactions as in Smog." McDonnell Douglas, Los Angeles, Paper 5298, 1968.

77. E. A. Ulbrich, "A Hybrid Computer Simulation Investigating the Cost Effectiveness of Air Pollution Control Over a 10-Year Period." McDonnell Douglas, Los Angeles, Paper 4902, 1968.

78. Air Management Research Group, "Report on Models for Prediction of Air Pollution." Organization for Economic Cooperation and Development, Directorate for Scientific Affairs, Paris, 1970.

79. R. E. Larson and W. G. Keckler, "Applications of Dynamic Programming to the Control of Water Resource Systems." *Automation* 5, 1969.

80. Robert E. Kohn, "Linear Programming Model for Air Pollution Control: A Pilot Study of the St. Louis Air Shed." *J. APCA* 20(2), 1970.

81. "Air Quality Display Model." TRW, Washington, D. C., November 1969.

82. J. Golden, "The Air Quality Display Model Applied to Cook County, Illinois." The MITRE Corporation, MTR-4148, July 1970.

83. H. R. Hickey, W. D. Rowe and F. Skinner, "A Cost Model for Air Quality Monitoring Systems." *J. APCA* 21(11):689-693, 1971.

84. "Air Quality Implementation Program Planning Program." TRW Systems Group, Washington, D. C., November 1970.

85. C. H. Chilton *et al*, "A Cost Availability Model for Fossil Fuels." Battelle Memoral Institute, December 27, 1970.

86. "An Economic Model System for the Assessment of Effects of Air Pollution Abatement." CONSAD Research Corp., May 15, 1971.

87. S. Poh, "General Description of Seven Available Mathematical

Models for Water Quality Management." The MITRE Corp., WP-7845, July 21, 1971.

88. H. W. Streeter and E. B. Phelps, "A Study of the Pollution and Natural Purification of the Ohio River." Public Health Bulletin 146, U.S. Public Health Service, Washington, D. C., 1925.

89. W. E. Dobbins, "BOD and Oxygen Relationships in Streams." *J. Sanitary Engineering Division Proceedings ASCE,* Vol. 90, 1964.

90. R. G. Quimpo, "Autocorrelation and Spectral Analysis in Hydrology." *J. Hyd. Div.* (ASCE) 303-371, March 1968.

91. Rodriquez-Iturbe and C. F. Nordin, "Some Applications of Cross-Spectral Analysis in Hydrology: Rainfall and Runoff." *Water Res. Res.* 3, 1969.

92. R. A. Deininger, "Linear Programming for Hydrologic Analysis." *Water Res. Res.,* October 1969.

93. D. P. Loucks, *et al,* "Linear Programming Models for Water Pollution Control." *Mgmt. Sci.,* December 1968.

94. D. P. Loucks, "Computer Models for Reservoir Regulations." *J. Sanit, Eng. Div.* (ASCE), August 1968.

95. C. S. Revelle, D. P. Loucks and W. R. Lynn, "Linear Programming Applied to Water Quality Management." *Water Res. Res.,* February 1968.

96. John C. Liebman, "A Branch and Bound Algorithm for Minimizing the Cost of Waste Treatment, Subject to Equity Constraints." Proceedings IBM Scientific Computing Symposium on Water and Air Resources Management, 1968, pp. 193-202.

97. C. S. Beightler and W. L. Meier, "Dynamic Programming in Water Resources Development." Prog. Natl. Symp. on the Analysis of Water Resources Systems, Denver, Colo., July 1-3, 1968, pp. 64-71.

98. O. R. Burt, "Optimal Resources Used Over Time with Application to Ground Water." *Mgmt. Sc.* 11, 1964.

99. W. A. Hall and N. Buras, "The Dynamic Programming Approach to Water Resource Development." *J. Geophys. Res.* 66(2):517-520, 1966.

100. W. A. Hall, W. S. Butcher and A. Esogbue, "Optimization of the Operation of a Multiple Purpose Reservoir by Dynamic Programming." *Water Resources Res.* 4(3):471-477, 1968.

101. M. B. Fiering, "Queing Theory and Simulation in Reservoir Design." *J. Hyd. Div.* (ASCE) November 1961.

102. W. B. Langbein, "Queing Theory and Water Storage." *J. Hyd. Div.* (ASCE) October 1968.

103. M. Gablinger and D. P. Loucks, "MARKOV Models for Flow Regulation." *J. Hyd. Div.* (ASCE) January 1970.

104. R. V. Thomann, "Time Series Analysis of Water Quality Data." *J. San. Eng. Div.* (ASCE) February 1967.

105. P. Roger, "A Game Theory Approach to the Problem of International River Basins." *Water Res. Research,* August 1969.

106. D. M. Berthovex and L. C. Brown, "Monte Carlo Simulation of

Industrial Waste Discharges." *J. San. Eng. Div.* (asce) October 887-905, Oct. 1969.

107. G. K. Yound, "Finding Reservoir Operating Rules." *J. Hyd. Div.* (asce) November 1967.

108. Gerald J. Nehls, Donald H. Fair and John B. Clements, "National Air Data Bank Open for Business." *Env. Sci. Technol.* 4(11):902-905, 1970.

109. Phllip L. Taylor, Clarence W. Tutwiler, Charles S. Conger, "STORET—A Data Handling System in Water Pollution Control." asce Annual Meeting, October 13-17, 1969.

110. P. Thomas, L. Dowell, Jr., "The Natural Resource Information System." Center for Advanced Computation, University of Illinois at Urbana.

111. R. H. Langford and W. W. Doyel, "Coordination: The Key to Effective Water Data Management." National Symposium on Data and Instrumentation for Water Quality Management, Wisconsin, July 21-23, 1970.

112. "Design Characteristics for a National System to Store, Retrieve, and Disseminate Water Data." Federal Interagency Water Data Handling Work Group, Dept. of Interior, Washington, D. C., August 1971.

113. R. P. Ouellette, Jr., Golden J. and R. S. Greeley, "The nadis Concept," The mitre Corp., M71-11, February 1971.

114. R. P. Ouellette and R. S. Greeley, "The Design and Use of an Ambient Air Quality Data Bank." 2nd International Clean Air Congress, Washington, D. C., December 8, 1970.

115. Phillip L. Taylor, "Experience with a Water Pollution Control Storage and Retrieval System (storet)." National Symposium on Data and Instrumentation for Water Quality Management, Wisconsin, July 21-23, 1970.

116. William T. Sayers, "Measurement Problems Associated with Water Pollution Control Activities." 14th Annual Meeting of the Federal Statistics Users Conference, Washington, D. C., November 18, 1970.

CHAPTER **6**

THE SYSTEMS APPROACH TO THE SPECIFICATION AND ACQUISITION OF COMPUTER SYSTEMS IN ENVIRONMENTAL SCIENCE

DEFINITION OF THE SYSTEMS APPROACH

The choice of computers and the design of automated or semi-automated systems in environmental applications—whether it be for monitoring, process control, laboratory analysis, other scientific work, or administration—involves the analysis of a set of complex inter-related factors. The systems approach, in which these relationships are carefully specified and evaluated in terms of the cost and effectiveness of providing the desired output, is required to ensure that the components match, are sized for the intended jobs, and can be purchased under competitive conditions.

The systems approach starts with a "requirements analysis":

1. Why is a system or a set of activities needed in the first place?
2. What basic problem is required to be solved?
3. Is there a legal, regulatory, economic, or other justification or rationale for the capability?
4. To what uses will the system be put?
5. Who will use the system?
6. What are the basic objectives or performance requirements that must be met to provide this capability?
7. What is the desired or required scope of the system in terms of geographical and temporal coverage?
8. What are the constraints that must be placed on the system, such as financial, manpower, or schedule limitations?

197

In answering these questions, the responsible officials will be forced into examining the basic issues from the outset. Many serious problems in system implementation would be avoided if this were done before any computer or computer-system purchase. There is a recorded case of a county in the U. S. purchasing and installing an expensive automatic air-monitoring system without providing for a device for printing out the results. In addition, the response time of the system was far faster than any decision could be legally made by the county officials. No "requirement analysis" had been conducted.

The second step is to conduct a systems analysis. In this step, the objectives and scope of the system are converted into a quantitative system-level design or set of alternative designs within the constraints. This analysis will involve estimates of data-input amounts and rates; calculation of transmission rates, buffer and storage capacities, and processing speeds; identification of input and output formats; and checks for consistency of design throughout the system. Tradeoffs among system capabilities will be made, including geographic coverage, capacity, response time, error rate, component redundancy, output-display capability, and cost.

Frequently, and particularly in the case of a complex system, the tradeoffs are too numerous to evaluate for every permutation and combination of components or alternatives. In this case two, three, or more baseline alternative systems are designed and tradeoffs evaluated within each alternative. For instance, "minimal," "moderate," and "full-capacity" systems may be designed and their costs and performance estimated. Or a phased approach may be designed, starting with a limited system and adding capacity in increments over time. The result of this second step should be a fully evaluated design or set of designs, fully costed, from which the responsible officials can select a particular design for further implementation.

The third step is the preparation of system specifications to be included in a request for proposals (RFP) to system manufacturers or suppliers. The system-level design and system specifications are not synonymous. The former will be stated in terms of general, though quantitative capabilities and certain common elements such as station power supply, buildings, specific locations, etc. would be omitted. The latter must be general enough to permit true competitive bidding, but specific enough to ensure that the performance requirements are met and that all required services and supplies are provided at the precise locations desired. Frequently, in the purchase of computers, standardized "benchmark" programs are provided by the purchaser for demonstration testing on the vendor's machine. Of particular importance is the specification of the reliability required in each component and in the system as a whole. Many systems can be designed to "fail safe" (e.g., not lose important data during a power failure) and to degrade partially (e.g., have component redundancy) rather than "crash" when a minor component fails.

The fourth step consists of the evaluation of the system configurations that respondents (vendors) have selected to meet the requirements set forth in the system specifications.

It is essential in evaluating RFP responses to use a repeatable, traceable, and quantifiable procedure to compare the overall system configuration as well as each major subsystem among the competing vendors.

A procedure based on mapping measurable parameters (quantitatively or qualitatively) onto an equivalent dollar scale or a dimensionless value to the user scale is recommended. The procedure allows for subsequent aggregation of the different value parameters of system value versus value for each vendor. Then comparison of system value versus procurement cost permits a rank ordering of vendor systems and the final selection of the most cost-effective candidate.

The fifth step, or implementation, really starts at the time the RFP is issued and consists of a number of planning and preparatory steps (site planning, training, personnel acquisition, etc.) up to the final acceptance testing of the delivered system.

Figure 6.1 is a chart illustrating the full system implementation cycle for acquisition of an air-quality monitoring network.[1] The various activities and timing are generally common to most system acquisitions. Of particular importance to the system purchaser and/or operator is to prepare a well-thought-out request for proposals (RFP), a plan for evaluating them competently and fairly and selecting the most cost-effective proposal, a financial plan, a system-design review procedure, a system-installation inspection procedure, and a system test and acceptance program. Prior to system acceptance, a system operations manual should be available, an operations team assembled, and the operators and maintenance personnel trained. User orientation should start with system testing, and all users should be aware, at least, of the system's full capabilities when it is declared operational. Frequently the system contractor is retained for a period up to a year by the permanent operating team to assist in making the system fully operational.

The following sections will describe a recommended approach to the requirement analysis, system analysis, specification, and acquisition of a large administrative-scientific computer system.

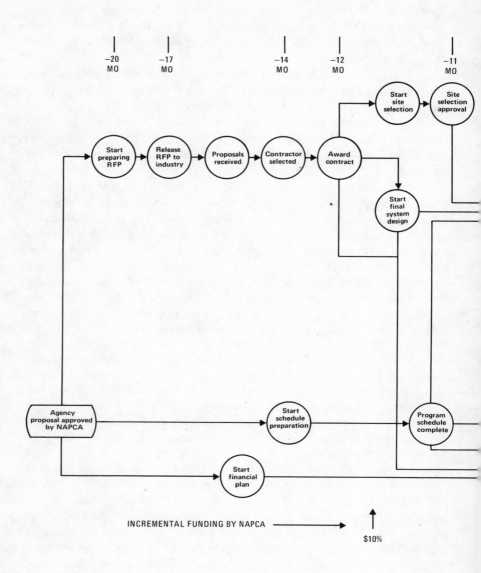

FIGURE 6.1.   Air-quality network acquisition circle.

200

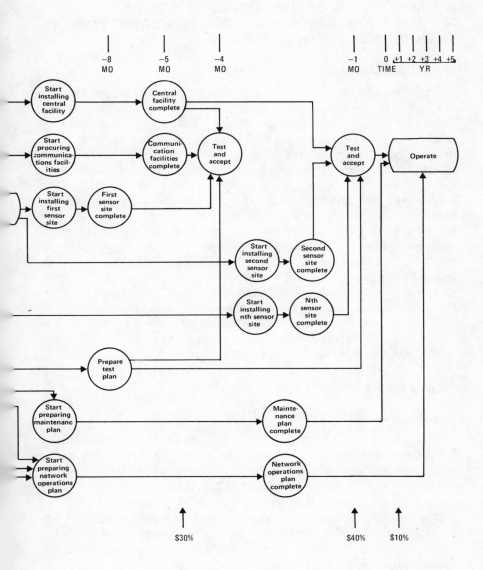

-8
MO

-5
MO

-4
MO

-1
MO

0
TIME

+1 +2 +3 +4 +5
YR

Start installing central facility

Central facility complete

Start procuring communications facilities

Communication facilities complete

Test and accept

Test and accept

Operate

Start installing first sensor site

First sensor site complete

Start installing second sensor site

Second sensor site complete

Start installing nth sensor site

Nth sensor site complete

Prepare test plan

Start preparing maintenance plan

Maintenance plan complete

Start preparing network operations plan

Network operations plan complete

$30%

$40%

$10%

AN APPLICATION OF THE SYSTEMS APPROACH
FOR THE ACQUISITION OF A LARGE ADMINISTRATIVE-
SCIENTIFIC COMPUTER SYSTEM

Study Case Description

In 1970 the government agency then responsible for air quality, the National Air Pollution Control Administration (NAPCA), recognized that its automatic data processing (ADP) capabilities were becoming a limiting factor on its ability to perform its mission. A requirements and a systems analysis were conducted. Next, system specifications were prepared; finally, a new, large administrative-scientific computer system was approved for implementation. The system was subsequently installed by the successor agency to NAPCA, the Environmental Protection Agency. The urgency of the situation was such in 1970 that the systems analysis led EPA to adopt an interim strategy and set up a medium-size computer at their new Technical Center in Research Triangle, North Carolina in 1971. Thus an effective requirements and systems analysis allowed sufficient expansion of ADP capabilities to meet an immediate critical need and to initiate the acquisition of a larger system to meet longer range needs.

The following sections give a summary of these analyses and the systems specifications, vendor response evaluation criteria and the implementation schedule developed for NAPCA.

Requirements Analysis [2]

System Objectives and Principal Applications

The objectives of a new NAPCA data processing system were to meet large and growing requirements for automatic data processing (ADP) capabilities essential to perform functions related to the achievement of the NAPCA missions. Included missions were defining and measuring air quality, defining the effects of pollutants, controlling motor-vehicle and stationary pollutant sources, and control-program operation and administration. System requirements included sorting large files in a highly structured fashion and providing for their manipulation in a user-oriented language, accurate handling of computational problems, rapid turnaround time, and time-sharing and teleprocessing capabilities. The principal nature of data processing workload included (1) conducting ecological, surveillance, and effects studies; (2) gathering, storing, and retrieving air-quality and emission data; (3) conducting and analyzing results of motor-vehicle emission tests; (4) performing grants administration and control; (5) conducting air-quality and implementation planning studies and providing fuel-additives registration; (6) providing bibliographic and administrative support services; (7) supporting process-control studies; (8) analyzing motor-vehicle combustion processes and photochemical reactions; and (9) performing meteorological support studies. As can be seen, these requirements attest to the need for a large centralized ADP system providing rapid access to users for scientific and data-retrieval applications.

Limitations of the Present System

The ADP needs of NAPCA were previously met through the use of a number of computers in four different geographical locations.

While NAPCA was utilizing the equivalent of approximately 340 hours of IBM Model 50 time, their data processing requirements were still in the embryonic stage. Moreover, due to the lack of their own large-scale equipment, NAPCA had been lagging for some time in meeting current requirements, and this was having a deleterious effect on progress toward substantive objectives. Their efforts were fragmented, and various kinds of equipment were being used. This situation was cumbersome and costly, not an efficient way to accomplish the agency's objectives.

Thus, NAPCA could not meet near-term increased demands for data service, needs for a growing data base, requirements of a sophisticated technology, and expanded missions without an immediate increase in data processing capability.

An investigation of the ADP capabilities existing prior to 1970 (the time at which the study was conducted) at NAPCA revealed the following specific weaknesses: inadequate capability to handle existing requirements; fragmented service capability, since variation in types of equipment and organization provide no focal point for integration; little room for expansion of most equipment; and misallocation of analytical and ADP manpower to accomplish missions due to organizational and geographic dispersion.

These system weaknesses were having varied effects on every operating bureau and division. These weaknesses had the following consequences: often information was received late or not at all; new development experienced time lags with respect to the state-of-the-art; some new research programs could not be initiated; and laboratory analyses were frequently delayed with a resulting buildup of work backlog. For example, the analysis and dissemination of air-quality data was often delayed by several years. Consequently, the efficiency of NAPCA was impaired by the inability to meet time-critical demands and its leadership potential was put at risk.

Requirements for the NAPCA ADP System

To determine quantitative requirements for a computer system configuration that could solve the problems of current ADP limitations, the then current size and projected growth (to 1974) of ADP input and output workload, data base, and computer usage for all of NAPCA was estimated. These system workload requirements are shown in Figures 6.2 to 6.5. Requirements for intermediate years assumed linear growth, although they were likely to increase more rapidly in earlier years. For example, Figure 6.5 indicates that computer utilization in 1971 will exceed 500 hours per month. Extra requirements for program conversion to new equipment would place temporary strain on the available capacity. The requirements growth depicted in Figues 6.2 to 6.5 is summarized:

	1970	1974 Estimate	Growth Factor
Input (char/mo)	1.16 billion	4.20 billion	3.6
Output (char/mo)	0.16 billion	1.88 billion	11.7
Data base (char)	0.85 billion	7.60 billion	8.9
Computer usage (360/50 hrs/mo)	339	1319	3.9

The NAPCA mission can be separated into nine functional application areas related to 33 specific ADP-oriented functions. These functions were analyzed with respect to their ADP characteristics. These functions are distributed into traditional ADP classifications as follows:

ADP Characteristics	Percent of Functions
File management	70
Scientific processing	54
Administrative processing	13

The total exceeds 100 percent since many functions exhibit more than one characteristic. It can be seen that scientific-processing and file-management characteristics dominated NAPCA's ADP needs.

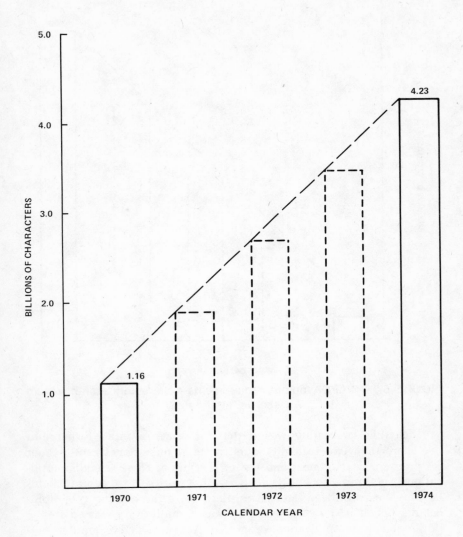

FIGURE 6.2.   NAPCA input requirements—characters/month. *(From J. Garrison,* et al, *ref. 2)*

205

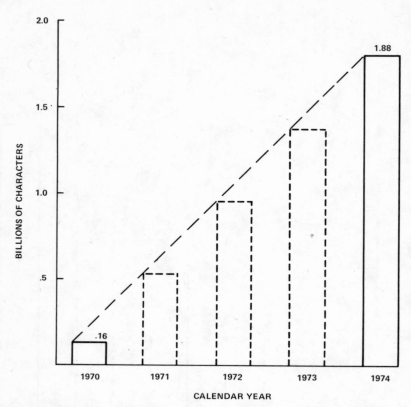

FIGURE 6.3.   NAPCA output requirements—characters/month. *(From J. Garrison,* et al, *ref. 2)*

Scientific processing was required to have a rapid turnaround (no more than two to eight hours for most operational runs, sooner for program development and testing). Many of these scientific applications required statistical analyses that needed to access simultaneous noncentralized data bases. Because of the existing geographical dispersion and equipment mix, much duplication existed in the development of application programs. A centralized computer network and central coordination of all ADP services would tend to eliminate this duplication.

A large number of the ADP functions required file update, data retrieval, and report generation utilizing a common data base; consequently, there was a requirement for a flexible data base management system that could meet the needs of most users.

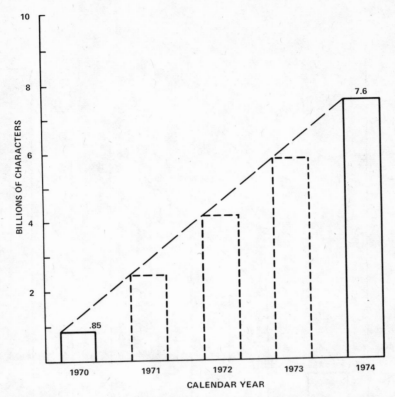

FIGURE 6.4. NAPCA data-base requirements. *(From J. Garrison,* et al, *ref. 2)*

Systems Analysis

Description of the Proposed ADP System for NAPCA

To meet the requirements described in the preceding paragraphs, it was decided that NAPCA needed a large-scale centralized data processing facility supplemented with separate data-acquisition and -reduction subsystems in critical areas. The facility should be capable of accommodating input/output terminals from remote locations to service time-sharing and remote-batch needs of the users. Internal memory speeds comparable to those available with current large-scale, third-generation equipment were required. Scientific as well as administrative applications would need to be performed effectively. System characteristics had to include:

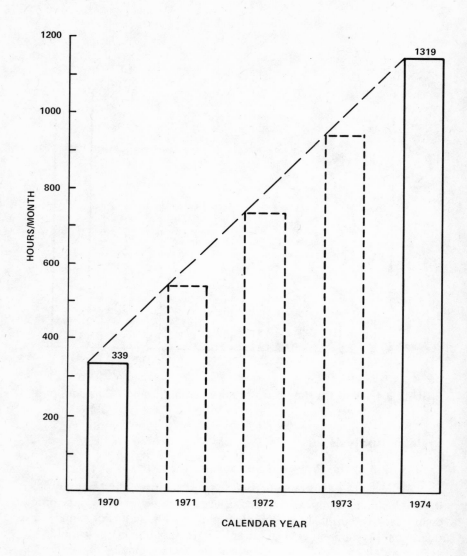

FIGURE 6.5.   NAPCA computer usage—360/50 equivalent. *(From J. Garrison,* et al, *ref. 2)*

208

1. Hardware
   a. 1–3 million-byte main memory
   b. Adequate selector and multiplexor i/o channels
   c. A wide complement of peripheral i/o equipment to include high-speed card reader and punch, high- and low-speed line printers, and paper tape reader and punch
   d. Rapid-access storage units capable of modular expansion from one billion bytes initially to four billion bytes and larger as the need arises
   e. High-speed, high-density magnetic tape drives
   f. 20–30 i/o terminals to allow for both data and program entry
   g. Interface transmission control
   h. Suitable data sets
2. System software
   a. Executive system control monitor with multiprogramming capability
   b. Spooling capabilities
   c. Versatile job control
   d. Utility programs for dump, restore, update, etc.
   e. Sort/merge capability for tape and disk
3. Applications software
   a. Statistical package providing tabulations, distributions, mean and standard deviation, linear and nonlinear multiple-regression analysis
   b. Standard mathematical routines (e.g., square root, sine, cosine, exponential) and large-scale matrix inversion
   c. Data- and file-management system
   d. Continuous and discrete system simulation language
   e. High-level languages, including standard FORTRAN IV, COBOL, RPG, PL-1

A primary criteria in the analysis was that the detailed design should consider the technical and economic aspects of interfacing the new processor with the existing Model 50.

Since NAPCA had plans to consolidate a substantial portion of its research staff and other organizational elements, a central facility had economic and technical advantages over a network-connected system. To permit timely access by scientists and managers in their own working environment, time-sharing terminals need to be strategically located to make the computer power available. The characteristics of the system, then, are that it was technically oriented to supporting scientific-programming and sophisticated file-management operations.

A list of detailed objectives to be achieved by the new ADP system was arranged in order of priority. These objectives were to be met within five years of the system implementation. These objectives are the benefits that were used in a cost/benefit analysis of the current and the proposed systems. A relative priority had been assigned each objective as a measure of the worth or value of the capability to the user. This priority ranking was considered in the subsequent system hardware and software evaluation. The specific rankings assigned to the individual performance capabilities are summarized in the following table.

Performance Capability	Priority
Provide rapid turnaround time:	1
2-8 hours for scientific jobs	
Within 2-24 hours for high priority requests	
Timely response for scheduled requests	
More extensive coverage of the population at risk	1
Provide basis for action during episodes	1
Integrated Data Bank, increase the value of the data	
by cross usage and coordination	2
Data output of high utility, including management	
information, quality control, etc.	2
Current data, i.e.,	
Immediate to telemetered data	
Daily update of special problems	
Monthly update on routine data	
Automated data handling keep personnel at minimum level	3

In Chapter 2 we presented in some detail a procedure for conducting a systems analysis of alternatives. This will not be repeated here. Rather, the few candidate alternatives that were identified will be briefly described together with the selected alternative. The emphasis in this chapter will be on the development of the associated systems specifications, the evaluation methodology, and the schedule for implementing the selected system configuration.

Alternative Solutions to Meet the NAPCA ADP Requirements

Th existing NAPCA ADP capability was inadequate. A temporary solution was to transfer an IBM 360/50 to the centralized research facility. This solution would eliminate the pressing need for a system decision and enable the staff to complete a detailed analysis of long-term alternatives. Three alternatives were considered:

1. Purchase computer time from external sources (service bureau, universities, or government)
2. Upgrade and augment the existing equipment
3. Design and acquire a new system free of the constraint of using existing equipment.

Alternative 1 would be employed to overcome the projected lack of capacity of the present equipment by 1971. This was a viable alternative only on a temporary basis. However, this alternative was not a good long-term solution.

The second alternative was marginally feasible. Present equipment could not be expanded to the extent required when one considers the aspects of economics and efficiency. It did not have adequate software and hardware characteristics to provide efficient time-sharing, remote-batch, and batch-processing capabilities required to meet NAPCA's application needs; these processing capabilities were required for effective operations. To meet the short-term need, it would be necessary to increment the memory capacity on the 360/50 to allow for terminal connection and to meet additional processing and storage needs.

Conclusions

A major conclusion was that the only way in which NAPCA can meet a four-and-one-half-fold growth in input/output processing, a ninefold growth in storage requirements, and a fourfold growth in computer usage within three point five to four years would be by taking the necessary steps immediately to acquire a large dedicated central facility that would provide the focal point for timely support of NAPCA technical and administrative applications.

Recommendations

In order to meet NAPCA's ADP requirements, which were shown to be closely related to the effective attainment of its missions, the following recommendations were made:

- Issue immediate approval for acquisition of a centralized ADP system with supporting data acquisition and reduction equipment and input/output terminal devices.

- Prepare a request for procurement incorporating functional specifications for the detailed design and procurement of the proposed system.

System Specifications

System specifications are traditionally oriented toward identifying strict standards of hardware and software performance and for the effective integration of subsystem components. The specifications do not use specific vendors or model identification, as this practice would tend to preclude potential vendors from responding.

The specifications for the NAPCA ADP center were based on a detailed analysis of functional requirements. The objective in developing the functional specifications was to use them as the system requirements section of a request-for-proposal (RFP) from vendors to provide a system capable of meeting the stated requirements. With this objective in mind, the specifications are written such that they could be used by prospective vendors in preparing competitive bids.

The RFP contains specifications for mandatory requirements and desirable features of computer hardware, computer software, and the operation of the total computer system. Also specified are details such as vendor support, schedules for training, procedures for program conversion and data conversion, installation dates, preinstallation test schedule, and other events and tasks necessary for full system implementation.

In describing the system specification of the RFP, we have employed the wording and format consistent with many RFPs. This has been done to give the reader an idea of how system specifications actually appear in RFPs. All RFPs for ADP equipment will generally contain the same categories of specifications. The details of the specifications obviously must be tailored specifically to the requirements derived from application.

Mandatory System Requirements [3]

The following paragraphs prescribe mandatory system requirements for which compliance is required. In responding, the vendor's ability to fulfill each mandatory requirement listed must be made in the proposal. All costs associated with any requirement listed below will be reflected in the proposal. Equipment proposed by the vendor must consist of components selected from an integrated group of off-the-shelf ADP equipment systems. Equipment types, the minimum number of components, and the characteristics of the components are given in Table 6.1.

TABLE 6.1

ADP Hardware Characteristics Summary

Equipment Type		Storage Capacity/No. of Components Minimum Acceptable Configuration
CPU		2
Primary storage exclusive of resident executive (bytes)		1 million
Immediate	Fast	7 million
access	Medium	1.25 billion
storage	Slow	210 million
(bytes)	Very slow	400 million
Type drives		15
Operator console, CRT and keyboard for hard copy		3
Printer (high-speed) 1100 LPM		3
Card reader/punch		2
CRT displays		10
Keyboard inquiry device and terminal		20
Remote job entry printer, card reader/punch, keyboard device		7

SOURCE: Garrison, ref. 3.

Central Processor Unit

PRIMARY STORAGE. A minimum primary storage capacity of one million bytes exclusive of system storage is required. The primary storage must be capable of expansion up to three million bytes by the addition of storage modules of similar speed. Additionally, the vendor must provide excess storage capacity to handle the executive software described in the section on mandatory software.

An effective cycle time cannot exceed 750 nanoseconds. Parity checks must be performed on all data transfers to and from primary storage, the main processor, and I/O channels.

ARITHMETIC HARDWARE. Arithmetic hardware must perform fixed-point arithmetic and floating-point arithmetic having a minimum of six digits in single precision calculation and 12 digits in double-precision calculation. The hardware must permit numeric values to range from 10^{-30} to 10^{+30}.

REAL-TIME. One real-time clock shall be provided. Its resolution must be at least 1/64 second.

IMMEDIATE ACCESS STORAGE (IAS). Four categories of immediate-access storage are required. Their characteristics and the minimum acceptable capacities are shown in Table 6.2. Parity checking on all read accesses is required.

TABLE 6.2

Immediate-Access Storage Characteristics

Category	Average Access Time (Milliseconds)	Minimum Transfer Rate (Bytes/Second)	Minimum Capacity (Bytes)
Fast	No greater than 4	1.5 M	7 M
Medium	60–100	300 K	1.25 B
Slow	100–250	100 K	210 M
Very slow	500–600	60 K	400 M

B = Billion
M = Million
K = Thousand
SOURCE: Garrison, ref. 3.

The ability physically to remove the medium, slow, and very slow storage medium when it is not used by the central processing unit is a requirement. If the vendor does not have removable storage, a method must be suggested for maintaining data integrity and for a logical disconnect of the storage medium from the CPU. The vendor will be rated on this proposed method.

MAGNETIC TAPE. The vendor must provide a minimum of 15 tape units with the following capabilities:

at least one unit that can record seven tracks at a density of 556 and 800 bytes/inch (bpi)

at least one unit that can record nine tracks at a density of 800 and 1600 bpi

all remaining units must be able to record at least nine tracks at a density of at least 1600 bpi

The minimum data-transfer rate between CPU and the storage shall be at least 90K bytes/second. Programmatic density selection is also required.

CARD READER/PUNCH. At least two card-read and card-punch units are required. Each must have the capability to read and punch standard 80-column 12-row punch cards and must be fully buffered. The card readers and card punches speed for reading/punching 80-column cards must be at least 800 cpm and 250 cpm respectively. The unit must have the ability to read and punch both hollerith and column binary.

PRINTERS. Two high-speed printers must be provided. High-speed printers will be on-line devices and must be capable of printing at least 1100 lmp. Additionally, each printer must:

be fully buffered

have a minimum of 132 print positions per line

be capable, under program control, of single-space printing, double-space printing, controlled multiple-line skipping, and page eject

A form stacker or its equivalent is required. The standard, alphanumeric character set will be provided for high-speed printers, all typewriterlike devices, CRT displays, and remote job entry printers.

REMOTE TERMINALS AND CONSOLE SUBSYSTEMS. Three types of remote access terminals are required. The number of each type of terminal required is listed in Table 6.3. Each type is described below.

TABLE 6.3

Remote Terminals and Consoles Summary

Type		Name	Number of Terminals	
			Initial	Expanded
Type 1		Typewriterlike terminals		
	a	Remote (Dial-up switched)	5	15
	b	Local	10–20	30
Type 2		Cathode-ray tube consoles		
	a	CRT/keyboard/hard copy terminal	5	10
	b	CRT/keyboard terminal	5	10
Type 3		Remote job entry terminal		
	a	Dial-up	2	2
	b	Leased line	4	4
	c	Hard wired	1	1

SOURCE: Garrison, ref. 5.

216 COMPUTER TECHNIQUES IN ENVIRONMENTAL SCIENCE

Type 1a. Low-speed, typewriterlike devices will be located at local and state air pollution control centers in each of the ten Air Pollution Control Regions. These 10 devices must print approximately 15 characters/second and must operate on half-duplex lines. These terminals must print and transmit the full standard character set.

Type 1b. Anywhere from 10 to 20 local low-speed, typewriterlike devices will be required for supporting the operating divisions located in the immediate vicinity of the NAPCA computer center. These terminals must be hard-wired, low-speed devices to provide a convenient means of developing programs and interrogating the data base in a conversational mode. Typically, these terminals will be used when low output volume is expected and quick turnaround is desired.

Type 2—CRT/Keyboard. Five medium-speed local CRT display terminals (up to 2,000 bps) with no hard copy capability are required. The line printers will be used if hard copy is needed, by requesting printout at the computer center. Five additional CRT terminals with hard copy capability are required. These will be placed in buildings surrounding the computer center. All ten CRT devices will be hard-wired, and the vendor will supply the wiring.

Type 3—Remote Job Entry Terminals. The required remote job entry terminal charatceristics are:

Printer; 300 lpm, 132 print positions, standard character set
Card reader, 250 cpm
Card punch, 75 cpm
Capability for half or full duplex lines
Typewriterlike device for operator messages between the computer center and the remote facility.

Mandatory Software Requirements

The following paragraphs prescribe the mandatory software requirements. A statement concerning the vendor's ability to fulfill each mandatory requirement listed below is required and will be considered in the proposal evaluation.

Operating System (Executive Control) Requirements

Each application program must be executed under the control of the operating system with regard to loading, sequence and priority in the job queue, I/O and library calls, resource allocation, and program termination activities under all processing conditions. The operating system must control the organization and regulation of the flow of work through the entire proposed system. The operating system will also contain a basic usage accounting system.

The operating system shall have a multiprogramming capability. The operating system shall supervise the execution of batch processing jobs in a continuous flow but must allow for interruption of programs-in-progress to receive jobs and process input/output requests with remote terminals.

In the event of i/o unit failures, ias unit failures, channel failures, the operating system will provide capability for fallback and recovery processing.

Data Management (on System Level)

Techniques and procedures must be provided to enable users the ability to create files, perform file maintenance, and selectively retrieve data from files.

The data-management system must provide for the structuring and formatting of data files from either source (input) data or data contained in existing data base files. Further, the system must provide the capability to store file descriptor-parameters such that subsequent file access need not entail redefining the file format to the system. The data management system must permit user-supplied subroutines that process input file items to be stored.

The data-management system must provide file-maintenance capabilities including adding new data; modifying existing file data (this includes the capability for the user to define which data needs to be modified and in what manner it must be modified); deleting existing file data; and restructuring files in the systems data base (this capability must provide for reformatting and datum conversion). The data-management system must have a generalized capability to retrieve data from files in the systems data base.

The data-management system would include a high-level language capability to (1) provide the data-management system with control information such as data file descriptions, data item maintenance specifications, retrieval specifications for jobs that are performed periodically, and so forth; (2) specify job requests (when such requests do not already reside in the system); (3) to modify user-supplied control (data description, subroutines, job specification, etc.) of information residing in the system to specify requests to the system either batched on-line or not on-line.

Programming Systems

The computer center requires a set of varied programming languages to satisfy its needs for business-oriented and scientific computation, internal development of system software, report generation, and on-line conversational applications. These include COBOL and FORTRAN, machine-oriented mnemonic language, RPG, and general utility programs.

COBOL AND FORTRAN. Both COBOL and FORTRAN IV must be usable in batch and interactive processing modes.

Machine-Oriented Mnemonic Language. An assembler or other machine-oriented language is required to facilitate extensions to operating system and to facilitate the development of special-purpose software with a measure of efficiency not usually found in compilers. This language must (1) permit programmer definition of macroinstructions (or object code routines inserted in the basic assembler); (2) permit the calling of separately generated object coding; (3) produce, after assembly, relocatable object programs, with absolute addresses assignable by the operating systems; and (4) provide machine-oriented instructions or macroinstructions for operations upon both words and characters, character-by-character searches within memory, transfer of variable-length data blocks within memory, and decimal arithmetic operations.

Report Program Generator (RPG). An RPG (or COBOL report writer) must be provided. The report writer language must operate under the control of the operating system and generate an object code that can be loaded, initiated, and executed by the operating system. The report writer must produce an object program capable of the following: obtaining data records from single- or multiple-input files contained within the storage media; performing such calculations as addition, subtraction, multiplication, and division of data obtained from input records and data constants in the object program; editing and writing printed reports with the ability to suppress specific information such as leading zeroes; writing output tape files; checking the sequence-input records; assessing specific tabular entries; branching within calculations; and writing output to IAS files.

General Utilities. General utility programs must perform these functions: tape-to-tape, tape-to-printer, card-to-tape and tape-to-card, tape-to-IAS and IAS-to-tape, card-to-IAS and IAS-to-card, IAS-to-printer, IAS-to-IAS, main-storage-to-printer, card-to-printer, and tape compare.

Equipment diagnostic routines must be available to facilitate maintenance and error checking.

A dump routine is required, which will display selected areas of memory and registers by symbolic address or reference on request of the application program. Trace and snapshot capability, as well as compiler diagnostic support, during on-line program development are required.

A sort/merge capability for the magnetic tapes and for the IAS proposed by the vendor is required. These programs must be callable through and must operate under the control of the operating system. They must allow sorting by single and multiple keys, in ascending or descending order or numerical magnitude and collation sequence. There must be a capability of performing arithmetic or logical operations on the data being sorted. The ability to include other object code sequences within the sort programs to call and exit to other preprogrammed routines is also required. The relevant sort algorithm of the sort programs must be described.

A basic display utility package (macros, subroutines, or combinations) that will operate under control of the operating system is necessary. It must perform, as a minimum, the following functions: conversion of data from character or byte strings to proper format for display output and initiate the output and conversion of data from display format to a specified character or byte string and store the origin and status of the display device sending the message.

Desirable Features

The items and features listed below are *not* mandatory; however, if they are provided, they will receive special consideration during the evaluation of proposals. A statement concerning the vendor's capability to fulfill all or a segment of each desirable feature listed must be made in the proposal.

Present workload projections indicate that computer usage will be the equivalent of eight-hour IBM 360/50 work shifts by 1974. The mandatory system requirement is to reduce this to a two-shift/day operation or a 4:1 reduction in workload processing time.

It is desirable that the system be operational 12 months after notification is given to the selected vendor. The cost-value of early and late delivery will be determined by projecting the cost of leasing additional facilities to process the expanding workload, plus estimating the dollar value of the inconvenience this will cause.

It is also desirable that the proposed system be housed in an area containing no more than 4,200 square feet. A cost-value penalty will be assessed based upon the modifications required (e.g., removal of wall partitions, additional raised floor, additional space, etc.).

Languages providing a capability for discrete and continuous simulation of real events are desirable, and proposal of such languages will constitute quality evaluation factors. Languages proposed must operate under the operating system to be acceptable. The number of qualifying languages will be used for evaluation, along with the following criteria for each language: extensiveness of the built-in function capability and ability to add, through subroutines or subprograms, additional functions.

A system of mathematical statistical programs is desired. These will be capable of providing all or any part of the following:

1. The ability to support statistical analyses
   a. Polynomial regression
   b. Multiple linear regression
   c. Elementary statistics
2. Matrix manipulation
   a. Inversion
   b. Systems of linear algebraic equations
   c. Eigenvalues and eigenvectors
3. Numerical integration
4. Special functions

A CAUTIONARY NOTE. As can be seen from the above, the preparation of system specifications is a laborious and tedious task. However, the performance of the acquired system is directly related to the quality of the specifications.

PROPOSAL EVALUATION AND SELECTION CRITERIA

Some aspects of the methods of evaluation of a vendor's proposal are discussed in this section. To receive consideration for selection, it is imperative that a proposal meet the mandatory requirements.

The Cost-Value Technique

A useful method for evaluating and selecting an ADP system is the cost-value technique. This method is based on Joslin's procedure.[4] The cost-value technique is a means of scoring or ranking vendor proposals by using a "cost-value accounting scheme." From the total cost of the proposed system, the cost-value of optional but desirable features is deducted. This assures that all vendors will be evaluated on the same basis. Any vendor not meeting the full mandatory system requirements is eliminated from further evaluation. If only the mandatory system is desired, final vendor selection is based on the lowest derived cost (which is the difference between total system cost and cost-values of desirable features).

Table 6.4 depicts items to which cost-values are to be assigned.

TABLE 6.4

Cost-Value Accounting Table

Items	Vendor Proposal 1 (Dollars)	Vendor Proposal 2 (Dollars)	Vendor Proposal 3 (Dollars)	. . .
0. Normalized Total System Cost				
Value Items				
1. Workload capability				
2. IBM 360/50 software compatibility				
3. Vendor program test time				
4. Equipment delivery				
5. Space				
6. Paper tape reader/punch				
7. Optical mark page reader				
8. Simulation languages				
9. Mathematical program system				
Total value of desirable features				
Total cost of mandatory requirements				

SOURCE: Garrison [3]

Item 0, Total System Cost, reflects the total system cost based on a specified system life-cycle. Items 1 through 9 reflect the optional but desirable features the vendor included in his response. The difference between Item 0 and the sum of Items 1 through 9 represents the cost of the mandatory system.

Procedures for Evaluating Vendors Including Desirable Features

The costs associated with the additional, but desirable, features of a system proposed by a vendor are easily identified. The benefits derived by the procuring agency by having these additional capabilities vary according to the type and characteristics of the capability proposed. If all vendors would propose the same amount, or level, of capability, no problem in evaluating the vendor proposals would result. However, this situation is rarely encountered. When vendors differ in their proposed capabilties, the procuring agency must quantify the relative worth of each capability to its need.

This is accomplished by "cost-value" mapping function. Figures 6.6 through 6.9 present examples of the general shape of such cost-value functions. Only the general shape of the cost-value mapping function is presented. The agency procuring this system must supply its own quantitative values based on its judgment regarding the capabilities utility to the requirements.

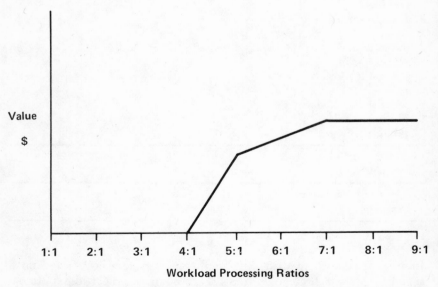

FIGURE 6.6.   Cost-value chart. *(From J. Garrison,* et al, *ref. 2)*

System Implementation

The NAPCA staff planned to standardize data processing systems, equipment, and programming to the extent that such standardization would be practical from an operational point of view. The installation schedule for the system described above in the specification is shown in Figure 6.10. Obviously, specific configuration and installation data would be negotiated during the proposal cycle.

As can be seen from Figure 6.10, there are three major areas of activity. The first area includes those tasks associated with the RFP cycle—the release of the RFP, proposal submission, and its evaluation. The second area represents those tasks relating to the internal review and contract approval cycle of the procuring agency. The third area includes those tasks more directly associated with the actual installation of equipment. The third area includes three main tasks: preinstallation testing, training of agency personnel, and program/data conversion. The specific activities associated with the first two of these main tasks are described below. The third does not need a detailed discussion.

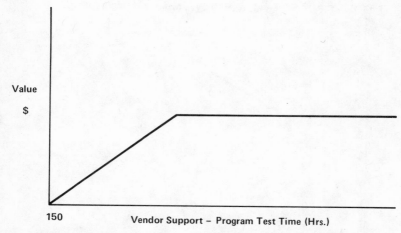

FIGURE 6.7.   Cost-value chart. *(From J. Garrison, et al, ref. 2)*

Preinstallation Test Schedule

The selected vendor provided preinstallation test facilities for the compilation and testing of system software and application programs at a site mutually agreed upon by the procuring office and the vendor.

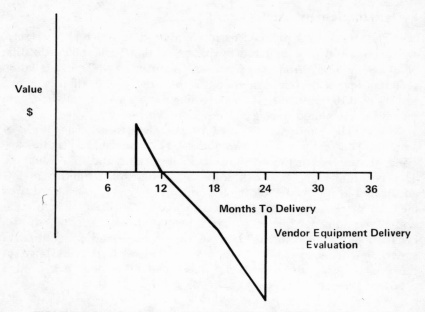

FIGURE 6.8.   Cost-value chart. *(From J. Garrison,* et al, *ref. 2)*

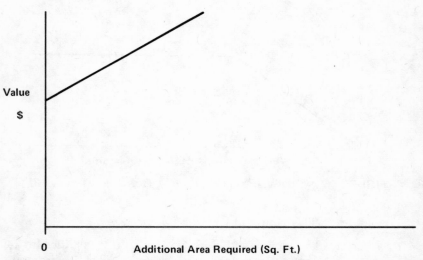

FIGURE 6.9.   Cost-value chart. *(From J. Garrison,* et al, *ref. 2)*

This activity began four months prior to the scheduled installation date. The selected vendor provided approximately 150 hours of compilation and test time, spread over the four-month period. The facilities used for this purpose consisted of hardware and software completely compatible with the systems that were to be installed.

Training

The selected vendor provided an orientation/training course on the selected ADP equipment for key agency personnel. The course consisted of an instruction period of approximately one week. The cur-

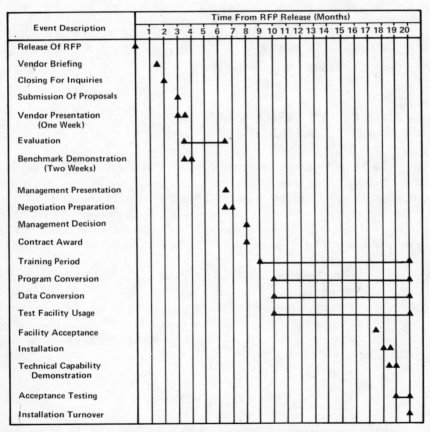

FIGURE 6.10. ADP system implementation schedule. *(From J. Garrison, et al, ref. 2)*

riculum design was reviewed and approved by the procuring agency. The selected vendor was responsible for conducting the first such course and for training personnel so that they were able to present continued orientation courses. Presentation of the orientation course was 30 days prior to the installation.

The selected vendor provided for the training of analysts and programmers. Training for systems analysts included sufficient coverage of equipment and support software to permit efficient systems design and adequate communication with programmers.

The selected vendor furnished training for operators to support the equipment installation. This training included instructions on operation of system software and on the operation of each component. All classroom training commenced early enough to allow for operation of equipment immediately after installation. Hands-on operator training consisted of approximately 80 hours of system time. The selected vendor trained two full shifts of operators so that the system could be placed in operation 16 hours a day.

RESULTS OF THE SYSTEMS APPROACH
IN COMPUTER ACQUISITION

The large administrative-scientific computer system described in some detail above has been purchased by EPA and was recently installed in the Technical Center, Research Triangle, North Carolina. This new system appreciably augmented the limited interim capability at the Center, and indeed improved EPA's ability, particularly from the standpoint of rapid, large-scale data handling and ease of user access.

This latter point is extremely important. Since the EPA staff, EPA regional offices, and state environmental agencies can be more easily and rapidly served with this new system, decisions on environmental policies and programs have been and will continue to be much more effective than in the past, when decisions were based on information a year or more old.

REFERENCES

1. R. B. Shaller, "A Systems Approach for Acquiring Air Monitoring Networks." The MITRE Corp., M70-18, RW1, April 1970.

2. John Garrison, *et al,* "Functional Requirements for an Automatic

Data Processing System for the National Air Pollution Control Administration." The MITRE Corp., MTR-4150, Vol. 1 & 11, August 1970.

3. J. Garrison, R. Helfand, F. Skinner, "A Preliminary System Specification for an Automatic Data Processing System for the National Air Pollution Control Administration." The MITRE Corp., WP-7396, December 1970.

4. Edward O. Joslin, *Computer Selection*. Addison-Wesley Publishing Co., 1968.

CHAPTER 7

THE ROLE OF COMPUTERS IN NATIONAL ENVIRONMENTAL POLICY- AND DECISION- MAKING

In December 1970 the U. S. House of Representatives passed a bill [1] providing for an environmental monitoring data system to "serve as the central national coordinating facility for the selection, storage, analysis, retrieval, and dissemination of information, knowledge and data relating to the environment so as to provide information needed to support environmental decisions in a timely manner and in a usable form." The bill did not come to a vote in the Senate in the closing days of 1970, but the idea of a national environmental data system has frequently been discussed in both Houses ever since.

As it is envisioned, the national environmental data system would serve the Council on Environmental Quality, the Environmental Protection Agency, the National Oceanic and Atmospheric Administration, the Agriculture and Interior departments, and other administrative agencies concerned with the environment at the Federal level, as well as the Congress and the Federal Courts. Most probably, computers will play a major role in the operations of such a system. Mention has been made in previous chapters of the computerized SAROAD and STORET systems of the Environmental Protection Agency. Other large environmental data-gathering and -processing activities are conducted using computer tools by the National Center for Health Statistics, HEW; and the Environmental Data System of NOAA, which includes the National Weather Records Center, the National Oceanographic Data Center, and the National Geophysical Data Center. The Census Bureau maintains a wide variety of environmentally related data on tape. The U. S. Geological Survey and other bureaus of the Department of Interior maintain extensive data banks. The National Aeronautics and Space Administration gathers in digital form extensive data from the Earth Resources Technology Satellite and numerous aircraft outfitted with multispectral cameras. The Department of Agriculture maintains perhaps the largest store of environmentally related activities.

In the following paragraphs, we will investigate the benefits that would result from automation methods of integrating the data bases. Typical parameters that would be measured in comprehensive national environmental data system include: quality, quantity, and pollution effects, natural effects, resources, and social-aesthetic factors. By 1976 the number of measurement sites for each parameter is expected to be in the thousands. For instance, natural resources, land use, and other natural effects would be reported on a county basis, or even finer grid. As many as 10,000 stations are expected to be needed for full coverage of the nation for air and water quality, emission and effluent quantities, and other pollution effects. Each neighborhood is expected to be monitored for social-aesthetic factors. The data rate per site has been estimated,[2] in a very general way, from the number of characters required per measurement (100 to 1,000), the number of measurements per month (1 to 720), and the number of instruments at each site (1 to 20). The maximum number of characters per month to be reported per site would be 10^4 but generally lower figures are expected. If original data are forwarded to the federal level for storage and processing by the responsible agencies, the data rate for most parameters would be 10^8 to 10^9 characters per month. The total data storage required for just a year's worth of data would be 10^9 to 10^{10} characters and might ultimately reach upward to 10^{11} characters for long-term historical purposes. Table 7.1 lists these data flow rates and storage requirements.

These data rates do not include multispectral imagery from air- and space-born sensors for monitoring natural resources. Also, these numbers do not include a wide variety of data needed by each agency to carry out its operational responsibilities. In fact, the total amount of environmentally related data already existing at the federal level in a file of data banks is probably nearing 10^{12} characters. Therefore, from a system requirements standpoint, very effective data acquisition, data transmission, and data storage capabilities would be required to implement a national system.

It is instructive to imagine what such a system would look like today and to understand how the country has been able to get along since 1970 without it.

TABLE 7.1

Environmental Data Flow

	Quality	Quantity	Pollution Effects	Natural Effects	Resources	Social-Aesthetic	Total
Typical parameters	Air quality Water	Air emissions Water effluents Solid waste	Respiratory Diseases	Severe storms	Climatology Minerals Fuels	Odors Noise Housing	
No. meas. sites (1976)	10^3–10^4	10^3–10^4	10^3–10^4	3000	3000	10^3–10^4	
Data rate per site (characters per month)	10^3–10^6	10^4	10^4	10^3	10^5	10^4	
Data rate to federal level (characters per month)	10^8	10^8	10^8	10^7–10^8	10^8–10^9	10^7–10^8	10^9
Data storage (characters)	10^{10}	10^{10}	10^{10}	10^9–10^{10}	10^{10}–10^{11}	10^9–10^{10}	10^{11} *

* Plus Air/Space Multi-Spectral Imagery
SOURCE: Ouellette, Rosenbaum, & Greeley, ref. 2.

231

THREE TYPES OF NATIONAL ENVIRONMENTAL DATA SYSTEMS

It is possible to envision three basic types of national environmental data systems.[3] A *centralized* system configuration would have all environmental data stored in a national environmental data bank. A *categorical* system configuration would have environmental data in each category of air, water, land, resources, health, social-aesthetics, etc., reported to the responsible federal agency for storage, analysis, and calculation of the indices. A *geographical* system configuration would have data gathered and validated at the local level, reported to state agencies, which would summarize and forward the data to the regional agencies, which would, in turn, send aggregated data to the federal agencies for calculation of the indices.

Centralized System Configuration

In the centralized system (Figure 7.1) all federal, state, and local agencies together with private institutions and industrial organizations would transmit their validated data to the national environmental data bank. The flexibility of this system configuration would be excellent because of the centralized control of the data. However, its responsiveness would be poor because of the separation of the data bank from the responsible operating agencies and also from the sheer physical size of the data base to be handled. Because of the large environmental data bases already existing in the federal government to meet particular operational uses, a centralized system would still require a large number of storage memories within an interconnected network. The computer network of the Advanced Research Projects Agency (ARPA) of the Department of Defense is an example of a large-scale, interconnected system. An operational goal of the ARPA network is to allow a person sitting at a console connected to any one of the computers in the network to use the hardware and software of any other computer of the network with the same facility with which he could use his own. Thus, many different and separate computers appear to each user to be, in fact, a dedicated computer. The ARPA network, however, is still in its initial stages as a research tool and is several years away from being useful as an operational tool for the sort of program considered here. An alternate in this direction is to set up a central data repository, with interconnected data banks, to handle as much of the data as is technically possible. This would

ENVIRONMENTAL DATA FLOW

	QUALITY	QUANTITY	POLLUTION EFFECTS	NATURAL EFFECTS	RESOURCES	SOCIAL AESTHETIC	TOTAL
Typical parameters	● Air quality ● Water	● Air emissions ● Water effluents ● Solid waste	● Respiratory diseases	● Severe storms	● Climatology ● Minerals ● Fuels	● Odors ● Noise ● Housing	
No. meas. sites (1976)	$10^3 - 10^4$	$10^3 - 10^4$	$10^3 - 10^4$	3000	3000	$10^3 - 10^4$	
Data rate per site (characters per month)	$10^3 - 10^6$	10^4	10^4	10^3	10^5	10^4	
Data rate to Federal level (characters per month)	10^8	10^{8*}	10^8	$10^7 - 10^8$	$10^8 - 10^{9*}$	$10^7 - 10^8$	10^9
Data storage (characters)	10^{10}	10^{10*}	10^{10}	$10^9 - 10^{10}$	$10^{10} - 10^{11*}$	$10^9 - 10^{10}$	10^{11}

* Plus Air/space multispectral imagery

FIGURE 7.1. Centralized system configuration. (From R. P. Ouellette, D. M. Rosenbaum, & R. S. Greeley, ref. 2)

234 COMPUTER TECHNIQUES IN ENVIRONMENTAL SCIENCE

have the effect of forcing the operators of the system to decide which of the data are most important for acceptance into the bank.

However, present experience with remote access and time-sharing systems serving a large number of users requiring access to large data bases has indicated extensive downtime, significant delays during peak daytime periods, and high cost of rapid access storage. Also, the organization difficulties of establishing a central data bank would be quite large. Discussions with federal, state, and local personnel have made it clear that transferring all of the environmental data to a group not within their responsibility is acceptable only under extensive constraints to permit the originating agency to analyze and publish its own data before transmitting them to the central data bank. Therefore, the apparent dollar economies of scale and flexibility of a centralized configuration may be outweighed by the technological and organizational difficulties.

Categorical System Configuration

The categorical configuration (Figure 7.2) is most nearly the way most environmental monitoring is now acomplished. The "environment" is divided among federal agencies within categories of air, water, health, etc. Each agency gathers data directly from private institutions and industrial organizations or from local and state agencies within its own category of responsibility. This configuration has excellent response within categories, but there is poor coordination across categories. For instance, "land" data gathering is divided among Office of Solid Wastes in EPA; the U.S. Geological Survey, Bureau of Recreation, Bureau of Land Management, Bureau of Mines, National Park Service, and Bureau of Reclamation in the Department of the Interior; the Forest Service in the Department of Agriculture; and a number of bureaus in other departments. This type of system has not been responsive historically to the needs of local and state agencies for information. The flexibility of such a configuration will also tend to be poor since changes in the type or amount of data required by the Council on Environmental Quality, for instance, will involve changing capabilities among the agencies or reassignment of responsibility. Most of the information stored by the federal, state, and local agencies will be used to support operational needs rather than national policymaking and overall environmental control. Such a configuration is technically within the current state of the art and the cost to upgrade current capability into a national environmental information system is probably moderate.

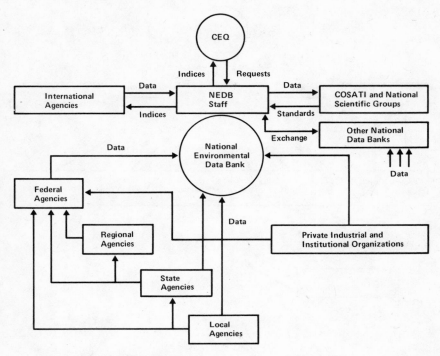

NEDB = National Environmental Data Bank
CEQ = Council on Environmental Quality
COSATI = Council on Scientific and Technical Information

FIGURE 7.2.   Categorical system configuration. *(From R. P. Ouellette, D. M. Rosenbaum, & R. S. Greeley, ref. 2)*

Geographic System Configuration

In the geographic configuration (Figure 7.3), the basic data originates in the field with private institutions, industrial organizations, and local agencies. The local agencies forward validated data to the state agency so that the state is aware of all environmentally related conditions within its boundaries. It is envisioned that the ten federal regions shared by EPA, HEW, and HUD, and the Labor, Interior, and Transportation departments, will become strong organizations with sufficient computer power and professional data processing personnel to carry out effective environmental monitoring and control programs. Eventually, the regions may be interconnected with an

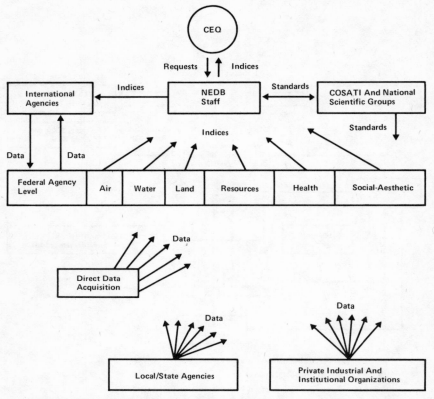

FIGURE 7.3.   Geographic system configuration. *(From R. P. Ouellette, D. M. Rosenbaum, & R. S. Greeley, ref. 2)*

ARPA-type computer network. Each state is entirely within one of these federal regions, and categorical areas, such as river basins or air-quality control regions, could be assigned to whichever of these regions is most convenient. The federal regional centers would receive appropriate processed data from the states and, in turn, would process and transmit aggregated data to the parent federal agency.

The advantage of this concept is that information would be stored in the area and at the level at which it was generated and would be most useful; at every level there would be an agency that had an overall grasp of conditions at that level and below. One disadvantage of this scheme is that a categorical area such as weather, with a nationwide observing system and a centralized electronic processing center supporting regional forecast offices, does not fit appropriately. The geographical concept would have excellent response within categorical areas at each level of data aggregation and responsibility. To the extent that local, state, and regional agencies were established in categories to consider the overall environment, this system would become more responsive and flexible in providing the information needed. The system is technically within the state of the art, and its dollar cost would depend, primarily, upon the degree of sophistication of the data-acquisition and -processing capability provided.

CURRENT NATIONAL ENVIRONMENTAL DATA SYSTEMS

The current systems [5, 6] for handling environmental data exist as the "categorical" configuration, as noted above. However, no "national environmental data bank" (NEDB) exists, no procedures exist for collecting, formatting, and reporting data to the Council on Environmental Quality or international agencies; for sharing data amongst federal agencies or even within agencies; for reporting data back to states and localities except through normal published reports, generally at least a year behind the date of measurement. Clearly, no "system" in the ordinary sense of the term exists.

The situation is not systematic in other important aspects. Some of these are as follows:

PARAMETERS TO BE MEASURED. Agreement has not been reached on what pollutants and environmental effects should be measured.

MEASUREMENT TECHNIQUES. Methods and equipment for measuring many pollutants have been standardized, but many more hazardous and potentially hazardous substances are not covered by agreed-upon techniques. The failure to have an adequate technique for measuring nitrogen oxides in the air has prevented a standard from being set and has caused major consternation in the automotive industry.

SITING STRATEGIES. No adequate guideline exists as to where to situate samplers.

DATA VALIDATION. No procedures or standards exist for ensuring that data are valid.

DATA TRANSMISSION AND REPORTING. No standards have been set for timeliness, allowable error rate, nor format for getting data from the measurement device to the user.

DATA PROCESSING. No agreement has been reached on methods, algorithms, or standards for handling the data, even to ensure good common statistical practice.

DATA USAGE. The use of environmental data is marked by the absence of standard or agreed-upon indices, baselines, thresholds, and other relevant characteristics.

Many of these shortcomings have been recognized. The original hearings on the proposed national environmental data bank [1] discussed them in some detail. The Study of Environmental Quality Information Programs (SEQUIP), carried out by the Office of Science and Technology in 1971, also recognized most of these problems.[7] The Environmental Protection Agency has been developing an integrated nationwide environmental monitoring system [8] to handle environmental data from a "systems approach." [9] EPA also has addressed, specifically, the problem of data validity with a major program of "quality assurance." [10] The U. S. Geological Survey has initiated a "Resource and Land Information Program" to "provide key information on land and other natural resources . . ." in a form usable by decision-makers and has established the Earth Resources Observations Center in Sioux Falls, South Dakota.[11] The Council on Environmental Quality, through its annual reports and a special director on federal monitoring efforts, has attempted to indicate what data are needed for national policymaking.[12, 13]

On the other hand, essentially every policy decision and environmental standard has been made on the basis of extremely inadequate data and analysis. The current controversy over automotive emission standards is a case in point.[14] The cost of implementing the federal standards has been estimated to be nearly $48 billion over the period 1971–80 [15] and, yet, measurements of ambient air concentrations for automotive-related pollutants have been made only in Los Angeles since before 1970 and even now are made sporadically in many cities. The health effects of automotive-related pollutants are inadequately known, and the relation of pollution-control devices to resulting ambient air quality has not been shown. Cost-benefit studies of alternative approaches to achieving ambient air quality have been extremely limited in scope. The same limited approach is true for other air-pollution and for water-pollution standards. In all of these cases, computer techniques, as described in chapters 4 and 5, would be very useful to format and validate data, reduce the data into convenient graphs and indices, model and simulate strategies or alternatives, and produce summary statistics.

PROPOSED NATIONAL ENVIRONMENTAL DATA SYSTEM

The need still exists for a more coordinated approach to the gathering and use of environmental data, particularly for policy- and decision-making. A formal, "hard-wired" system is undoubtedly out of the question, at least for the foreseeable future. However, the establishment of an organization similar to that shown in Figures 7.1, 7.2, and 7.3 as "NEDB staff," appears to be warranted. This group would propose answers to the problems raised in Nos. 1 to 7, noted above, concerning measurements and standards, for action by the President's Council on Environmental Quality, the Congressional Office of Technology Assessment, and others. The group would also have sufficient computer resources to carry out analyses of the impact of alternative pollution-control policies and regulations. The group would calculate indices showing the status and trends of environmental quality and prepare background information for enforcement activities, standard setting, criteria preparation, standard compliance monitoring, following progress of implementation plans, baseline establishment, identifying nondegradability of the background, scientific investigations, planning, budgeting, and management.

The group would also play a coordinating role, including the following tasks: catalog existing data systems in terms of acquisition, transmission, storage, processing, and usage; assist in exchange of data among agencies and across media and political jurisdictions; establish commonality in code exchange procedure, quality control, standards, data system, etc.; develop a glossary of terms; standardize formats, symbols, notations, nomenclature, and units; and organize a dissemination program for the catalog of data.

The computer resources of the organization should be obtained following the procedure outlined in Chapter 6. A fairly large computer will probably be needed to handle the activities noted above. Careful delineation of the interfaces with STORET, SAROAD, RALI, EROS, and other large data bases will have to be made during the requirements and systems analyses. The organization and its computer must not take over the responsibilities of EPA, USGS, and other agencies, but must complement their capabilities and assist the entire "environmental establishment" in carrying out its responsibilities of protecting and preserving our natural heritage.

REFERENCES

1. HR17436, HR17779, HR18141.

2. R. P. Ouellette, D. M. Rosenbaum and R. S. Greeley, "National Environmental Data Systems." The MITRE Corp., MTP-353, July 19, 1971.

3. R. P. Ouellette, D. M. Rosenbaum and R. S. Greeley, "Is There a System for Pollution Madness?" *Datamation,* April 15, 1971.

4. R. Pikul, *et al,* "Monitoring the Environment of the Nation; a System Design Concept." The MITRE Corp., MTR-4176, October 1970.

5. G. J. Nehls, D. H. Fair and J. B. Clements, "National Air Data Bank Open for Business." *Env. Sci. & Technol.* 4 (11), 903-905, 1970.

6. P. L. Taylor, C. W. Tutwiler and C. S. Bonger, "STORET—A Data Handling System in Pollution Control." ASCE Annual Meeting, 1969.

7. Hearings before the Subcommittee on Fisheries and Wild Life Conservation of the Committee on Merchant Marine and Fisheries, House of Representatives, Serial No. 91-29, June 2, 3, 25 and 26, 1970.

8. Environmental Protection Agency, personal communications.

9. S. M. Blacker and J. S. Burton, *Environmental Protection Agency's Monitoring Program.* U.S. EPA, Office of Research and Development, Washington, D. C., August 1973.

10. A. Johnson and S. Stryker, "The U.S. Environmental Protection Agency's Quality Assurance Program." The MITRE Corp., M72-199, December 1972.

11. C. A. Bisselle, *et al,* "Resource and Land Information Program: System Concept, Implications and Development Plan." The MITRE Corp., MTR-6275, October 1972.

12. *Annual Reports on the Council on Environmental Quality.* U. S. Government Printing Office, Washington, D. C.

13. *The Federal Environmental Monitoring Directory.* U. S. Government Printing Office, Washington, D. C.

14. J. M. Heuss, *et al,* "National Air Quality Standards for Automotive Pollutants—A Critical Review," and D. S. Barth, "Discussion." *J. APCA,* 21:9, pp. 535-548, September 1971, and 21:12, pp. 788-789, December 1971.

15. *The Economic Impact of Automotive Emission Standards.* Turner, Mason and Solomon, Consulting Engineers, Dallas, Texas, March 31, 1972.

INDEX

CATAD: *see* Computer Augmented Treatment asd Disposal System
COM: *see* Computer output microfilm
CRT: *see* Cathode-ray tube
Cabling, Communications: *see* Communications cabling
Calibration regression 164
California mode emission test cycle 74
Cancer, Lung 4
Carbon, Total organic 134
Carbon monoxide 4
  air-monitoring networks 51
Carbon oxides 145
Carnegie-Mellon University 31
Cat-ox demonstration measurement points 59
Catalytic Oxidation Project 56
Categorical system 232, 234
Cathode-ray tubes 31
Cathode-ray tube terminal 32
CDC 3300 31
CDC 6600 31
Census Bureau 229
Central processor unit 213
Central station 89, 108
  Seattle 119
Centralized system 232
Chemical calibration 87
Chicago 157
  air monitoring 51
Chicago Central District Filtration Plant 122, 126
Chlorination 127
Clean Air Amendments 4, 43, 46, 47
Coal
  coke oven emission-control system 65
  soft 3
Coaxial cable 94, 95
COBOL 26, 218
COBOL F 167
Coke oven emission-control and monitoring system 65

Columbia Willamette
  air monitoring 51
Common Carrier Communications 18
Common-mode noise 93
Communications cabling 94
Commutator: *see* Input scanner
Computer augmented treatment and disposal system 8, 118
Computer control 117
Computer network 31
Computer output microfilm 32
Computer processes 12
Computers 11
  specification and acquisition 197
Condensation Nuclei Network 40
Congress 229
Congressional Office of Technology Assessment 239
Connecticut
  air monitoring 51
Continuous Air Monitoring Program 37
Continuous-balance: *see* Direct-comparison technique
Contour lines 154
Control Data Corporation 31
Controller
  central station 109
  remote station functions 89
Correlation matrix 157
Cost approximation model
  air quality monitoring 164
Cost-value technique 220
Council on Environmental Quality 1, 2
Cyanide 5
CYBERNET 31

DBM: *see* Data base management
Dade County
  air monitoring 51
Dallas 135
Data acquisition 12
Data-acquisition systems 84, 93
Data banks 178

Motor-vehicle emission monitoring 71

Motor vehicle pollution control 74

Multiplexer
remote station functions 87

Multiplexing 20

Municipal-waste 38

NABD: *see* National Aerometric Data Bank

NADIS: *see* National Aerometric Data Information Service

NAPCA: *see* National Air Pollution Control Administration

NASN: *see* National Air Surveillance Networks

National Aerometric Data Bank 6, 30, 43, 152, 178

National Aerometric Data Information Service 43, 47, 49

National Aeronautics and Space Administration 77, 230

National Air Surveillance Network Laboratory 7, 37

National Air Pollution Control Administration 202

National Center for Atmospheric Research and the Environmental Research Laboratory of the National Oceanic and Atmospheric Administration 7

National Center for Health Statistics 229

National Emission Data System 140

National environmental data systems 229, 232

National Environmental Policy Act 1

National Geophysical Data Center 229

National Oceanic and Atmospheric Administration 229

National Oceanographic Data Center 229

National Park Service 234

National Pesticides Monitoring Program 40

National Weather Records Center 229

Nassau County, Long Island 135, 151

Netherlands
air monitoring 51

Network analysis 151

New Jersey
air monitoring 51

New York, state
air monitoring 51
monitoring 6

New York, city
air monitoring 51

New York Department of Environmental Conservation
water monitoring 50

New York State Surveillance System 56

Nitrogen 134

Nitrogen dioxide
air-monitoring networks 51

Nitrogen oxides 4
air-monitoring networks 51

Noise 93

Noise
monitoring sites 39

Noise pollution 42

Nonbiodegradable wastes 173

North Carolina, University of 31

North Carolina State University 31

Nuclear power plants 6

Off-line storage 23

Office of Water Programs 8

Ohio River 54
monitoring and alert systems 6

Oil spills 5

Ontario
air monitoring 51

Operating systems 92
requirements 216

ORSANCO 50, 54